D0891522

The Johnson Years, Volume Two

The Johnson Years, Volume Two
Vietnam, the Environment, and Science

Edited by Robert A. Divine

 University Press of Kansas

© 1987 by the University Press of Kansas
All rights reserved

Published by the University Press of Kansas (Lawrence, Kansas 66045),
which was organized by the Kansas Board of Regents and is operated and
funded by Emporia State University, Fort Hays State University, Kansas
State University, Pittsburg State University, the University of Kansas,
and Wichita State University

Library of Congress Cataloging-in-Publication Data

The Johnson years.
  Includes bibliographies and indexes.
  Contents: —v. 2. Vietnam, the environment,
and science.
  1. United States—Politics and government—1963–
1969. 2. Johnson, Lyndon B. (Lyndon Baines), 1908–
1973. I. Divine, Robert A.
E846.J64 1987   973.923′092′4   87-6186
ISBN 0-7006-0327-1

British Library Cataloguing in Publication data is available.

Printed in the United States of America
10 9 8 7 6 5 4 3 2 1

In Memory of Chuck DeBenedetti
1943–1987

Preface

IN 1981 I EDITED a collection of essays entitled *Exploring the Johnson Years*, in which seven scholars surveyed major issues of the 1960s, ranging from the Vietnam War to the civil-rights movement, to demonstrate the rich veins of previously untapped material available in the Lyndon Baines Johnson Library. Although the essays dealt with many of the important themes that concerned the Johnson administration, they could not cover all areas of historical interest.

The present volume is designed to broaden and extend the coverage of the Johnson years by treating topics that were not included in the first collection. Once again, with generous support from the Lyndon B. Johnson Foundation and with close cooperation from the staff of the Johnson Library, the authors have searched through the files in Austin that are relevant to their subjects and then have related their archival findings to the existing literature. They have written both to extend our present understanding of significant aspects of the sixties and to point the way to topics and resources that scholars could profitably develop in the future.

Rather than force the authors into a standard format, I encouraged them to write their essays along whatever lines seemed most appropriate. As a result, their contributions fall into three categories. First, several have chosen to offer a general survey of the Johnson Library's holdings on a broad issue of national policy. Thus, in dealing with the opposition to the Vietnam War and environmental policy, Charles DeBenedetti and Martin Melosi have sketched out the larger issues of national policy and have pointed out the types of material available in the library for more detailed studies of these topics. Lewis Gould, Donald Kettl, and Clarence Lasby, on the other hand, have written much more intensive essays on more limited subjects to show how the library's holdings can be used to bring little-known but important aspects of national policy in the 1960s into focus. Finally, Burton Kaufman and I have combined these two approaches in writing essays that survey broad areas but also include some detailed coverage of selected portions. Despite the difference in method, the resulting essays all strive for the same goal—to demonstrate the wide variety of materials available and to encourage other scholars to join in exploring the Johnson Library so as to enhance our understanding of a stormy and controversial decade of the recent past.

While by design there is no single theme to the essays, two elements tend to appear with great frequency. The first is the Vietnam War. From the time of the escalation in 1965, it casts an ever-greater shadow over nearly all aspects of national policy, from the debate over tax policy to the funding of such areas dear to Lyndon Johnson's heart as health and space. Although only Charles DeBenedetti's essay on the antiwar movement deals directly with the Vietnam experience, nearly all reflect the growing absorption of Johnson and his staff with the war in Southeast Asia. By the late 1960s, Vietnam not only was creating a budget squeeze that hurt nearly every other administrative program; it also was distracting the White House from all other issues and was poisoning the administration's relations with Congress and the press.

The other unifying element in the essays is the elusive presence of Lyndon Johnson. He is the central figure in nearly all the essays, dominating his administration and setting priorities by the sheer force of his personality as well as the power of his office. At the same time, it is almost impossible to be sure what LBJ really felt and thought about the issues of his administration. The common dilemma facing all the authors is the absence of material in the library by Johnson himself. Vast numbers of memos and reports reflect the advice from the bureaucracy and his aides, but very few documents reveal Johnson's own personal reaction. Occasionally there is a scrawled handwritten comment at the bottom of a memorandum, indicating the president's pleasure or disfavor; usually, however, there is only a terse yes or no or a cryptic comment, such as "See me about this."

The difficulty lies with Johnson's personal style. Secretive by nature, he hated to reveal his innermost thoughts on paper. Instead, he favored oral communication, either by telephone or, preferably, in person, where he could question, cajole, flatter, or intimidate whomever he was dealing with. The scholar is thus forced to rely on the recollections of others, either in oral histories or in contemporary memoranda, on what Johnson told them and what they thought he really meant. Only very rarely does one find a document that indicates LBJ's private feelings and thoughts.

Yet despite this handicap, the essays in this collection do offer new insight into the character and leadership qualities of Lyndon Johnson. In particular, they cast doubt on the usual stereotypes of LBJ as the opportunistic wheeler-dealer, intent on building a legislative record though not caring about the issues, or the super hawk, ruthlessly pursuing a belligerent foreign policy. Instead, these essays reveal the complexity of Johnson as president and his genuine commitment to such diverse causes as the conquest of disease, the protection of the environment, and the exploration of outer space. The LBJ in these pages is a very human figure who understands the corrosive impact of the Vietnam War on his administration and who struggles to try to preserve the domestic programs that he fought so long and hard to achieve. By suggesting the contradictions that undercut so many of the positive aspects of Johnson's actions, the contributors to this volume add greatly to our knowledge of this deceptively elusive president. The ultimate success of these essays, however, will depend on the degree to which they challenge other historians to join in the effort to arrive at a fuller understanding of Johnson's vital but flawed legacy to the nation.

Contents

Introduction

1 | The Johnson Revival: A Bibliographical Appraisal

Robert A. Divine

IN THE FIRST DECADE after the death of Lyndon Baines Johnson, there were surprisingly few books published about this controversial president. Both biographers and historians seemed to share in the public's desire not to be reminded of a figure who had presided over such a stormy and disruptive period in American life. In the "me decade" of the 1970s, Johnson faded from memory, along with his Great Society and the trauma associated with the Vietnam War. The only book on LBJ to attract much attention was Doris Kearns's *Lyndon Johnson and the American Dream*, but even this well-written account achieved only brief popularity.[1]

The growing historical blackout came to an abrupt end in the early 1980s with a marked revival of interest in Johnson and his policies. The election of Ronald Reagan and the subsequent assault on many of the Great Society programs of the sixties led to new scholarly attention on Johnson's legislative program and its subsequent impact on American life. Even more dramatic was the renewal of interest in Vietnam, which was manifested in the striking popularity of the PBS series and Stanley Karnow's accompanying book, *Vietnam: A History*. As the American people began to come to terms with a war they had tried to forget, Johnson once again became a central figure. And finally, biographers began to take up the challenge inherent in chronicling Johnson's remarkable rise to power and his equally dramatic fall from grace. The realization that so little was known about a man who had played such a major role in recent American history helped to stimulate a new wave of Johnson literature.

The result was to subject Lyndon Johnson and his policies to a critical scrutiny that was long overdue. Most of these biographies and historical studies were hostile toward LBJ, portraying him in an unfriendly light and subjecting his motives and actions to very painstaking analysis. Yet, even Johnson partisans could take some comfort in the fact that the long years of neglect were finally over; their hero was at last getting the historical attention he had always craved and was no longer the victim of a collective scholarly amnesia.

I

The publication in 1982 of three books on LBJ's political career marked the beginning of the Johnson revival. Two were biographies that focused on his early career, primarily in Texas and in the House; the third was a memoir that concentrated on his Senate years. All three were by journalists who painted a bleak picture of Johnson as a scheming and unlikable politician, but there were notable differences in their approaches and conclusions.

By far the most ambitious work, and clearly the best written and most absorbing, was the first volume of Robert A. Caro's planned three-volume biography of Lyndon Johnson, *The Path to Power*. Using his skills as an investigative journalist, he combined extensive research in the materials at the Johnson Library with exhaustive interviews with everyone he could find who had known or worked with Johnson, including many who had never been interviewed before and were eager to tell their stories, which were often very critical of LBJ, to a sympathetic listener. The result was a book that offered a great deal of new information on Johnson's life and career through his first, unsuccessful Senate race in 1941 and that presented Johnson in a uniformly negative light.

Bothered at first by the secrecy with which LBJ surrounded himself, Caro finally found the theme that illuminated his entire political career, and then proceeded, in nearly 800 pages, to elaborate on it. The "dark thread" that Caro uncovered was Johnson's vaunting ambition, "a hunger for power in its most naked form, for power not to improve the lives of others, but to manipulate and dominate them, to bend them to his will." Caro discovered that once the secret was out, the mystery of Lyndon Johnson disappeared: LBJ was a man of great political skill who used his talents solely to advance his own career without regard to ideas, principles, or friendships. By the end of the 1930s Johnson had "displayed a genius for discerning a path to power, an utter ruthlessness in destroying obstacles in that path, and a seemingly bottomless capacity for deceit, deception and betrayal in moving along it."[2]

The key to understanding Johnson, Caro argues, is to focus on his extraordinary ambition, which he hid so carefully from contemporaries. Yet it is the revealing observations of some of those around Johnson who confided in Caro that he relies on so heavily. Thus, several times the reader is reminded of the comment of a childhood playmate that Johnson as a boy was already a "natural born leader," but "if he couldn't lead, he didn't care much about playing."[3] And the statement by a secretary in the 1930s, when LBJ was a congressional assistant, that Johnson possessed "a burning ambition to be somebody," is repeated later, along with the added comment, "He couldn't stand not being somebody—just could not *stand* it." "He wanted to be *somebody.*"[4] Caro uses such observations to conclude that from the time LBJ first arrived in Washington as a powerless young congressional aide, he was bent on a secret plan to advance through the House and the Senate to become president.

Caro uses the various incidents in Johnson's early career to plot out the methods and techniques that LBJ used to fulfill his hidden agenda. From his first plunge into political maneuvering in college through his first great setback in the 1941 Senate race, Johnson is portrayed as a ruthless, deceitful, and utterly immoral man, intent only on his own advancement. Asserting that LBJ cared nothing about ideology, Caro argues that he supported the New Deal purely out of expediency and repudiated it after 1941, when it no longer suited his political purposes. Friendships were equally dispensable; people, from worshipful aides such as Gene Latimer, who was driven to drink by working overtime for Johnson, to powerful patrons such as Sam Rayburn, were cast aside or subtly undermined when their usefulness was at an end.

The difficulty with this interpretation of Johnson is Caro's failure to explain LBJ's success. The reader is left to wonder why only Robert Caro, years later, could discern so clearly the evil nature of Lyndon Johnson and why so many contemporaries were taken in by Johnson's apparent duplicity. Nor does Caro succeed in explaining how LBJ was able to build up such a network of loyal and hard-working associates, men who stayed with him despite bad treatment and few tangible rewards and were crucial elements in his political advancement. The suggestion that some men like to be bullied or dominated hardly explains Johnson's appeal to the talented band of associates he gathered about him from his college days and his service as director of the National Youth Administration (NYA) in Texas. The failure to consider any more-human qualities that Johnson may have possessed, aside from naked ambition and the power to manipulate, casts considerable doubt on the dark portrait that Caro paints.

The second biography that appeared in 1982, Ronnie Dugger's *The Politician*, offers an equally critical view of LBJ, but one that differs considerably from Caro's account. Dugger is also a journalist but, unlike Caro, a crusading one who had opposed Johnson in the 1950s and was fascinated by what made his adversary tick. Relying on Texas newspapers, selected files in the Johnson Library, some interviews, including key ones with the president himself in late 1967 and early 1968, and the existing Johnson literature, Dugger writes a critical account of Johnson's career through the early fifties, with a few flashes ahead to Vietnam, which he explains as a result of LBJ's embodiment of such frontier values as pride and false courage. Dugger's main concern, however, is with ideology as he attempts to explain why Johnson did not live up to Dugger's own liberal principles.

In contrast to Caro, Dugger views Johnson as a genuine New Dealer, a man with principles who abandoned them under the spur of ambition. Thus he portrays LBJ as a "true crusader" in his days as director of the NYA in Texas and, unlike Caro, not simply as using his NYA position for a stepping stone to Congress.[5] Dugger is particularly impressed that during the thirties, Johnson was willing to aid blacks with educational support and public housing at a time when it was not politically advantageous, a topic that is reserved for a later volume in Caro's biography.

The tragedy, as Dugger sees it, is that Johnson's commitment to the New Deal and to humanitarian reform was not strong enough to withstand the pull of ambition. Claiming that Johnson had no long-range goals but, rather, that he was a man of impulse who reacted instinctively to opportunity, Dugger traces LBJ's fortuitous partnership with Herman and George Brown and his subsequent corruption as a "back-sliding liberal" who became enmeshed in helping Brown and Root become a huge government contractor by giving them inside information and assistance.[6] Caro, aided by a key interview with George Brown, had traced this same development; but Caro saw it as a predictable part of the larger pattern of LBJ's path to power.

Thus, though both Dugger and Caro view Johnson as an opportunistic politician who had abandoned the New Deal by the 1940s, their interpretations are quite different. Dugger regrets that LBJ had become an ardent Cold Warrior, engaging in Red-baiting and anti-union activities, while Caro finds it perfectly understandable. Dugger sees Johnson as a flawed but potentially decent political leader, a complex man who was both vindictive and compassionate, both charming and vicious, both selfish and generous—a man who, he says, "was everything that is human." And his great regret is that Johnson had not chosen a different course, "one that lay latent in him," and thus turned against the New Deal and the peaceful world that Dugger hoped would be possible after World War II.[7] In other words, Dugger writes more out of sorrow than out of anger as he describes a Johnson who betrayed his own best instincts.

The third 1982 book on LBJ was George Reedy's *Lyndon B. Johnson: A Memoir.* Less ambitious than either Caro or Dugger, Reedy was content to try to think through his own ambivalent feelings toward a man he had served as a Senate aide and presidential press secretary. Reedy agreed with many of the negative aspects of Johnson's character, but he also found in LBJ some redeeming qualities. Trying to explain how he could work so long and hard for a man he often detested, Reedy said it was Johnson's occasional acts of courage and genuine legislative achievement that made it all worthwhile. In the 1950s, Reedy explained, several times he was ready to leave his vulgar and insensitive boss when LBJ "would do something so magnificent that all of his nasty characteristics would fade."[8] In particular, Reedy cites Johnson's role in arranging for the censure of Joe McCarthy and LBJ's skillful maneuvering in behalf of the 1957 Civil Rights Act as examples of genuine statesmanship.

The key to Johnson's appeal, according to Reedy, was his dynamic personality and his many-sided nature. LBJ's contradictions fascinated Reedy: "He was a tremendous figure—a combination of complexities and simplicities that bewildered all observers." At times very shrewd, he could also be "astoundingly gullible in the selection of his personal advisers."[9] As one who worked for him, Reedy admits that LBJ was "a miserable person—a bully, sadist, lout, and egotist"—who took "special delight in humiliating those who had cast in their lot with him." But most of all Reedy was impressed by the sheer audacity and force of Johnson's personality: "He may have been a son of a bitch but he was a colossal son of a bitch."[10]

Unlike both Caro and Dugger, however, Reedy does view Johnson as a man who cared about issues. He admits that Johnson did not formulate any coherent ideology and that he preferred always to talk tactics rather than strategy, but he senses in him a profound kinship for the underdog in society. Rebutting the charge that LBJ cared only about his own political fortunes, Reedy said such a feeling was not "shared by blacks or Appalachians or Chicanos or by poor people generally. They could see much of themselves in him."[11] For all of LBJ's concern with mastering the political currents of his time, Reedy believes, "he usually tried to ride them in the direction of uplift for the poor and downtrodden." Unpleasant as he was in his dealings with individuals, he genuinely tried "to do something for the masses."[12]

But even Reedy does not try to suggest that Johnson espoused any definable ideology beyond a vague desire to " 'be for the people—spelled pee-pul.' "[13] For all LBJ's skill at political maneuvering, he lacked any clear sense of purpose or a vision of what he hoped to achieve. Reedy echoes Dugger, who notes that Johnson was so caught up in the present that he never speculated about the future. One reason for his cultivation of political patrons such as Alvin Wirtz, Sam Rayburn, and Franklin D. Roosevelt, beyond immediate political opportunism, Reedy suggests, may have been to share in their larger vision of what was desirable. Without dreams of his own, LBJ had to borrow those of the men he admired most. Yet, even though he lacked the ability to chart a course for the nation to follow, he possessed remarkable skills in making government work effectively, skills that led Reedy to conclude that of all our presidents, Johnson "should be rated as the master tactician of all times."[14]

II

Historians as well as journalists have taken part in the Johnson revival. Interested more in LBJ's record in the White House than in his earlier political career, they have focused on two broad areas—the Great Society and the Vietnam War. Scholars have probed both into Johnson's attempts to carry out a broad program of domestic reform and into his flawed efforts to contain communism in Southeast Asia. Like the biographers, they have adopted a critical stance that has led to some very hostile judgments.

There has been one major effort to assess the entire sweep of the Johnson administration at home and abroad—Vaughn Davis Bornet's *The Presidency of Lyndon B. Johnson.* Bornet's book, part of a series on individual American presidencies, is based on both the body of Johnson literature and on research in the files of the Johnson Library. Written before much of the newer work on Johnson had appeared, it is an uneven book that does not reach any coherent or persuasive conclusions. Yet Bornet's survey does succeed in capturing the breadth of the Johnson administration's efforts to bring about change in American life; it is particularly helpful on the various Great Society programs.

The book's main weakness is the author's ambivalence toward Johnson. Bornet leans over backwards in his effort to be fair, but the result is an awkward balancing of positive and negative judgments. Thus, on the Great Society, Bornet credits Johnson with good intentions, along with substantial achievements in a few areas, notably education and civil rights. But he thinks that the Great Society failed because Johnson promised far more than he could deliver. Even the record of legislative output is misleading, Bornet argues, because as a result, "so many impractical and/or untested laws emerged, laws that much later would require modification, amendment, abandonment, or repeal." He thinks LBJ was guilty of "overpromising of utopia," but at the same time he credits him with "at least trying to strike effective blows against injustice, extremes of poverty, and the failure to educate the young."[15]

Similarly, Bornet sees "great virtue" in LBJ's attempt to halt communism in Southeast Asia, calling the effort in Vietnam "definitely worth trying." But Bornet faults Johnson for not doing enough and for failing to be honest with the American people. According to Bornet, Johnson "was unwilling to use much of the power the nation had and . . . would not take risks that real escalation of the war seemed to entail."[16] Once more LBJ is praised for his good intentions but damned for his failure to follow through. "Johnson cautiously avoided full commitment of his and the nation's resources," Bornet charges, "to any of the expensive causes he espoused, at home or abroad."[17] Yet it can be argued that it was not Johnson's caution and restraint that were at fault but that it was his more fundamental failure to think through both his sweeping legislative programs and his foreign-policy adventures.

Johnson's greatest difficulty, it would appear, was the absence of a definable ideology. Intent on passing bills in Congress and on fighting communism, he lacked a set of principles to guide him in these activities. Yet Bornet dodges this whole question, commenting only that LBJ's ideology "is not easy to capsulize."[18] In failing to probe into the impact of Johnson's ideological weakness, Bornet is unable to offer a consistent explanation of why, despite his good intentions, LBJ could not either sustain his Great Society or win in Vietnam. Bornet's long chapter on Johnson's concern over the state of his health dictating his decision to step down in 1968, while interesting, still does not offset the fact that Johnson had lost the confidence of the American people on both domestic and foreign-policy issues. The contrast between the initial success of a new president stepping in to restore the nation's faith after the tragic Kennedy assassination and the scorn heaped on a failed leader rejected by a disillusioned nation calls for a more incisive explanation than poor health. Instead, Bornet concludes with the contradictory observation that the Johnson presidency was a "brilliant tour de force" yet one that "saw the nation in turmoil, with loss of faith in the system itself."[19]

III

The Great Society, which is often viewed as Johnson's most substantial achievement as president, came under critical fire in the early 1980s. Two assessments, one by a historian and one by a social scientist, challenged the traditional belief that LBJ had presided over a period of remarkable social progress at home.

Allen J. Matusow, writing from a New Left perspective yet also drawing upon conservative attacks on liberalism, has offered a broad-ranging critique of the Great Society and of LBJ's War on Poverty in particular in *The Unraveling of America.* Although his conclusions were damaging to Johnson, Matusow's main target was mainstream American liberalism, not LBJ. Indeed, unlike Caro, Matusow was willing to concede that despite past inconsistency in ideology, President Johnson was a sincere advocate of reform who was out to "confound his critics by doing good" and to prove that he could be a more effective occupant of the White House than either Kennedy or Roosevelt.[20] Matusow gives LBJ especially high marks in the area of civil rights, calling his actions in passing the 1964 and 1965 Civil Rights Acts "the greatest achievement of his tenure."[21] LBJ's only failure in this area, the author contends, was when he failed to support the effort to end educational and economic discrimination in the North.

It is liberalism, not Johnson's character, that Matusow sees as fatally flawed. LBJ, like Kennedy, was a "corporate liberal"—one who "unashamedly asserted the benevolence of large corporations and defended the existing distribution of wealth and power in America." The clearest example of this devotion to bolstering the existing corporate structure of America was the tax cut proposed by Kennedy and enacted by Johnson in 1964. This measure, Matusow argues, "sought no redistribution of wealth and power"; its sole purpose was "lubrication of the system, not its reform."[22]

Matusow's primary concern is with the War on Poverty. The problem, he contends, lay not in Johnson's excessive rhetoric but in a faulty concept of the nature of poverty in America. Democratic liberals saw it as a fixed condition, defined in 1963 as any family with an income below $3,000. In reality, poverty was a relative state that embraced 20 percent of the population—the one in five American families who did not share fully in the nation's abundance. By 1968 the poverty line had moved up to $7,500, but 20 percent of the population fell below that mark of "relative deprivation." The only way to eradicate poverty, according to Matusow, was to move against its source—namely, inequality of income. "It followed that, to attack poverty, the government would have to reduce inequality, to redistribute income, in short, to raise up the poor by casting down the rich." "By American standards," Matusow concludes, "this was radicalism, and nobody in the Johnson White House ever considered it."[23]

Instead of a genuine onslaught involving income transfers to ensure that the lowest 20 percent of the population would receive more than 5 percent of the national income, Johnson engaged in ameliorative programs to train poor youth, to provide better educational opportunities, to furnish health care for the aged and the poor, and to improve housing in the slums. None of these programs proved successful, according to Matusow, because none was aimed at the fundamental problem of income redistribution. Unwilling to take risks or to anger important interest groups, LBJ waged a crusade without casualties and therefore without victories. "This then," Matusow concludes, "may serve as the epitaph of the famous War on Poverty— 'Declared but Never Fought.' "[24]

Contrary to the conventional view that the Vietnam War doomed the poverty effort, Matusow believes that Vietnam proved to be "an inefficient but highly successful antipoverty program, the only one in the Johnson years that actually worked."[25] The military effort helped the poor by stimulating a demand for labor that particularly helped unskilled workers and blacks. Unfortunately, the resulting inflationary pressures eventually eroded the short-term benefits and contributed to the economic malaise of the 1970s, which proved to be equally hard on the poor and on the well-to-do.

Long before then, however, the triumph of liberalism had led to its demise. In 1968, Hubert Humphrey received almost 12 million fewer votes than Johnson had in 1964. The repudiation of the Democrats was due to far more than an unpopular war or a failed president, Matusow contends. It represented the "massive defection of the electorate from the liberalism that had guided the country since 1960. Liberals had once promised to manage the economy, solve the race problem, reduce poverty, and keep the peace. These promises not only remained unfulfilled; each of them would be mocked by the traumatic events of this election year."[26]

Powerful as is Matusow's indictment of the liberal failure in the 1960s, it is lacking in a realistic understanding of what was possible. His arguments for more sweeping reform and the large-scale redistribution of income ignore the nature of the American political system. Much like the similar New Left critique of Franklin Roosevelt's New Deal, Matusow's commitment to a more radical agenda, one that called for structural change rather than piecemeal reform, clashes with what was historically feasible. Yet his indictment of liberalism and of LBJ's faithful devotion to it helps to explain the tragedy that overcame both the nation and Lyndon Johnson during this tumultuous decade.

An equally provocative critique of Johnson's domestic social program has come from the opposite end of the political spectrum. In *Losing Ground*, Charles Murray, a neoconservative, contends that it was precisely the policies that Matusow advocates—attempts to transfer income—that interrupted slow but steady progress in the lessening of poverty. Surveying social policy from 1950 to 1980, Murray contends that the percentage of Americans who were mired in poverty had declined from 30 percent in 1950 to 13 percent by 1968. But then changes in the welfare program that began under Johnson led to a leveling off in the poverty level, so that by 1980, 13 percent of all Americans were still below the poverty line.[27]

Unlike Matusow, Murray focuses, not on the familiar Great Society legislation, but on changes in social policy that began during the last years of the Johnson administration and reached their full impact during the 1970s. He blames, not LBJ, but the intelligentsia, primarily academics and journalists, for fostering an "elite wisdom," which called for changes in social programs that made welfare more attractive than low-paying jobs. The greatest shift, however, was in favor of transfer payments, such as supplemental security income, food stamps, and other forms of welfare for working people. The changes that began under LBJ were often small in scale, but they would snowball in the future. Thus the number of people who were eligible for food stamps, which had increased from less than 0.5 million in 1963 to 2.1 million by 1968, had reached 21.1 million by 1980.[28]

Murray has relatively little to say about Johnson's impact on social policy. He glides over most of the Great Society programs, not even mentioning the historic changes in health care that were brought about by Medicare and Medicaid. He is equally vague on precisely who was responsible for the change in rules that he claims made it "profitable for the poor to behave in the short term in ways that were destructive in the long term."[29] And he fails to show how and why welfare policies that were designed to alleviate poverty suddenly included the kind of transfer payments that Matusow found so alien to Johnson's Great Society approach.

Despite their sharp ideological differences, Murray and Matusow agree that the War on Poverty failed. Neither author blames Johnson personally for this failure; rather, both see it as the product of flawed ideology. For Murray, the villains are "the upper echelons of academia, journalism, publishing, and the vast network of foundations, institutes, and research centers" who in the late 1960s reached agreement on a new social policy that "represented an abrupt shift with the past." Matusow is much more precise in assigning responsibility, stating that "the War on Poverty was destined to be one of the great failures of twentieth-century liberalism."[30]

The irony is that Lyndon Johnson, the man whom Robert Caro and many others have accused of lacking any ideology, is now seen as the man whose reform program floundered because of the liberal ideas that he followed as president. In waging war on poverty and in trying to use the power of government to create a Great Society, LBJ failed, not because of compromise or manipulation, but solely out of devotion to ideas and principles that proved to be fatally flawed.

IV

The revival of interest in Johnson reached its peak on the most controversial of all his policies—the Vietnam War. In the early 1980s, scholars began a careful reconsideration of Johnson's decisions in regard to Vietnam, one based on an examination of the evidence rather than on the emotional reaction that had colored so many of the earlier studies. Although nearly all the authors were still critical of Johnson, holding him responsible for America's failure in Vietnam, he began to be seen, not as the villain, but as yet another victim of this great tragedy.

Larry Berman, a political scientist, offered the most revealing new assessment of Johnson's Vietnam policy in his 1982 book, *Planning a Tragedy*. Using recently opened materials at the Johnson Library, Berman narrowed his focus to the critical decision in July, 1965, to commit the United States to full participation in the ground fighting in South Vietnam by authorizing the dispatch of another fifty thousand troops. Berman was particularly intent on examining the advisory process that Johnson had employed in reaching this critical decision, notably the dialogue between Undersecretary of State George W. Ball, who advocated a "tactical withdrawal," and Secretary of Defense Robert S. McNamara, who favored open-ended military escalation.[31]

Berman concluded that the president had used the advisory process to reach a prearranged decision for the controlled escalation of the conflict. Convinced that Johnson sincerely believed that South Vietnam was of vital strategic interest to the United States, Berman believes that LBJ never had any intention of pulling out of Vietnam. During the debate, the entire burden of proof was placed on those like Ball, who argued for withdrawal, and not on those who favored staying on, thereby preventing any fair weighing of the alternatives. At the same time, however, LBJ signaled to his national-security adviser, McGeorge Bundy, his desire to avoid an all-out military commitment in Vietnam.[32]

The picture of Johnson that Berman paints is one of a "master of consensus," a leader who was gifted in manipulation engaged in a "delicate exercise of political juggling." The whole elaborate process of meetings and discussions raised crucial questions, including the likelihood of a war that would last at least five years and might involve as many as six hundred thousand troops. But the purpose of the advisory process was not to consider these possible consequences, Berman explains, but "to legitimize a previously selected option by creating the illusion that other views were being considered."[33]

Johnson's most difficult task was putting a rein on the military. In a crucial meeting with the Joint Chiefs of Staff, he had to secure their agreement to his concept of a controlled and limited American military effort in Vietnam. One by one he turned down the suggestions of the service chiefs for calling up the reserves, for putting the nation on a wartime footing, for making extensive air and naval attacks on North Vietnam. Johnson finally asked each of the military leaders if he agreed with the policy of limited escalation, and each reluctantly nodded agreement. Calling this scene "an extraordinary moment," Berman likens Johnson to a "lion tamer dealing with some of the great lions."[34] This virtuoso performance led to disaster. "The president committed the United States to fight a limited war against an enemy totally committed to revolutionary war," Berman points out. "He had weighed all the costs and then used his great talents to forge a marginal consensus—enough to get the United States into war, but insufficient for war termination."[35]

The reason for this grave misjudgment, Berman thinks, is LBJ's devotion to the Great Society. In July, 1965, Congress had already passed thirty-six major pieces of legislation, but twenty-six others, including Medicare and civil rights, were still awaiting action. Reluctant to withdraw from Vietnam, LBJ was also unwilling to sacrifice his domestic reforms for victory abroad. So he opted for a middle course in Vietnam, one that he thought he could pursue without destroying the Great Society. "In holding back from total commitment," Berman observes, "Johnson was juggling the Great Society, the war in Vietnam, and his hopes for the future." The result, Berman concludes, was inevitable: "the Great Society would crumble," and he would lose in Vietnam to an enemy that was waging "a total, not limited war." Lyndon Johnson "was the cause of his ultimate undoing"; the master manipulator had finally undertaken a political juggling act that was beyond even his great skill.[36]

Berman's critical but sympathetic analysis of Johnson's failure in Vietnam provided a basis for another, a more ideological, interpretation of that conflict. Beginning in 1978 with Guenther Lewy's *America in Vietnam*, a group of revisionist writers had been defending the American involvement in Vietnam in reaction to the prevailing historical condemnation. Now they could develop the argument that the American defeat in Vietnam was self-inflicted, and thus did not prove that the effort was wrong from the outset.

Military strategist Harry Summers was one of the first to argue that the United States could have prevailed in Vietnam. Challenging the conventional view that the American army unwisely used traditional methods in an antiguerrilla war calling for new counterinsurgency tactics, Summers claimed that the real enemy had been the North Vietnamese regulars, not the Vietcong guerrillas. Had the United States used World War II–type tactics and taken the strategic initiative, he claims, America could have prevailed in Vietnam.[37]

Summers blamed Johnson for imposing political restraints that forced the army to fight a defensive war that was bound to end in failure. Johnson's attempt to wage a limited war, his refusal to ask Congress to declare war, and, above all, his decision to "commit the Army without first committing the American people"—all led to disaster. In trying to protect the Great Society, he neglected his major responsibility. "The failure to invoke the national will," Summers wrote, "was one of the major strategic failures of the Vietnam war." But he claimed that the fault was not Johnson's alone. The refusal of the Joint Chiefs of Staff to insist on taking the strategic offensive in Vietnam, even to the point of threatening to resign and to challenge the president in a public debate, was equally unfortunate.[38]

Other Vietnam revisionist writers were more solicitous of Johnson in making the same basic point. Herbert Y . Schandler, a retired colonel whose earlier book had offered a dispassionate analysis of Johnson's 1968 decision not to seek reelection, added to the revisionist analysis in a contribution to a symposium on the Vietnam War in 1984. Drawing on the work of both Summers and Berman, Schandler analyzed the impact of "the Johnsonian compromise" on the conduct of the war. Schandler depicts Johnson as being caught between the hawks in the military, who wanted to wage unlimited war, and the doves in the peace movement at home, who were calling for American withdrawal; this resulted in a gradual military escalation that led, not to victory, but to a prolonged stalemate. Far from being a villain, Johnson became the victim of his own policies of moderation, "a careful President who weighed the alternatives as he saw them, limited each response, and took into account the opinion of the public."[39]

Neoconservative Norman Podhoretz defended Johnson's decision to fight to contain communism in Southeast Asia, but he regretted the fact that LBJ "was trying to save Vietnam on the political cheap." Johnson's refusal to jeopardize the Great Society by asking for a tax increase hurt, but even more damaging was his failure to use his powers of persuasion on the American people. "To be fought successfully," Podhoretz wrote, "the war had to have a convincing moral justification, and the failure to provide one doomed the entire enterprise."[40]

A specialist in communications theory, who was not associated with the Vietnam revisionists, provided the most acute analysis of LBJ's dilemma in waging a limited war. In *Lyndon Johnson's Dual War: Vietnam and the Press*, Kathleen J. Turner used the extensive files in the LBJ Library to trace the president's concern with the way in which the media treated the war. At first, LBJ hoped the press would ignore the war and concentrate on the Great Society; after the escalation began in 1965, however, he was caught in what she describes as a "double bind—an inability to convince a large portion of the population that America was doing enough for Vietnam coupled with an inability to convince another large element that America was not doing too much." Trying to hew to a middle path in Vietnam, she argues, "Johnson's statements were neither sufficiently aggressive nor sufficiently conciliatory."[41]

The result was the emergence of the "credibility gap." Reporters thought that Johnson was deliberately holding back on the extent of the American involvement in Vietnam, when in reality he was trying to restrain public opinion in order to avoid a call for an all-out effort there. Thus he downplayed his July, 1965, decision to send an additional fifty thousand troops to Vietnam, vetoing an evening televised speech to the nation and instead announcing it at the opening of an afternoon press conference. "I think we can get our people to support us without having to be too provocative and warlike," he told his aides. As Turner points out, this policy led only to confusion and dissent. "The United States was engaged in military conflict, but hadn't declared war; . . . there was a wartime economy, but little austerity or sacrifice was required," she observes. "It simply didn't make sense to a growing proportion of the population."[42]

The most recent book on Johnson's Vietnam policy, *Intervention*, by George Kahin, a political scientist who specializes in Southeast Asian affairs, is surprisingly sympathetic to LBJ. Although Kahin is highly critical of the decision to escalate in 1965, he blames Johnson's predecessors in the White House, especially Dwight D. Eisenhower and John F. Kennedy, for making commitments that LBJ felt forced to honor. In addition, Kahin accuses the advisers Johnson inherited, notably McGeorge Bundy, Maxwell D. Taylor, and Robert S. McNamara, for failing to give him alternatives other than escalation or withdrawal, usually labeled as "bugging out." Kahin even accuses these men of deliberate deception, such as holding back the true facts on the Gulf of Tonkin incident and not giving the president George Ball's initial proposal for a negotiated withdrawal from Vietnam. Kahin suggests that the advisers may well have confused what was best for the United States with what was best for their own careers. "It was usually not too difficult for these men to equate the U.S. national interest with their own reputations."[43]

Instead of the bloodthirsty hawk of legend, Johnson emerges from Kahin's book as a prudent, even cautious, leader who has grave doubts about escalation. Told that it is necessary to bomb North Vietnam to save a tottering government in the South, LBJ objects, informing the chairman of the Joint Chiefs of Staff that he "did not wish to enter the patient in a 10-round bout, when he was in no shape to hold out for one round." And in the July, 1965, debate over troop commitment, it was the president, not his advisers, who kept raising the critical questions, asking at one point, "Are we starting something that in two or three years we simply can't finish?"[44] Thus Kahin portrays Johnson as the last dove in his own administration, the man who raised the right questions but received the wrong answers.

V

The portrait of Lyndon Johnson that is emerging from the recent literature is a very confused one. Unsympathetic biographers portray LBJ as an ambitious and amoral politician who either ignored or betrayed ideological concerns in advancing his career. Yet those who focus on the Great Society see in Johnson a genuine attempt to carry out the liberal program of his party and of such predecessors as Kennedy and Roosevelt. The failure that they document comes much more from flaws in the ideas than from defects in Johnson's character.

The new interpretation of Johnson's mistakes in Vietnam is even a greater departure from the conventional wisdom. Rather than being seen as a bloodthirsty and unrepentant war hawk, Johnson comes across as a reluctant warrior, a president who tried to find a middle path between all-out war and surrender in an area that he believed was vital for American security. Yet his efforts at moderation proved disastrous both for himself and for the nation. As Larry Berman comments, "Lyndon Johnson's greatest fault as a political leader was that *he chose* not to choose between the Great Society and the war in Vietnam."[45]

Even though Johnson's stature as a human being and as a statesman has not risen with the new scholarship, his failure takes on a more tragic dimension. The harder he tried to carry out what he perceived to be his mission in the White House—reform legislation to improve the quality of life at home and an active foreign policy to protect the national security abroad—the more he met with scorn and rejection. LBJ must have sensed the underlying irony of the dilemma in which he found himself, saying to a journalist in 1967, "If history indicts us for Vietnam, I think it will be for fighting a war without trying to stir up patriotism."[46] Had Johnson abandoned the Great Society and had he embraced the war in Vietnam as a great national crusade, much as Wilson and Roosevelt had done with domestic reform during the two world wars, then he might have saved his presidency, and perhaps even his historical reputation. But driven on by his enormous ego, he tried to triumph both at home and abroad, and he lost out in both endeavors, thereby jeopardizing his place in history.

Notes

1. For an evaluation of the earlier body of books on Lyndon Johnson see my essay "The Johnson Literature," in *Exploring the Johnson Years*, ed. Robert A. Divine (Austin: University of Texas Press, 1981), pp. 3–23. The most complete bibliography of books, articles, and dissertations on LBJ is the volume compiled by Craig Roell and members of the staff of the Johnson Library, *Lyndon B. Johnson: A Bibliography* (Austin: University of Texas Press, 1984).

2. Robert A. Caro, *The Years of Lyndon Johnson: The Path to Power* (New York: Knopf, 1982), pp. xix, xx.

3. Ibid., pp. 71, 457, 552.

4. Ibid., pp. 229, 552.

5. Ronnie Dugger, *The Politician: The Life and Times of Lyndon Johnson: The Drive for Power, from the Frontier to Master of the Senate* (New York: Norton, 1982), p. 184.

6. Ibid., p. 254.

7. Ibid., pp. 12, 15.

8. George Reedy, *Lyndon B. Johnson: A Memoir* (New York: Andrews & McMeel, 1982), p. xiv.

9. Ibid., p. 9.

10. Ibid., pp. 157, 158.

11. Ibid., p. 78.

12. Ibid., p. 158.

13. Ibid., p. 14.

14. Ibid., p. 159.

15. Vaughn Davis Bornet, *The Presidency of Lyndon B. Johnson* (Lawrence: University Press of Kansas, 1983), pp. 120, 341, 342. Hugh Davis Graham offers a detailed and critical view of Johnson's contributions to educational reform in *The Uncertain Triumph: Federal Education Policy in the Kennedy and Johnson Years* (Chapel Hill: University of North Carolina Press, 1984). While crediting the Great Society with giving enormous assistance to higher education, Graham is more critical of LBJ's efforts on behalf of elementary and secondary education. Johnson's decision in 1965 not to alter the aid-to-impacted-areas formula for funneling government aid to impoverished school districts resulted in legislation that "disproportionately aided the children of the middle class and even those who were well-to-do," rather than "the children of the poor." Graham attributes this decision to LBJ's fear that a more progressive formula might antagonize key figures in Congress and thus "would jeopardize the entire education bill" (*Uncertain Triumph*, pp. 75–76).

16. Bornet, *Presidency of Lyndon B. Johnson*, pp. 337, 331.

17. Ibid., pp. 331–32.

18. Ibid., p. 339.

19. Ibid., p. 348.

20. Allen J. Matusow, *The Unraveling of America: A History of Liberalism in the 1960s* (New York: Harper & Row, 1984), p. 133.

21. Ibid., p. 180. Steven F. Lawson gives Johnson equally high marks for his insistence on implementing the 1965 Voting Rights Act; between 1966 and 1968, the number of blacks who were eligible to vote in the Deep South rose from 41 percent to 61 percent (see *In Pursuit of Power: Southern Blacks and Electoral Politics, 1965–1982* (New York: Columbia University Press, 1985), p. 39.

22. Matusow, *Unraveling*, pp. 33, 59.

23. Ibid., p. 220.

24. Ibid., p. 270.

25. Ibid., p. 175.

26. Ibid., p. 395.

27. Charles Murray, *Losing Ground: American Social Policy, 1950–1980* (New York: Basic Books, 1984), pp. 57–58.

28. Ibid., pp. 43, 48.

29. Ibid., p. 9.

30. Ibid., p. 42; Matusow, *Unraveling*, p. 220. For a persuasive dissent from the view that the Great Society failed to overcome the problem of poverty see John E. Schwarz, *America's Hidden Success: A Reassessment of Twenty Years of Public Policy* (New York: Norton, 1983). Schwarz argues not only that poverty fell from 18 percent in 1960 to below 8 percent by the end of the 1970s but also that this achievement came as a result of deliberate government policy, not as a by-product of economic growth. Moreover, Schwarz contends that the uneven economic development of the 1970s, including the double-digit inflation, was the result of absorbing the baby-boom generation into the work force and was not a consequence of heavy government spending for either the Vietnam War or the Great Society. Between 1965 and 1980, some 29 million new workers joined the work force, thereby creating strains that Schwarz thinks the American economy handled remarkably well. Although he does not focus specifically on Lyndon Johnson and the Great

Society, Schwarz does offer a vigorous rebuttal to the claims of Matusow and Murray that the Great Society was a failure (*America's Hidden Success*, pp. 32, 39, 124–26, 131–32, 139).

31. Larry Berman, *Planning a Tragedy: The Americanization of the War in Vietnam* (New York: Norton, 1983), pp. 79–87.

32. Ibid., pp. 51, 93–94.

33. Ibid., pp. 112, 145.

34. Ibid., p. 126.

35. Ibid., pp. 93, 149.

36. Ibid., pp. 144, 145, 147, 149, 150.

37. Harry G. Summers, Jr., *On Strategy: A Critical Analysis of the Vietnam War* (New York: Dell, 1984), pp. 22–26. For a briefer statement of these views see Harry G. Summers, Jr., "Lessons: A Soldier's View," in *Vietnam as History: Ten Years after the Paris Peace Accords*, ed. Peter Braestrup (Washington, D.C.: University Press of America, 1984), pp. 109–14.

38. Summers, *On Strategy*, pp. 35, 43, 168.

39. Herbert Y. Schandler, "America and Vietnam: The Failure of Strategy, 1965–67," in *Vietnam as History*, pp. 26, 32. Schandler's earlier book was *The Unmaking of a President: Lyndon Johnson and Vietnam* (Princeton, N.J.: Princeton University Press, 1977).

40. Norman Podhoretz, *Why We Were in Vietnam* (New York: Simon & Schuster, 1982), pp. 80, 107–8.

41. Kathleen J. Turner, *Lyndon Johnson's Dual War: Vietnam and the Press* (Chicago: University of Chicago Press, 1985), p. 6.

42. Ibid., pp. 146–50, 164–65.

43. George McT. Kahin, *Intervention: How America Became Involved in Vietnam* (New York: Knopf, 1986), p. 245.

44. Ibid., pp. 239, 383.

45. Berman, *Planning*, p. 150.

46. Larry Berman, "Waiting for Smoking Guns: Presidential Decision-making and the Vietnam War, 1965–67," in *Vietnam as History*, p. 21.

Part 1 | The Impact of Vietnam

2 | Lyndon Johnson and the Antiwar Opposition

Charles DeBenedetti

FOR AMERICANS, the Vietnam War was most extraordinary in that it was not so much a fight against enemies abroad as it was an internal struggle over their own national identity. Vietnam in American history meant—and still means—a struggle among Americans over the nature of their interests, their values, and the very meaning of their country and their purpose. If ethnocentric, this understanding of the war is consistent with the fact that the Vietnam question in the United States turned recurrently around three realities: first, Vietnam existed as a vital American national interest because—and as long as—Washington policy makers said that it was; second, the nature and the cost of the U.S. commitment in Vietnam were always arguable issues in the United States after 1963; and, third, the domestic debate over Vietnam embraced more a cluster of historical, geopolitical, and moral symbols than any question of America's literal survival. Americans argued about Vietnam in historical terms drawn from the meaning of Munich and Korea, the Cuban missile crisis, and the Nuremberg war-crimes trials. They argued in geopolitical terms about the meaning of dominoes, enclaves, and wars of national liberation. And most of all, they argued in moral terms over the significance of Vietnam to perceptions of American perseverance and reliability and to substantive matters of correct policy formation, the proportion between ends and means, and the proper bounds of individual conscience, democratic debate, and official accountability. For ten years, Americans waged over Vietnam a war by metaphor for the sake of symbols of meaning to themselves. They saw Vietnam as a "proving ground," a "showcase," an "experiment," and, most especially, a "test" of what the American people could and should do. They believed that the real stakes in the war centered upon the question, as Dean Rusk once put it, of "what kind of people we are."[1]

From beginning to end, Lyndon Johnson tried to steer the United States down what he conceived to be a middle course of involvement in Vietnam. Claiming an inherited national commitment, the president sought to maintain an anti-Communist regime in Saigon at the same time as he shunted aside demands either to carry the war beyond Vietnam or to undertake military de-escalation and early peace negotiations. Inevitably, Johnson's course produced domestic discontent. On the Right, a powerful constellation of critics urged the president to unleash the U.S. military to conduct more massive bombing campaigns throughout Indochina, a blockade of North Vietnam, an invasion of the North, and, if necessary, war against China and Russia. On the Left, a less powerful but surprisingly vocal combination of critics called for decreased U.S. military involvement and a greater effort toward a negotiated peace, if not immediate U.S. withdrawal, on the grounds that the American intervention was morally unjustifiable, corrupting of American democracy, and grossly disproportionate in cost to the peoples of Indochina and to America's broader security interests. This was the antiwar opposition. Too diverse and fractious to sustain an ongoing movement, antiwar critics improvised an opposition that involved an unusually broad range of disaffected citizens on two levels of action. They made up a political force that questioned the workability and morality of U.S. policy; and they galvanized a cultural rebellion that joined dissatisfied blacks, women, students, and undifferentiated others in attacking the assumptions and priorities of Cold War life in the United States. The purpose of this paper is to review the origin, dimensions, and workings of this opposition and then to consider how Lyndon Johnson and his administration tried to come to terms with it during the course of the president's struggle to vindicate the value of the U.S. intervention and to emphasize the unbreakability of his determination to prevail in Vietnam.

I

The antiwar opposition was a multilayered, many-sided phenomenon that originated in dissent against Washington's deepening involvement in Vietnam from 1962 to 1964, crystallized in protest against the initiation of the U.S. air war against North Vietnam in 1965, and proliferated with the escalation over the next four years of U.S. involvement in ground combat. Politically informed and highly articulate, this opposition began first among tiny bases of policy dissent seeded throughout American public life. One base existed among such dissident members of the nation's policy-shaping elite as journalist Walter Lippmann and Senate Foreign Relations Committee chairman J. William Fulbright. European in their orientation and conservative in temperament, these elite critics believed that the U.S. involvement in Vietnam was marginal to our true security interests, subversive of improved Soviet-American relations, and needlessly provocative to China. They favored multilateral negotiations toward the neutralization of all Indochina, a more modest enunciation of claimed U.S. commitments in Asia, and a strengthened American naval presence in the Western Pacific. Fundamentally, they saw Vietnam as irrelevant to America; and they tried to change U.S. policy by winning the president to their ways by means of their words and influence.

A second base of antiwar opposition gathered across a broad range of internationalists, liberals, and pacifists who were ordinarily identified as Adlai E. Stevenson Democrats, eastern establishment Republicans, or Democratic Socialists in the style of Norman M. Thomas. Some, such as the *Catholic Worker*'s Dorothy Day, were religious pacifists who were committed in conscience to the ways of active nonviolence. Others, such as the editor Norman Cousins, were well-known advocates of a strengthened United Nations. Many, such as the pediatrician Benjamin M. Spock and the housewife Dagmar Wilson, were concerned citizens who had first participated through such new-fashioned organizations as SANE (National Committee for a Sane Nuclear Policy) and Women Strike for Peace in more recent public-policy debates over a treaty to ban atmospheric nuclear tests and over the possibilities of a Soviet-American détente.[2] Terrified by the Cuban missile crisis and then encouraged by the 1963 Partial Test-ban Treaty, this collection of peace liberals had rallied to support Lyndon Johnson against the anti-Communist crusade of Barry M. Goldwater in 1964 and had looked, with Johnson's victory, toward a real improvement in cold-war tensions. Instead they got Vietnam. Outraged by the initiation of Johnson's war against North Vietnam, this mélange of housewives, businessmen, intellectuals, clergy, and students condemned the U.S. military escalation for having diverted the country from America's preeminent interest in eased cold-war tensions and in progress toward real disarmament. Peace liberals generally accepted the president's claim that the United States had both a national commitment and a moral right to intervene in Vietnamese affairs. But they wanted the president to subordinate American military power to social and political attempts that would effect a reformed pluralist South Vietnam that could successfully negotiate its own peace with the Communists. Fundamentally, they saw Vietnam as a distraction from America's larger interests in détente and disarmament; they tried to change U.S. policy by lobbying, letter writing, and demonstrating until Washington would see the rightness of their way.

A third base of antiwar opposition collected about a tiny but influential band of war resisters who looked to A. J. Muste and groups such as the War Resisters for direction in their personal commitment to overturn the war system and to promote social justice. Steeped in an individualistic ethic of nonviolent civil disobedience, war resisters such as the Catholic priests Philip and Daniel Berrigan saw no essential moral difference between the American and the Soviet power states; they assailed great-power interventionism in the Third World for containing the necessary advance there of revolutionary social change. Convinced that the United States had no moral right to intervene in Vietnamese life, they ignored demands for negotiations and called instead for an immediate American withdrawal from Vietnam. Fundamentally, they saw Vietnam as a crime and a sin; and they tried—as political moralists who believed that means determined the ends—to change U.S. policy by inspiring a revolution in national values through nonviolent acts of resistance and through disruption that would turn people away from war and toward the pursuit of justice.[3]

A fourth base of antiwar opposition centered about a radical Left that gained force at the beginning of the 1960s with the spreading southern civil-rights movement, increased student dissidence, and deepening impatience with the cost at home and abroad of continuing the cold war. In large measure, this renascent Left operated organizationally through Old Left sectarian Marxist groupings such as the pro-Soviet Communist party, the pro-Peking Progressive Labor party, the Trotskyist Socialist Workers party, and their various youth affiliates. In practice, however, the rising Left was identified with more eclectic action-oriented inventions of the New Left, such as the Student Nonviolent Coordinating Committee and Students for a Democratic Society, which combined a propensity for nonviolent direct action with a commitment to free the American people from racism and corporate bureaucratization for the sake of genuine participatory democracy. Advocates of radical domestic change who supported revolutionary Third-World socialist regimes such as Castro's Cuba, these leftists naturally attacked the U.S. involvement in Vietnam as an evasion of the need for domestic change and as a typical capitalistic attack upon impoverished colored peoples in rebellion. Fundamentally, they saw Vietnam as a mirror of American life; and they tried to change U.S. policy by fomenting, through local organizing, mass demonstrations, and the politics of provocation, a social revolution that would overturn the prevailing order of power and privilege in American life and, with it, the whole of the country's policy-making structure.[4]

Finally, beyond the active bases of antiwar discontent, there existed in the United States a sizable reservoir of unorganized but popular antiwar sentiment. Throughout the war years, public-opinion pollsters reported consistently high levels of support for peace negotiations, the one demand that was supported by the broadest range of antiwar critics. In addition, a number of other factors—including the general expectation that the war only would end in a compromise settlement anyway, contempt for America's South Vietnamese allies, and confusion over the very purposes of the war—aggravated the popular dislike for the war in ways that provided a large working space for vigorous expressions of antiwar opposition. Yet the general tolerance for dissent that was bred by popular distaste for the war never suggested popular approval of antiwar activism. On the contrary, poll data repeatedly indicated that if anything was more unpopular than the war, it was antiwar protesters.[5] Identified in the popular mind with discontented blacks and rowdy students, antiwar protesters were viewed as troublemaking deviants who took to the streets either because they were Communist dupes or because they simply wanted to let off steam. At worst, antiwar activists succeeded in provoking otherwise passive Americans into rallying in support of the president. At best, their efforts appeared irrelevant to the job of re-forming popular attitudes toward the war.[6]

In the light of widespread popular contempt for antiwar protesters, it seems reasonable to wonder why the opposition was never overwhelmed in a wave of popular antagonism. Certainly Lyndon Johnson wondered. Partly, it appears, the very social diffuseness of the opposition allowed it to survive the broad and abiding popular resentment that it encountered. Despite the popular stereotypes of protesting hippie youths, public-opinion analysts determined that the most remarkable feature of antiwar disaffection was the way in which it spread so evenly throughout the American political and social order, with noticeable strength only among women and blacks.[7] This democratic character of the dissent gave it a fluidity that frustrated antiwar activists in their attempts to organize a coherent mass opposition. Yet it also frustrated prowar nationalists in their attempts to single out and crush an identifiable opposition.

In a connected way, the irrepressibility of antiwar activism arose from the fact that it seethed with a greater popular rebellion against prevailing social codes and orthodoxies that caught up diverse people in protracted struggles over questions of rights and power in matters of race, sex, age, and class. From the local to the national level, Americans during the 1960s argued bitterly over such issues as welfare rights, dormitory regulations, equal employment opportunities, and beauty pageants. Inevitably, antiwar activists became identified in the popular mind with other demonstrating deviants in a development that both strengthened and contained the force of their dissent. "Beards are beards. Marches are marches," wrote one reporter; and both beards and marches were detested by most of the population.[8] Yet the very popular identification and detestation of deviant antiwar activists allowed them to swim with other social dissidents in a larger sea of "pluralistic intolerance."[9] Because popular antagonism toward all deviants was sharp but diffuse, antiwar dissidents managed to avoid any devastating concentrated attack until significant chunks of elitist sentiment had turned against the war and had thus granted them fuller legitimacy and even protection.

In practice, members of the antiwar opposition manifested their differences with the administration's policies through tactics that ranged from individual letter writing to nationally coordinated mass protests. At first their efforts were mostly educational or attention-grabbing attempts to demonstrate the existence of other ways of resolving the American predicament in Indochina. In 1965, critics wrote protest letters, gathered at teach-ins, or joined in a few mass marches that were sponsored by young radicals in the Students for a Democratic Society or by older liberals in SANE. Some critics tried to communicate their horror with U.S. war policy more graphically. At least three pacifists immolated themselves in 1965 to demonstrate symbolic unity with Vietnamese Buddhist protest suicides. A number of American intellectuals, inspired by a similar action taken by French intellectuals during the Algerian War, circulated a public letter denouncing the U.S. war effort and pledging to withhold their support from that effort. Housewives and students in the San Francisco Bay area tried, by means of nonviolent direct action, to block the movement of troop trains to the Oakland Army Terminal. Bands of radical pacifists and war resisters organized well-publicized rituals to burn draft cards.

Early in 1966 the opposition's educational impetus received a powerful boost when Senator Fulbright led the Senate Foreign Relations Committee in a nationally televised inquiry into U.S. policy in Asia that broadcast the antiescalation sentiments of elitist policy critics such as George F. Kennan and retired army General James M. Gavin. The Fulbright hearings made dissent all the more legitimate and the public questioning of U.S. war policy all the more acceptable. Shortly afterwards, a New York–based coalition of antiwar activists collected in the Spring Mobilization Committee to End the War in Vietnam, which poured fifty thousand people into a one-day street protest against administration policy and established a pattern of seasonal antiwar rallies in different cities from New York to the Bay area.

Meanwhile, on different college campuses, local antiwar dissidents worked to convert visceral antidraft resentment into antiwar activism; and young white radicals, who were being shoved out of the civil-rights movement by the exclusionary drive of black-power nationalism, pressed forward in their attempts to adapt the spirit of the country's spreading ghetto uprisings to American universities and to antiwar dissent. Overwhelmingly, however, antiwar opponents persisted during 1966 in the ordinary work of education, witness, and conversion. They collected protest petitions, conducted public vigils in open expression of their concerns, and tried to encourage congressional antiwar critics, mostly in the liberal wing of the Democratic party.

Early in 1967, radicals within the antiwar opposition talked of moving "from protest to resistance," while liberals worked to preserve the opposition's tactical nonviolence and to prepare for the 1968 presidential election. Cheered by the rise of a white hippie counterculture, which gathered in defiance of all authority, and convinced that ghetto uprisings were producing a revolutionary black guerrilla movement in the United States, radical leftists such as David Dellinger and Jerry Rubin tried to rally individual resistance to the war in disruptive antidraft actions, campus sit-ins against corporate and military recruiters, and, in October, a climactic March on the Pentagon to Confront the Warmakers. Partly theatrics and partly a *cri de coeur*, the confrontation at the Pentagon between some thirty-five thousand protesters and some three thousand U.S. troops and marshals featured many speeches, more confusion, and some sporadic clashes between radical adventurers and baton-wielding officials. The Pentagon was saved. But the mood of the country became more sour, and fear of greater social convulsions became more palpable.

Distressed over intensifying domestic tensions, peace liberals struggled in their attempts to organize a political challenge to the president until early December, when Minnesota's Senator Eugene McCarthy announced his intention to contest Johnson and his war policies in the Democratic presidential primaries. Aside from some speculation as to its relationship to Robert Kennedy's intentions, McCarthy's candidacy made little impression upon top party planners and pundits who were involved in serious thinking about the 1968 campaign. But it lent a new dimension—and a sharper polarity—to the country's organized antiwar opposition. While peace liberals rushed to the senator's support, radical activists denounced McCarthy's candidacy as a trap and a diversion from the prior need for disruptive direct action in the streets. It was time, they said, for politics of deeds, not words. Angry and divided, antiwar dissidents thus raced into the winter of 1968 with a sense of fresh hope that was swathed in fear and desperation. After thirty months of struggle, they had won neither concentrated popular sentiment nor significant partisan support to their side. But they had survived; and they did stand ready to make and exploit new opportunities of the kind that came rushing across the country with unexpected ferocity in 1968.[10]

II

Lyndon Johnson and other members of his administration contended with the antiwar opposition in light of their conception of the opposition, which derived, in turn, from their conception of the war. For all practical purposes, these conceptions were defined by the president, who approached the matter of war and peace in accordance with a number of axioms drawn from his Texas upbringing and from a generation of experience in national politics. First among these axioms was Johnson's faith in the American national mission to secure world peace through military strength and demonstrated toughness. An intense nationalist whose pride in his country bordered on nativism, Johnson not only believed that the United States possessed a redemptive mission in the world but also that individual Americans drew the literal possibility for eternal life from the blessing of their nationality. The " 'only thing' " that an ordinary person has, he once told Bill Moyers, " 'that gives him immortality other than his belief—he may be an atheist—is his citizenship.' " When " 'you say I am an American, you're saying I'm as immortal as this Republic.' "[11]

Most commonly, Johnson's vision of peace through American national success expressed itself in his reverence for America's armed forces and in his more personal commitment to stand tough. A martial Texan who took such pride in his own military service that he always wore the emblem of his World War II Silver Star on his suit lapel, the president believed that American military forces represented the real instrument of peace in his time.[12] He was an ardent proponent of the need for peace through superior armed strength; and in a reciprocal way, he had a deep fear of showing any sign of irresolution or weakness. "If there was anything that Johnson feared during his White House residence," wrote reporter Hugh Sidey, "it was that the historians might say he was not a brave leader." He worried incessantly that if he did not lead his country to victory in Vietnam, he would be revealed as " 'a coward. An unmanly man. A man without a spine.' " If Johnson was sure of anything, it was that he was not " 'going to go down in history as the first American President who lost a war.' " He would never be "an appeaser President."[13]

In Johnson's mind, American national pride, as manifested in military strength and personal toughness, was the historically proven prerequisite for international peace. As a New Deal loyalist during the 1930s, the president believed that Washington's prewar attempts at the diplomatic appeasement of nazism had only encouraged the totalitarian aggressors, postponed the coming of World War II, and made it more costly because of the delay. He was not about to let the history of the thirties begin again in Vietnam. "The central lesson of our time is that the appetite of aggression is never satisfied," he once declared; "to withdraw from one battlefield means only to prepare for the next."[14] Determined to stand tough on one battlefield, Johnson insisted that the United States must fight on in Vietnam, not only to repel totalitarian aggression but also to preclude any sign of weakness that might mistakenly tempt the aggressors into further adventures, rouse a wrathful America, and set off World War III.

A second axiom that was basic to the president's thinking on questions of war and peace involved his fear of right-wing power in American politics and his own limited faith in popular democracy. As a Texas Democrat who had observed first-hand the sweep of McCarthyism, the crazed partisan quarrel over who had "lost" China, and the subsequent rise of the Sun Belt Right of Barry Goldwater, Johnson properly appreciated the power of right-wing forces in national politics, particularly in Congress and the Republican party. He had, conversely, little respect for the political effectiveness of the American Left. In fact, Johnson insisted throughout his presidency that any American failure in Vietnam would unleash a right-wing backlash that would destroy the Left and thereby any standing hopes for domestic reform in the United States. In part, his repeated warnings of the danger of right-wing frustration was a tactic designed to undercut left-wing antiwar sentiment. In part, too, however, Johnson believed it. He believed that American democracy was vulnerable to destructive divisions that were being worked by political extremists; and he believed that rightists overwhelmingly possessed the necessary means to do the job.

In a related way, Johnson loved democracy with an intensity that was offset only by distrust in its good sense. The president felt real compassion for social underdogs and weaker people, whether at home or abroad; nevertheless, he felt an equally powerful skepticism toward the practical implications of popular rule. Remembering his early hero, Louisiana's Democratic Senator Huey P. Long, Johnson craved the chance to do good for the sake of the little people. But with Huey still in mind, Johnson feared that uncontrolled democratic rule would produce the kind of demagoguery that would foment mob irrationality and the worst threats to orderly constitutional democracy. Johnson preferred to let America's sleeping democracy lie. He did not, however, want it to lie too soundly. Convinced that the American people were vacillating between ethnocentric passivity and exploitable aggressiveness, the president feared that if left to its own instincts, American democracy would revert to the kind of dangerous isolationism that had misled the dictators and had brought on World War II. At the same time he worried that if excited too much, the democracy would become inflamed by right-wing nationalists in a neo-McCarthyite crusade that would wreck the Democratic party and the American system itself. He therefore intended, once more, to steer the middle course. He intended to fight a war for peace in Vietnam that would rouse the American people from their instinct for isolationism at the same time that he was containing any demagogic right-wing attempt to rally popular blood lust against domestic enemies. There were only three requirements for success in such an effort: the war would have to be short, victorious, and undisturbed by complaints from left-wing critics.[15]

Johnson's fear of the Right and his distrust of democracy combined with his established success as a legislative operator to fashion the third axiom that governed his attitude toward the antiwar opposition: the belief that what happened in public life was the result of hidden scheming, elitist manipulation, or malevolent conspirators. As a man who had grown up in a political family and who had spent most of his life in legislative wrangling, Johnson had little reason to believe that political issues sprang fully clothed from the breast of the people. Shrewd and suspicious, he rather assumed that politics was the realm of shakers and movers, who operated through fronts, agents, and dupes. Temperamentally disinclined to consider the possibility of historical accident or ambiguity, Johnson could not believe that political events and developments took place without an identifiable (if well hidden) cause. Instead, he was prone toward suspecting that conspiratorial forces commonly worked their effects in everyday life; and his own working habits reinforced this mind set. As a Senate leader who understood that knowledge was power, Johnson had a notorious appetite for information relating to politicians' private lives, which he used to good advantage; and he carried this habit into the White House for the same purposes. Hubert Humphrey once observed that Johnson was " 'a walking FBI,' " with a preference for more salacious and salable gossip.[16] Politics, for this president, was a highly personal, ill-regulated arena of bartering and bashing that blended naked self-interest with loyalty to the larger system. It was no place—unless inspired by craven elitist factions or Communist manipulation and direction—for the serious questioning of life-and-death matters such as the war in Vietnam.

Johnson never developed any coherent understanding of the anti-war opposition. His attitudes and approaches toward critics of the administration were rather fragmented, inconsistent, and sometimes hallucinatory; and they varied in their expression according to precisely who was issuing the criticisms and, therefore, who, according to Johnson, was really behind the attack. Within his official family the president brooked no serious opposition to policies. Johnson accepted dissenting views among his advisers during the months prior to the Americanization of the war in summer 1965. But once U.S. air power and ground troops had been committed, he steam-rolled any internal expressions of doubt or disaffection. Undersecretary of State George Ball, a policy adviser who had distinguished himself during administration policy debates by his opposition to the Americanization of the war, tried quietly to advance his "heretical views within a limited circle" at the White House.[17] But publicly he avowed his loyalty to the president's ways by attacking antiwar critics and by insisting that " 'the one thing we have to do is to win this damned war.' "[18]

While Johnson demanded loyalty within his administration, he felt and acted toward other expressions of opposition in a surprisingly wide variety of ways. Senate majority leader Mike Mansfield sent stacks of memoranda that were critical of administration policy to the White House; but his criticisms were customarily cast aside because he was personally withdrawn and politically inoffensive. Oregon's Democratic Senator Wayne Morse freely excoriated the president for his Vietnam policies. Yet Johnson treated Morse as a high-minded maverick and worked comfortably with him on other matters of mutual interest. Senator Fulbright, however, presented a special case. A former Rhodes scholar who had meshed his cosmopolitan interests with the crude provincialism of Arkansas politics, Fulbright figured in Johnson's eyes as the lead running dog on Capitol Hill for the dissident eastern establishment elite, which was centered around Walter Lippmann, the *New York Times*, and the Georgetown crowd of diplomatic professionals. According to Johnson, these eastern upper-crust dissenters were chronic complainers who looked up to Europe in awe and down on Asia with racist contempt. Fixing his anger upon

Fulbright, the president dismissed him as Senator Halfbright, the "stud duck of the opposition," and a "frustrated old woman" who gossiped with the elite while voting in the Senate for the "sweatshop and racism."[19] Johnson professed to expect nothing better from the country's foreign-policy establishment. Justly or not, the president believed that because of its prejudices against his southern birth and his mediocre schooling, the northeastern elite would never approve of him, his presidency, or his policies. They opposed him in Vietnam because they wanted him to lose.

Sometimes Johnson's resentment toward dissenters in the northeastern elite would spread into wholesale attacks upon the communications media. More commonly, however, the president's suspicions of antiwar media critics were limited to certain columnists, such as Joseph Kraft or Mary McGrory, who were identified as being sympathetic to Johnson's real *bête noire* and most feared antiwar critic, Robert F. Kennedy. Sniped at after 1966 by Kennedy loyalists such as Richard Goodwin and Arthur M. Schlesinger, Jr., and always anxious over latent pro-Kennedy sentiment within the Democratic party, the president showed acute apprehension after 1966 with the softly critical views of New York's junior senator (or, as he was commonly called around the White House, " 'The Little Shit' ");[20] and he deeply feared that Kennedy's emergence as an antiwar candidate would fracture the party and interfere with the administration's prosecution of a successful war effort.

Johnson expected criticism from members of the country's policy-shaping elite and from ambitious figures such as Robert Kennedy. The president did not expect, however, an irrepressible rash of antiwar street protests, and he was temperamentally unprepared to cope with the anger and frustrations that boiled through various public demonstrations, especially among radical college students. He resented antiwar street demonstrations mounted by older Americans, who should have known as well as he the history lessons of the 1930s. But he was amazingly tolerant of youthful protesters, partly because he attributed their opposition to ignorance born of generational differences and partly because of simple bafflement with their behavior. " 'The young people that my daughters bring around are not like that,' " he told one friend. " 'I just can't believe it.' "[21] On one occasion the president asked national-security adviser Walt Rostow how one generation could simultaneously yield brave fighting marines and hippie protesters; and Rostow, characteristically enough, came up with a comforting answer: "If many of the dissidents actually were in Vietnam and faced the reality of the problem, they would change."[22]

Mostly, however, Johnson accepted youth protest as an inexplicable fact of his presidential life. When the subject came up at the family dinner table, his brother remembered, "Lyndon would wearily nod his head and look away with a baffled expression in his eyes."[23]

Johnson's tolerance of youth protest was all the more remarkable in view of his fundamental hatred of open and serious dissent over policy. The president abhorred the public airing of disagreements over major policies. According to Senator Frank Church, Johnson's primary objection to the 1966 Senate Foreign Relations Committee hearings on Vietnam was that they were being conducted under media klieg lights that generated wide public attention. He could not "understand why Americans who dissent can't do their dissenting in private," where they could be brushed off with kind words and claims to having superior intelligence information.[24] "If all these people," the president once said in reference to congressional and clerical dissidents, "wanted to help their President they would come in here and say to me privately what they are saying to the press" and would not broadcast their criticisms " 'through my intelligence bulletin via Peking, or Hanoi, or Moscow.' "[25] Periodically, Johnson's fundamental loathing and suspicion of antiwar dissent erupted into wild charges that his critics were really active instruments of Communist subversion. In the gentler versions of these harangues, the president declared that his domestic enemies went on " 'jags' which pretty much originate in the Communist world" and then "find their way to American dissidents."[26] On other occasions, his attacks would degenerate into fantastic conspiratorial claims that it was " 'the Russians who are behind the whole thing.' " Soviet agents were in " 'constant touch with anti-war senators,' " he confided at one White House meeting, and " 'think up things for the senators to say.' " Wasn't it funny, he said to another listener, that the Soviet ambassador's car was always in front of the home of *New York Times* columnist James Reston " 'the night before Reston delivered a blast on Vietnam?' "[27] Johnson always claimed that he, the FBI, and the CIA knew what was " 'really going on.' " But his claims and charges only aggravated the concern, among attentive listeners, over his grip on reality and his capacity to deal with the real strength of the dissent.[28]

In practice, Johnson's attempts to deal with the antiwar opposition changed between 1963 and 1969 from grudging tolerance to outright attacks and then to pained acceptance. In the process, the president's reaction to the opposition careened unpredictably between his proud contention, on the one side, that domestic dissent was the price of working democracy and his dark suggestions, on the other side, that the opposition was a Communist plot. In the beginning, the president appeared patient and generous. During 1963 the Johnson White House politely dismissed expressions of opposition that were voiced by such elitist critics as Lippmann and such peace liberals as Norman Thomas, and it ignored altogether the few scattered street protests that were mounted by radical pacifists and leftists. In August 1964, shortly after the Tonkin Gulf raids, national-security adviser McGeorge Bundy warned the president of "mutterings around the edges" that the administration was not "doing as well as we should with the very first team of businessmen, bankers, et al."[29] Otherwise, the administration did not expect any serious expressions of domestic opposition that could not be managed with the right combination of intimidation and moderation.

Early in 1965, after the inauguration of the U.S. air war against North Vietnam, the administration continued to treat its domestic critics more as a nuisance than as a serious factor in policy. The State Department dispatched a "truth team" to different university campuses to offset the criticisms that had been generated by different antiwar teach-ins; and it lent covert support, in "a major agit-prop effort," to a prowar citizens group called the American Friends of Vietnam, which was headed by Wesley Fishel, a former CIA station chief in Saigon and now a professor at Michigan State University.[30] The State Department paid deference to prominent antiwar critics such as Walter Lippmann and Norman Cousins; and it politely met with petitioning pacifists whom White House aides privately dismissed as "very limp young men."[31] Altogether, the administration played its response to the domestic opposition in a very low key. Expecting quick military success in Vietnam, the White House left the management of antiwar critics in 1965 to local prowar enthusiasts, such as New York State's VFW commander, Vincent DiMattina, who tried to make a citizen's arrest of a draft-card-burning pacifist, and to Connecticut's Democratic Senator Thomas Dodd, who led the Senate Internal Security Committee in arguing that the teach-in movement was manufactured in Moscow.[32]

The president himself stood calmly above the fray, even though he privately champed at the bit for the chance to lash back at his critics. In the White House, he systematically strong-armed congressional skeptics with the renowned "Johnson treatment," nagging and cajoling them to withhold their criticisms for the sake of a united domestic front. In meetings with the press, he declined to describe his critics as appeasers, and he expressed doubt that domestic dissent was injuring the U.S. war effort. Instead, he defended dissent as one of the values that America was fighting for in Vietnam; and he refused to comment on charges that insofar as the opposition hinted of domestic disunity and a fatal lack of will, it falsely encouraged Hanoi to resist and thereby prolonged the war. Privately, however, the president complained that he could not act upon his deeper suspicion that the opposition was, at least, a source of false encouragement to the North Vietnamese or, at most, a Communist plot. He said at a cabinet meeting in June, 1965:

> We are confronted with a dilemma, unquestionably, that is difficult to face up to, as a result of the extremes of McCarthyism and the extremes of Goldwaterism. The people have more or less put the Communist menace on the back burner. You immediately become a dangerous character or suspect if you express strong feelings about the system and some question about the activities of Communists as a result of these other two extremes.
>
> I don't want us to get into that dangerous position. I love this system, and I don't want us to either be addicts of some other system or tools of some other system. The thing that troubles me more about our government than nearly anything else is that they will see a line from Peking, Hanoi and Moscow about a month ahead of the time I see it there. I see it being openly espoused by so-called devotees of our system. It is almost taken in text.[33]

Yet, for all his doubts about the sources of the opposition, the president declined at first to attack his critics more frontally, and with good reason. For one thing, he did not want to incite the Right and to jeopardize domestic gains in civil rights in building the Great Society. For another, he wanted to "be careful not to get the country on an anti-communist binge because it would tear up what we had gained" with the Soviets in arms-control negotiations and in prospects for détente.[34] It was "hard to wage a major war against one communist group without having the public oppose all communists." As it was, the president thought it was "amazing" that the American people were so willing to fight Communists in Vietnam without clamoring for war against Communists everywhere.[35] Finally, Johnson did not want to lead a popular crusade against an antiwar opposition that was already the object of general scorn and contempt, for fear of inflaming domestic politics beyond his own management and control. Johnson aimed to fight and win at home and abroad on his own terms. Like his personalized handling of the war, in which he refused to allow the Joint Chiefs of Staff full rein or even to establish a central directorate for strategic planning and operations, the president refused to attack his domestic critics with the kind of unrestrained force that might escape from his direction. He intended to lose control neither of the American position in Southeast Asia nor of American politics at home.

The American people in the meantime rallied impressively to support the war effort. Yet neither their numbers nor their enthusiasm slowed the growth of the war or the spread of antiwar opposition. Instead, the many illogical claims and unanswered questions that the White House raised during the 1965 U.S. intervention in the Dominican Republic and that it accentuated during the winter 1966 bombing pause over North Vietnam helped to broaden the "credibility gap" that dogged the president in his attempts to quiet dissent and to fashion a united domestic front behind his policies. Persisting attacks from elitist figures such as Fulbright, demonstrated antidraft resentment on different campuses, and popular apprehensions over a great war with China only aggravated suspicions about the wisdom of Johnson's war and prompted the president into making more aggressive attacks on antiwar critics. In March, 1966, the president lambasted his critics as "Nervous Nellies" who were turning "on their leaders, and on their country, and on our own fighting men."[36] He lent support to the popular suspicion that dissenters were actually prolonging and working to help the failing Communists to "victory on a silver platter in Southeast Asia."[37] Then he abruptly pulled back from the attack, urging only that his critics "do their dissenting in private" and declaiming: "I am not angry; I am not even sorrowful. I sometimes think of the words, 'God forgive them, for they know not what they do.' "[38]

Johnson's zigzag approach toward the antiwar opposition during 1966 reflected differences within the administration over how to deal with White House critics. Some staff aides, such as Jack Valenti, wanted more aggressive attacks upon the diverse "doves, the [Yale University historian Staughton] Lynd-liners and the [New York] Times," whose criticisms were "all of a piece." "Slowly," he warned the president, "but like lava pouring over a volcano, the flow is resistless—first, one concession then another, and then another, and as we adjust to each new position, the Lynd-liners go onto the next retreat point" until Fulbright and his allies picked up "the new line" and cut deeper into the American position.[39] Other aides, however, feared that the opposition only indicated a problem that was far broader and more dangerous: namely, antiwar disaffection among "the relatively well-informed internationalist middle class," who had been the "strongest supporters" of every major U.S. foreign-policy initiative since 1940 and who were not convinced of the wisdom of Vietnam.[40] Indiscriminate attacks upon antiwar critics only aggravated the suspicion and uneasiness that was being felt among all those " 'suburban families with college-age kids' " who were " 'getting to be troubled about the war' " and who certainly did not like being called traitors.[41]

In the eyes of public-opinion pollsters, 1967 was "the year of the hawk." Popular support for a larger U.S. military effort rose so sharply that at one point during the spring, one out of four Americans favored a nuclear attack upon North Vietnam if that were what would be necessary for victory.[42] Popular resentment toward militant expressions of antiwar protest increased proportionately. Yet neither growing popular support for the war nor hostility toward its opponents cleared the way for Washington's success in Vietnam. On the contrary, for the Johnson administration, 1967 was the year of greatest challenge, with rampant domestic disorders, especially in the country's black ghettoes, rising to new levels of destructiveness at the same time as some of the president's key policy advisers were coming to the conclusion that the United States might be tied down for another five to ten years of war in Vietnam. With domestic turmoil spreading and with the war mounting in cost with no end in sight, the Johnson administration decided to persist in its prevailing war strategy in Indochina at the same time as it was opening a broader attack upon its domestic critics while trying to contain any right-wing onslaught that would only aggravate the country's racial and political crises and complicate Washington's plans for protracted war. It was a high-risk strategy; but it was the only one that Johnson saw available to him if he were to win at home and abroad.

During the first half of the year the president continued his zigzag approach to the opposition, righteously affirming the importance of "responsible" democratic dissent at the same time as he was blasting his critics for encouraging the Communists and for undercutting the GIs in Vietnam. Even as he zigzagged, however, Johnson shifted his approach in a more repressive direction. In April, shortly after Martin Luther King had declared both his final break with Johnson and his plans to connect the civil-rights movement and the antiwar opposition, a White House aide declared that King "has thrown in with the commies" and insisted that "the Communist origins of this operation must be exposed, the leaders discredited and the flag-burners and draft-card burners jailed."[43] Shortly after receiving a presidential summons to Washington, General William C. Westmoreland declared at a press conference that the enemy was on the verge of defeat in the field and that it took hope of ultimate success only because of the carping of antiwar critics. White House aide Robert Kintner received Johnson's encouragement in asking Attorney General W. Ramsey Clark to prepare a report "that would show that there was common planning throughout the United States of public demonstrations, riots in colleges," and related disorders, a report that might be shared with friendly media allies such as the *Washington Post*'s Benjamin C. Bradlee.[44]

During the second half of 1967 the administration launched its most serious attempt to subvert its domestic opposition and to rally popular sentiment behind its policies. The White House offensive advanced along several salients on two fronts. On the positive side, administration officials put together an interagency White House Vietnam Information Group, for the purpose of developing more favorable news coverage of the war. With the help of former Illinois Senator Paul H. Douglas, they also invented the prestigious Committee for Peace with Freedom in Vietnam, which boasted former presidents Dwight D. Eisenhower and Harry S. Truman as cochairmen and which purported to speak for the " 'silent center' " of prowar American opinion.[45] General Westmoreland returned once more under White House orders to tour the country, with hints that a victorious end to the war was within sight. And the president pressed his supporters to the attack on their critics. Gripped in the "sheer battering of emotions" in a White House that was nearly possessed by "a feeling of being under siege," Johnson told his cabinet that "it is time that this Administration stopped sitting back and taking it from the Vietnam critics." "Every day," he complained, "Senators attack us and return to the attack encouraged by our silence," while "professional agitators in our own party" were trying to wreck the party and others were spending "huge sums to set Labor against us . . . [and] set up Martin Luther King."[46] " 'We have got a psychological war as well as a military war on our hands,' " the president declared, " 'and the Communists are winning the psychological war with our help.' "[47] All that was going to change.

On the negative front, the administration also moved more aggressively to discredit and disrupt the opposition. In August, two years after the FBI had first started to compile derogatory dossiers on different antiwar dissidents, the president instructed the director of the CIA, Richard Helms, to begin monitoring the opposition in a program of surveillance (and, later, disruption) that would become institutionalized shortly thereafter as Operation CHAOS. Although the agency failed to document Johnson's belief in the subversive sources of the opposition, the president privately advised a group of congressmen that a secret CIA report demonstrated irrefutably that the opposition was Communist controlled. Led by House minority leader Gerald R. Ford, the congressmen publicly urged the president to publish the CIA report. But the administration declined to release the document, and it dodged questions as to whether it really believed that the opposition was Communist manufactured.[48] In the White House, however, the president made no secret of his suspicions of the hidden sources of increasingly disruptive antiwar activism. " 'I'm not going to let the Communists take this government and they're doing it right now,' " he said to his foreign-policy advisers in early November, 1967. " 'I told the Attorney General that I am not going to let 200,000 of these people ruin everything for the 200 million Americans. I've got my belly full of seeing these people put on a Communist plane and shipped all over this country. I want someone to carefully look at who leaves this country, where they go, and why they are going, and if they're going to Hanoi, how are we going to keep them from getting back into this country.' "[49] Shortly thereafter, the Justice Department indicted Dr. Benjamin Spock and four other prominent protesters on charges of conspiring to counsel and abet the defiance of draft laws.

Convinced that "the principal battleground is in domestic opinion," the president called together a number of eastern elitist figures, known as the Wise Men, who had first met in July, 1965, in order to counsel him on the effectiveness of U.S. war policy and on ways of rallying stronger popular support.[50] A few, such as Robert D. Murphy, declared that the country really needed "a hate complex directed at Ho Chi Minh similar to Hitler."[51] Former Secretary of State Dean G. Acheson proposed a nationwide network of prowar committees. Although unable to agree on a common strategy for rallying domestic support, the assembled advisers did agree that "one of the few things that helps us right now is public distaste for the violent doves."[52] They also agreed that "the most serious single cause of domestic disquiet about the war" was in "the prospect of endless inconclusive fighting," which continued to be the core of prevailing administration strategy and Washington's only current hope of success.[53] Unsure about how to rally popular support to a two-year-old policy of frustration, the Wise Men suggested that the president undertake two concurrent strategies. In the short run, they proposed that the administration seize the public-relations offensive by emphasizing U.S. military progress and the " 'light at the end of the tunnel' instead of the battles, deaths and danger."[54] For the long haul, they suggested that "the only effective way of changing public attitudes at home" was "a redirection of strategy and emphasis" in the war, which would "make it plain that we are over the hump" in Vietnam and would "establish a pattern of gradually decreasing cost that would be endurable for the *Five or Ten Years* in the long pull."[55] Paradoxically, the Wise Men endorsed the prevailing administration war strategy; but they did not know how to win the domestic struggle over that strategy except by radically altering it.

With the Wise Men's support, the president pressed the administration's counteroffensive throughout the winter of 1967/68, making the case for U.S. military progress while blasting antiwar critics for their "storm trooper tactics" and for their craven willingness to "surrender."[56] Public support for the president's position shot up impressively. Then, starting in late January, a triphammer series of incredible shocks—including the North Korean seizure of the U.S. intelligence ship *Pueblo* and the Communist Tet offensive in Vietnam—set off rocket fires of domestic anger and confusion. While U.S. and South Vietnamese forces were fighting hard to deal the Communists a costly military defeat, the political and psychological shocks of Tet, combined with the *Pueblo* humiliation, a gathering international economic crisis, the need for a tax increase to pay for the war without increasing inflation, the country's ongoing racial strife, and the onrush of presidential-year politics, had a shattering effect among both elitist policy shapers and the voting electorate. Early in March a rush of anti-administration resentment in New Hampshire handed Senator McCarthy 42 percent of the Democratic primary vote and a striking moral victory. Four days later, New York Senator Robert Kennedy, whom Johnson most feared as his rival on the antiwar Left, announced his entrance into the Democratic presidential sweepstakes. Along with the country's other major presidential candidates, both McCarthy and Kennedy disavowed the idea of unilateral U.S. withdrawal from Vietnam. But for the first time in three years of war, two major political figures presented themselves as advocates of military de-escalation and of a more aggressive attempt at a negotiated peace. They made the opposition into an electable commodity.

In Washington the president reacted to the crush of wintertime shocks with an anger that was compounded by initial uncertainty over the scope and meaning of the disastrous turn of events. At first, Johnson feared that Tet and the seizure of the *Pueblo* indicated the start of a world-wide Communist offensive. As these fears slowly dissipated, however, he made clear his determination to stand tough for the sake of success in Vietnam; and he launched expanded attacks upon his critics. While Secretary of State Dean Rusk scolded reporters by saying that "there gets to be a point when the question is whose side are you on," the president ripped away at "croakers and doubters" and warned that "a lot of people are really ready to surrender without knowing that they are following a party line."[57] Public sentiment hardly indicated that. According to pollsters, public opinion at first reacted to the Tet offensive with a belligerent eagerness for fuller military action. Then it settled into a resigned mood of malleability, waiting for presidential management and direction.

In practical terms, the administration's attention during the waning days of the Tet offensive came to center on General Westmoreland's request for another 206,000 GIs for Vietnam. Confronted with a planned escalation of such magnitude, incoming Secretary of Defense Clark M. Clifford ordered an exhaustive review of U.S. policy and strategy. When the Pentagon could not convince him of the need for further escalation, Clifford and like-minded figures within the administration conducted an extended campaign to win the president over in opposition to the military request and in favor of some kind of unilateral bombing halt that might draw the North Vietnamese to the negotiating table. To give fullest strength to his campaign, Clifford recalled the Wise Men to review the new situation. Pressed by the turn of events in the war, the suspension of public confidence, the need for a tax increase, and worries over the U.S. and international economies, the Wise Men, after prolonged deliberations, advised Johnson to place limits upon U.S. military involvement in Vietnam and to attempt a bombing halt in the hopes of opening negotiations and of bringing popular disaffection into more manageable proportions. "Unless we do something quick," declared Cyrus R. Vance, "the mood in this country may lead us to withdrawal."[58] Johnson was so shocked by their advice that he first insisted that they had been misled by State Department briefers. Then he caved in to the collective wisdom. On March 31 the president announced that he was establishing a ceiling on the U.S. troop commitment while preparing the South Vietnamese to take over their own defense and that he was ordering a halt in bombing over most of North Vietnam in hopes of bringing Hanoi to the conference table. He also announced that he would refuse to seek his party's presidential renomination in the hope that his withdrawal from office might bring an end to the country's domestic divisions.

The president's address on March 31 brought the dreams of the antiwar opposition for a major change in policy as close to reality as they had been in three years. Yet, even as the North Vietnamese were responding positively to Johnson's initiative, American life was shuddering through additional spasms of violent dislocation and disorder that shoved Vietnam to the background of national concerns. In early April, Martin Luther King, Jr., was assassinated in an attack that triggered massive uprisings in the ghetto. Two months later, Robert Kennedy was shot to death—a murder that also cut down the McCarthy campaign.[59] Reeling under the impact of these tragic events, peace liberals stumbled into the Democratic National Convention in Chicago in August, where they became caught up with antiwar radicals in riotous clashes with city police and state authorities. The conflict in Chicago proved to be the climax of a year that was marked by rising hopes and larger failures. Early in November, President Johnson announced a complete halt in bombing over North Vietnam and, a few days later, the commencement of four-sided peace talks in Paris in January. Shortly after Johnson's announcement, Richard M. Nixon squeaked through to a presidential victory on the strength of a narrow popular vote and upon the promise of ending the war in Vietnam. By the end of the year, leading figures within the country's antiwar opposition hobbled toward the sidelines of American life in a spirit that was both discouraged and cautiously hopeful. The war was far from over; yet their principal demands had either been effected or had been set in motion: the bombing of North Vietnam had been halted; formal peace negotiations were about to begin; and U.S. military de-escalation and disengagement had commenced. At the same time, Lyndon Johnson prepared to leave the White House feeling both dispirited and determinedly optimistic. Doggedly, Johnson reiterated his abiding opposition to a Communist success in Vietnam. Indeed, he declared, in his very last public pronouncement upon leaving Washington in January, 1969, that "an honorable peace is possible if we here at home remain steady."[60]

In the end, strangely enough, Lyndon Johnson had both lost and won. He had lost the presidency to the worsening domestic divisions that had been caused by his commitment to an escalating American involvement in a war of attrition on mainland Asia. But he had won out in his determination to stand by the presidential commitment to the maintenance of an anti-Communist regime in South Vietnam. When he left the White House, major violence continued to tear across Indochina, and Richard Nixon came to power with every intention of salvaging the executive commitment in Saigon. Yet the antiwar opposition stood quiescent and confused, while many critics started, for the first time, seriously to confront—as Johnson always warned that they must do eventually—the full logic of their position. They began to realize that their earlier demand for negotiations begged the question of what was to be negotiated. Slowly they came to the conclusion that the fundamental point of the negotiations was America's earliest possible—if not immediate—withdrawal from Vietnam. But that meant a naked acknowledgment of failure; and it took the opposition another eighteen months to accept the enormity of that realization and to act from it.

III

In history books, the debate over the relationship between the Johnson administration and the antiwar opposition began early in the 1970s, long before the end of U.S. intervention. Inevitably, the early onset of this debate tended to obscure the fact that both the nature of the U.S. war effort and of the antiwar opposition were changing, even as both were continuing to course through the Nixon-Ford presidencies. Basically, however, the lines of historiographical debate had been set down even before Lyndon Johnson's death in January, 1973; they tended to crystallize, predictably enough, around arguments as to whether the opposition had been a benign or a malignant force in recent American history.

For the makers and executors of U.S. policy, the opposition was plainly a most damaging development. According to the memoirs of Johnson and his associates, the antiwar opposition subverted national morale and self-confidence, hindered the proper application of American power, and encouraged the Communists to hold out for a collapse on the American home front that would allow them to gain the kind of victory that U.S. fighting forces had denied them on the battlefield. Antiwar dissidents had helped to deliver "a self-inflicted wound" upon America on its way toward victory, declared General Maxwell D. Taylor. "Every war critic capable of producing a headline contributed, in proportion to his eminence, some comfort if not aid to the enemy."[61] Lyndon Johnson ventured that "there is not the slightest doubt in my mind that this dissension prolonged the war, prevented a peaceful settlement on reasonable terms, encouraged our enemies, disheartened our friends, and weakened us as a nation."[62] Even the vaunted White House dove George Ball had little use for open expressions of antiwar opposition. How could anyone "publicly attack the war without giving aid and comfort to the enemy?" he asked in his autobiography. For his part, he was "repelled by the hysteria and crudity" of antiwar activists and "disgusted" by the protests of "fatuous intellectuals" and "muddle-headed instructors."[63]

Writing with a sense of even sharper moral urgency, other proadministration partisans have assailed the antiwar opposition for having eroded America's moral fiber and the country's necessary self-confidence in the rightful deployment of its global power. Centering their resentment on American liberals, engaged intellectuals such as Norman Podhoretz and Robert Scalapino have attacked the naïveté and cynicism that allowed so many Americans "to side with the enemy with complete impunity" in a war that was fundamentally right for the United States.[64] Podhoretz, especially, criticizes the Johnson White House for having allowed antiwar dissidents to dominate "the moral field" and for failing, because of its desire to fight the war on "the political cheap," to make the moral cause that might have neutralized or overcome the arguments of the antiwar movement.[65] Some former antiwar activists have joined in these attacks. The sociologist Peter Berger, an early leader of Clergy and Laity Concerned about Vietnam, has condemned "the hatred of America" that he has decided was "intrinsic" to the opposition and that contributed to "a widespread malaise" about America and "a broad-scale attack on the whole of American power."[66] The antiwar opposition caused America, in the minds of these moralists, to lose its way; and its work and legacy would best be purged through "a reaffirmation of American patriotism" and reinvested faith in the moral superiority of American power.[67]

From another direction, a number of writers view the antiwar opposition as a positive force in recent history that helped to allow the future of Vietnam to be determined among the Vietnamese and that worked in America to set limits "to what governments can do and to what men must bear."[68] Many of the defenders of the antiwar opposition were formerly active in its operation; most lend it value according to their particular political perspective. Antiwar socialists such as James O'Brien and Fred Halstead, for instance, have applauded the opposition as an exercise in political radicalization and popular empowerment. Populists such as Paul Joseph similarly value the opposition as a democratic exhibition of the fact that "people do make history."[69] The radical pacifist David Dellinger sees the opposition as an example of what ordinary people can do through the force of conscience and mass civil disobedience. The liberal Peter Marin praises the opposition for having injected moral vigor into a society that was all too accustomed to acquiescence bred out of conformity. Antiwar activism helped to make the 1960s, wrote Marin, "a decade of genuine moral heroism, serious moral speech," and intense inner debates over "the most serious questions human beings can face, those pertaining to obedience and rebellion, others' lives and deaths, the pull of conflicting allegiances, and the nature and cost of moral life."[70] It helped to cleanse a country that felt dirty without knowing why.

Strangely, however, defenders of the antiwar opposition are not as confident as its critics are in characterizing it as a success. Some sympathizers think that the opposition, by its very nature as a moral-intellectual protest, were "condemned to powerlessness."[71] "The dissenters really did not have a chance," thinks Leslie Gelb. "Given the force of consensus in American history and the politics of foreign policy, they were bound to be losers."[72] Most defenders of the opposition, however, contend that it was "a partial success" in the way that it aggravated popular war-weariness, challenged the ruling mystique of anticommunism, opened the way for emerging elitist dissenters, and served to constrain Washington's interest in intensifying or expanding the war.[73] The opposition did not stop the war, writes Thomas Powers; but it did create "the necessary conditions" that moved the Johnson administration "to *recognize* the failure" of its war policies and to cast about for other means of dealing with Vietnam.[74] Lyndon Johnson won the war at home over the question of whether to continue the U.S. struggle in Vietnam. As a result of the force of the antiwar opposition, however, he failed to establish in the war a cause that would justify its escalating cost in Vietnam or America.

In the quarrel over the role of antiwar activism during the Johnson years, both critics and defenders of the antiwar opposition look with special interest on the role of the news media in shaping attitudes toward the war and on the dissidents. According to proadministration partisans, the media, both for institutional and for ideological reasons, played a decisive role in magnifying the opposition and in turning popular opinion against the U.S. war effort. In the best documented expression of these suspicions, Peter Braestrup has argued that for several reasons, American journalists mistakenly portrayed the Communist military disaster at Tet as a defeat for the United States and consequently changed the very " 'climate' of public debate" in favor of elitist antiwar dissidents. Braestrup concedes that no hard evidence exists that might connect the media misconstruction of Tet with increasing popular antiwar sentiment. But he contends that "unmistakable reflections" of the negative media coverage cast a shadow upon the elitist policy debate in favor of antiwar critics and precipitated Johnson's decision to restrict the U.S. commitment.[75]

Almost reciprocally, writers who are sympathetic to the antiwar opposition complain that the media distorted the nature of citizen dissent. Daniel C. Hallin has demonstrated how television network news consistently misportrayed the country's complex antiwar opposition as a deviant social force.[76] In a provocative study of the interelationship between the media and of the rise and fall of the SDS, former SDS leader Todd Gitlin has detailed how the media used different "framing devices" to portray radical antiwar activists as politically marginal, numerically trivial, torn by internal dissension, and provocative of right-wing extremism.[77] The SDS grew significantly under the glow of media attention. Its members, however, preferred communication through media to strong internal organization; as the war continued and as the media kept demanding newer and more outrageous expressions of protest, SDS activists rushed through internal arguments toward ever-more-militant tactics that substituted the cult of the deed for the organization of a movement for change. The SDS came to life under the lights of media attention, and it died in the same way.

From all indications, the issue of media influences will long affect any attempts to assay the significance of the antiwar opposition during the United States–Vietnamese War. Yet, in the end, any considered assessment of the role of the opposition rests upon the way in which we address two interconnected questions: Was it the war or a Communist success that posed the greater danger to Vietnamese life? and Was it the war or the dissent that posed the greater danger to life and democracy in the United States? However these questions are answered, they must be considered once more in the light of the essentially symbolic place of Vietnam in recent American life and politics. Vietnam was a real place, with real people, real problems, and real importance. But in American eyes it was essentially a bloody backdrop against which people argued about American interests, identity, and purposes. An antiwar opposition formed and functioned in the United States because the United States–Vietnamese War provoked among Americans a struggle over the values and ends of their country. "The war was never worth fighting for Vietnam alone," Theodore Draper has written, "it always had to be subsidiary to a larger purpose."[78] For Americans that purpose was the meaning of their own country. And that is why they fought—and continue to fight—over the matter of Vietnam: so that they might recover from it some worth for America.

Notes

1. Dean Rusk, quoted by Townsend Hoopes in *The Limits of Intervention*, text ed. (New York: David McKay, 1970), p. 94.

2. Charles DeBenedetti, *The Peace Reform in American History* (Bloomington: Indiana University Press, 1980), pp. 160-74; Lawrence S. Wittner, *Rebels against War: The American Peace Movement, 1933-1983* (Philadelphia: Temple University Press, 1984), pp. 176-283. For a contrary view see Paul Boyer, "From Activism to Apathy: The American People and Nuclear Weapons, 1963-1980," *Journal of American History* 70 (Mar., 1984): 821-44.

3. Neil H. Katz, "Radical Pacifism and the Contemporary American Peace Movement: The Committee for Nonviolent Action, 1957-1967" (Ph.D. diss., University of Maryland, 1974); and Jo Ann Robinson, *Abraham Went Out: A Biography of A. J. Muste* (Philadelphia: Temple University Press, 1981).

4. Among the better studies that survey the relationship between the American Left and recent U.S. foreign-policy making are: Edward J. Baccaccio, Jr., *The New Left in America: Reform to Revolution, 1956-1970* (Stanford, Calif.: Hoover Institution Press, 1974); Milton Cantor, *The Divided Left: American Radicalism, 1900-1975* (New York: Hill & Wang, 1978), chaps. 10-12; Allen J. Matusow, *The Unraveling of America: A History of Liberalism in the 1960s* (New York: Harper & Row, 1984), chaps. 10-13; Kirkpatrick Sale, *SDS* (New York: Random House, 1973); Massimo Teodori, ed., *The New Left: A Documentary History* (Indianapolis, Ind.: Bobbs-Merrill, 1969); and George R. Vickers, *The Formation of the New Left: The Early Years* (Lexington, Mass.: D. C. Heath, 1975).

5. Milton J. Rosenberg et al., *Vietnam and the Silent Majority: The Dove's Guide* (New York: Harper & Row, 1970), pp. 35-36; and John E. Mueller, *War, Presidents and Public Opinion* (New York: John Wiley, 1973), p. 164.

6. Harris poll published in *Washington Post*, Dec. 13, 1965, microfilm reel Vietnam 63, Public Opinion, Jan., 1965-July, 1968, News Clipping and Analysis Service, Dept. of Defense, Washington, D.C.; William R. Berkowitz, "The Impact of Anti-Vietnam Demonstrations upon National Public Opinion and Military Indicators," *Social Science Research* 2 (1973): 3, 10; and E. M. Schreiber, "Anti-War Demonstrations and American Public Opinion on the War in Vietnam," *British Journal of Sociology* 27 (June, 1976): 23-32.

7. Sidney Verba et al., "Public Opinion and the War in Vietnam," *American Political Science Review* 61 (June, 1967): 325, 331-33.

8. Douglas Kiker, "Washington Reports: Exploiting Dissent on Vietnam to Domestic Political Advantage," *Atlantic Monthly*, July, 1967, p. 6.

9. John L. Sullivan et al., "An Alternative Conceptualization of Political Tolerance: Illusory Increases, 1950s-1970s," *American Political Science Review* 73 (Sept., 1979): 793.

10. Useful studies of antiwar activism during the Johnson years include: Fred Halstead, *Out Now! A Participant's Account of the American Movement against the Vietnam War* (New York: Monad Press, 1978); Irving Louis Horowitz, *The Struggle Is the Message: The Organization and Ideology of the Anti-War Movement* (Berkeley, Calif.: Glendessary Press, 1970); Jerome H. Skolnick, *The Politics of Protest* (New York: Simon & Schuster, 1969); Thomas Powers, *The War at Home: Vietnam and the American People, 1964-1968* (New York: Grossman, 1973); and Nancy Zaroulis and Gerald Sullivan, *Who Spoke Up? American Protest against the War in Vietnam, 1963-1975* (Garden City, N.Y.: Doubleday, 1984).

11. Moyers is quoted by Merle Miller in *Lyndon: An Oral Biography* (New York: Putnam's, 1980), p. 489.

12. J. Michael Quill, *Lyndon Johnson and the Southern Military Tradition* (Washington, D.C.: University Press of America, 1977). One of Johnson's biographers called him "the consummate militaristic politician" of cold-war America. I think it a fair judgment (Ronnie Dugger, *The Politician: The Life and Times of Lyndon Johnson: The Drive for Power, from the Frontier to Master of the Senate* [New York: Norton, 1982], p. 397).

13. Quoted by Hugh Sidey in *A Very Personal Presidency: Lyndon Johnson in the White House* (New York: Atheneum, 1968), p. 211; Doris Kearns, *Lyndon Johnson and the American Dream* (New York: Harper & Row, 1976), p. 253; *Public Papers of the Presidents of the United States: Lyndon B. Johnson, 1968-1969*, 2 vols. (Washington, D.C.: Government Printing Office, 1970), 1:154 (cited hereafter as *Public Papers*). See also Larry L. King, "Machismo in the White House: LBJ and Vietnam," *American Heritage* 27 (1976): 8–13.

14. *Public Papers*, 1:395.

15. George Reedy, *Lyndon B. Johnson: A Memoir* (New York: Andrews & McMeel, 1982), pp. 6–8; Wilson Carey McWilliams, "Lyndon Johnson and the Politics of Mass Society," in *Leadership in America: Consensus, Corruption, and Charisma*, ed. Peter D. Bathory (New York: Longman, 1978), pp. 184–89; and Chester L. Cooper, *The Lost Crusade: America in Vietnam* (New York: Dodd, Mead, 1970), pp. 424, 465.

16. Humphrey is quoted in Kenneth W. Thompson, ed., *Ten Presidents and the Press* (Washington, D.C.: University Press of America, 1983), p. 87.

17. George W. Ball, *The Past Has Another Pattern: Memoirs* (New York: Norton, 1982), p. 384.

18. Henry F. Graff, *The Tuesday Cabinet: Deliberation and Decision on Peace and Decision on Peace and War under Lyndon B. Johnson* (Englewood Cliffs, N.J.: Prentice-Hall, 1970), p. 73; also Hubert H. Humphrey, *The Education of a Public Man: My Life and Politics* (Garden City, N.Y.: Doubleday, 1976), pp. 321–25.

19. Quoted by Frank Cormier in *LBJ: The Way He Was* (Garden City, N.Y.: Doubleday, 1977), p. 191; Graff, *Tuesday Cabinet*, p. 100; and Cyrus Sulzberger, *Seven Continents and Forty Years* (Chicago: Quadrangle, 1977), p. 434.

20. Robert Sherrill, *The Accidental President* (New York: Grossman, 1967), p. 12. "Johnson's paranoia used to get on my nerves," remembered presidential aid John Roche. "There was not a sparrow fell from a tree but what he was convinced that was the intervention of a Kennedy. . . . The trouble is, he was right on a number of cases, and I was wrong" (John Roche, oral history interview, tape 1, p. 60, Lyndon B. Johnson Presidential Library—cited hereafter as LBJL).

21. Quoted by Elizabeth Goldschmidt in Miller, *Lyndon*, p. 489.

22. Walt Rostow to the President, July 13, 1968, White House central files, country file: Vietnam, box 233, LBJL.

23. Sam Houston Johnson, *My Brother Lyndon* (New York: Cowles, 1969), p. 204; also Lady Bird Johnson, *A White House Diary* (New York: Holt, Rinehart & Winston, 1970), pp. 395, 469–70, 574–93.

24. Frank Church oral history interview, p. 27, LBJL.

25. "Notes on the President's Meeting with Bob Lucas, Aug. 14, 1967," in office files of George Christian, box 1, folder: notes on meeting, President 1967, LBJL; and quoted in Cormier, *LBJ*, p. 191.

26. George Christian notes, "Meeting of the President with Hugh Sidey of *Time* Magazine," Feb. 8, 1967, p. 2, meeting notes file, box 3, folder: Feb.–Apr., 1967, meetings with correspondents, LBJL; also Kearns, *Lyndon Johnson,* p. 316.

27. Eric F. Goldman, *The Tragedy of Lyndon Johnson* (New York: Knopf, 1969), p. 500; Kearns, *Lyndon Johnson,* p. 317.

28. Goldman, *Tragedy,* p. 500.

29. McGeorge Bundy, memorandum for the President, Aug. 24, 1964, National Security file, aides files, McGeorge Bundy, memoranda for the President, box 1, LBJL.

30. Donald Ropa and Chester Cooper memorandum to Mr. Bundy, "The Week in Asia," Sept. 28, 1965, in National Security file, name file, Chester Cooper file, box 2, LBJL.

31. Donald Ropa and Chester Cooper memorandum to Mr. Bundy, Aug. 9, 1965, ibid.

32. *New York Times,* Oct. 17, 1965, p. 44; U.S. Senate, Committee on the Judiciary, 89th Cong., 1st sess., "The Anti-Vietnam Agitation and the Teach-in Movement: The Problem of Communist Infiltration and Exploitation" (Washington, D.C.: Government Printing Office, 1965).

33. Cabinet papers, box 3, folder: cabinet meeting, June 18, 1965, p. 33, LBJL; also Lady Bird Johnson, *White House Diary,* p. 262.

34. "Notes of the President's Meeting with Robert Manning of the Atlantic," Oct. 18, 1967, meeting notes file, box 3, folder: Oct., 1967, meetings with correspondents, LBJL.

35. Memorandum for the record, p. 4, meeting notes file, box 2, folder: Feb. 2, 1968, meeting with China experts, LBJL.

36. *Public Papers . . . 1966,* 1:519.

37. Ibid., p. 684.

38. Ibid., p. 693.

39. Jack Valenti memorandum for the President, May 13, 1966, office files of the President, box 7, folder: Jack Valenti, 1965–66, LBJL.

40. Bill Moyers memorandum for the President, Aug. 4, 1966, aides files, Bill Moyers, box 12, folder: BDM memoranda, July 12–Aug., 1966, LBJL; also Joseph Califano, Jr., *A Presidential Nation* (New York: Norton, 1975), p. 76.

41. Harry McPherson, quoted in Miller, *Lyndon,* p. 463; and Mueller, *War,* p. 126.

42. Harris poll in *Washington Post,* May 14, 1967, microfilm reel Vietnam 63, Public Opinion, Jan., 1965–July, 1968, News Clipping and Analysis Service, Dept. of Defense.

43. John Roche memorandum for the President, Apr. 5, 1967, confidential file, name file, box 5, folder: Ki; and Roche, memorandum for the President, Apr. 18, 1967, aides files, Marvin Watson, box 19, LBJL.

44. Robert E. Kintner memorandum for the Attorney General, May 19, 1967, confidential file, HU 4, box 57, LBJL.

45. Paul Douglas to John Roche, Aug. 21, 1967, confidential file, country file: Vietnam, box 72, LBJL.

46. Lady Bird Johnson, *White House Diary,* pp. 575, 584; notes of cabinet meetings of Oct. 4, Nov. 1, and Sept. 6, 1967, in cabinet papers, box 10, LBJL.

47. Note of cabinet meeting of Oct. 4, 1967, p. 9, ibid.

48. Charles DeBenedetti, "A CIA Analysis of the Anti-War Movement:

October 1967," *Peace and Change* 9 (Spring, 1983): 31–35; see also Frank J. Donner, *The Age of Surveillance: The Aims and Methods of America's Political Intelligence System* (New York: Knopf, 1980), pp. 252–53, 259–61; and Athan Theoharis, *Spying on Americans: Political Surveillance from Hoover to the Huston Plan* (Philadelphia: Temple University Press, 1978), pp. 147–48.

49. Jim Jones notes of luncheon meeting with Rusk et al., Meeting notes file, box 2, folder: Nov. 4, 1967, LBJL.

50. McGeorge Bundy memorandum for the President, Nov. 10, 1967, in President's appointment file, Nov. 2, 1967, LBJL.

51. Jim Jones notes of Nov. 2, 1967, meeting with Foreign Policy Advisors, p. 3, meeting notes file, folder: Nov. 2, 1967, LBJL.

52. Bundy memorandum for the President, p. 7, Nov. 10, 1967, in President's appointment file, Nov. 2, 1967, LBJL.

53. Ibid., p. 4.

54. Jim Jones notes of meeting with Foreign Policy Advisors on Nov. 2, 1967, p. 3.

55. Bundy memorandum, Nov. 10, 1967, pp. 6–7; emphasis in the original.

56. *Public Papers . . . 1967*, 2:1168, 1096.

57. Quoted by Herbert Y. Schandler in *The Unmaking of a President: Lyndon Johnson and Vietnam* (Princeton, N.J.: Princeton University Press, 1977), p. 85; *Public Papers . . . 1968*, 1:456; and Johnson, notes of luncheon meeting of Mar. 22, 1968, in meeting notes file, box 2, folder: Mar. 22, 1968, LBJL.

58. "Summary of Notes," meeting notes file, box 2, folder: Mar. 26, 1968, LBJL; see also Hoopes, *Limits*, pp. 215–16; Schandler, *Unmaking of a President*, p. 306; and Harry McPherson, *A Political Education* (Boston, Mass.: Little, Brown, 1972), pp. 433–34.

59. Cabinet papers, box 14, folder: Cabinet meeting, June 26, 1968 (1 of 3), LBJL; also Hoopes, *Limits*, p. 165.

60. *Public Papers . . . 1968–1969*, 2:1308.

61. Maxwell D. Taylor, *Swords and Plowshares* (New York: Norton, 1972), pp. 402, 408.

62. Lyndon Baines Johnson, *The Vantage Point: Perspectives of the Presidency, 1963–1969* (New York: Holt, Rinehart & Winston, 1971), p. 530.

63. Ball, *The Past*, pp. 432–33, 448.

64. Robert Scalapino, "The Open Society at War," *Society* 21 (Nov./Dec., 1983): 30; and Norman Podhoretz, *Why We Were in Vietnam* (New York: Simon & Schuster, 1982), p. 85.

65. Podhoretz, *Why We Were in Vietnam*, pp. 112, 124.

66. Peter L. Berger, "Indochina and the American Conscience," *Commentary* 69 (Feb., 1980): 35, 30; and Charles Horner, "America Five Years after Defeat," *Commentary* 69 (Apr., 1980): 56.

67. Berger, "Indochina," p. 38.

68. Michael Walzer, "The Peace Movement: What Was Won by Protest?" *New Republic*, Feb. 10, 1973, p. 26.

69. James O'Brien, "The Anti-War Movement and the War," *Radical America* 8 (May/June, 1974): 66–69; Halstead, *Out Now!* passim; and Paul Joseph, *Cracks in the Empire: State Politics in the Vietnam War* (Boston, Mass.: South End Press, 1981), p. 305.

70. David Dellinger, *More Power Than We Know: The People's Movement toward Democracy* (Garden City, N.Y.: Doubleday, 1975); and Peter Marin, "Coming to Terms with Vietnam," *Harper's*, Dec., 1980, p. 49.

71. Sandy Vogelgesang, *The Long Dark Night of the Soul: The American Intellectual Left and the Vietnam War* (New York: Harper & Row, 1974), p. 166.

72. Leslie H. Gelb, "Dissenting on Consensus," in *The Legacy of Vietnam: The War, American Society and the Future of American Foreign Policy*, ed. Anthony Lake (New York: New York University Press, 1976), p. 112; see also Leslie H. Gelb with Richard K. Betts, *The Irony of Vietnam: The System Worked* (Washington, D.C.: Brookings Institution, 1979), p. 366.

73. Walzer, "Peace Movement," p. 26; and Anthony Oberschall, "The Decline of the 1960s Social Movements," in *Research in Social Movements, Conflicts and Change: An Annual Compilation of Research*, ed. Louis Kriesberg, 2 vols. (Greenwich, Conn.: JAI Press, 1978), 1:281. For similar conclusions reached by official analysts see BDM Corp., "A Study of Strategic Lessons Learned in Vietnam," vol. 4: "U.S. Domestic Factors Influencing Vietnam War Policy Making" (ms., McLean, Va., 1980), available through Strategic Studies Institute, U.S. Army War College, Carlisle Barracks, Pa.

74. Powers, *War at Home*, pp. 318, xv; emphasis in the original. For a beginning historical analysis of the effectiveness of the antiwar opposition on the Johnson administration's policy making see Melvin Small, "The Impact of the Antiwar Movement on Lyndon Johnson, 1965-1968: A Preliminary Report," *Peace and Change* 10 (Spring, 1984): 1-22. For some propositions regarding the opposition's long-term importance see Charles DeBenedetti, "On the Significance of Citizen Peace Activism: America, 1961-1975," ibid. 9 (Summer, 1983): 6-20.

75. Peter Braestrup, *Big Story: How the American Press and Television Reported and Interpreted the Crisis of Tet 1968 in Vietnam and Washington*, abridged ed. (New Haven, Conn.: Yale University Press, 1983), p. 505; see also Robert Elegant, "How to Lose a War," *Encounter* 57 (1981): 81-88.

76. For dissenting views see Daniel C. Hallin, "The Media, the War in Vietnam, and Political Support: A Critique of the Thesis of an Oppositional Media," *Journal of Politics* 46 (Feb., 1984): 2-24, and *The "Uncensored War": The Media and Vietnam* (New York: Oxford University Press, 1986), pp. 195-205 and passim; and Robert MacNeil, *The Right Place at the Right Time* (Boston, Mass.: Little, Brown, 1982), pp. 238-45; Kathleen J. Turner, in *Lyndon Johnson's Dual War: Vietnam and the Press* (Chicago: University of Chicago Press, 1985), effectively reviews the president's attempts to shape media coverage of his policies and of his antiwar critics.

77. Todd Gitlin, *The Whole World Is Watching: Mass Media in the Making and Unmaking of the New Left* (Berkeley: University of California Press, 1980), p. 27 and passim.

78. Theodore Draper, "Ghosts of Vietnam," *Dissent* 26 (Winter, 1979): 40.

3 | The Economic Education of Lyndon Johnson: Guns, Butter, and Taxes

Donald F. Kettl

NO PRESIDENCY IN AMERICAN HISTORY had such exhilarating economic highs or such devastating economic lows as the Johnson administration. A generation of economists hailed the tax cut of 1964 as "the triumph of modern fiscal policy."[1] It was the high point of the "new economics," the end of balancing the federal budget for balance's sake, the rise of economists into unquestioned power in the White House, the final volley of "the fiscal revolution in America."[2] That triumph, however, proved to be disastrously short-lived. United States involvement in Vietnam grew enormously after June, 1965, but not until two years later did Lyndon Johnson submit a plan to increase taxes substantially, and not for another year after that did Congress finally pass the tax surcharge. Bill Moyers later called the delay in seeking the tax increase "the single most devastating decision in the Johnson administration." By overruling his advisers, who argued for a tax increase as early as December, 1965, while insisting on their loyalty, Johnson helped to undercut the base of his internal support. "It was the beginning of the end," Moyers said, "a time when he lost control of the administration, lost control of events."[3]

The three-year delay in getting a tax increase helped to fuel a booming economic growth and to unleash inflation, which had been relatively quiet since the Korean War. When the Federal Reserve Board triggered tight money to slow the boom, the economy started on a roller coaster that took another fifteen years to stop. The struggle over the tax surcharge was the keystone of Lyndon Johnson's tragedy: great hopes, a stormy struggle for consensus, and dashed dreams.

Perhaps no account of this struggle is better known—or more harsh—than David Halberstam's article in the September, 1972, *Atlantic Monthly*, "How the Economy Went Haywire," which he repeated in *The Best and the Brightest*.[4] To Halberstam, Johnson was "a magician who lied." Johnson's own economists, especially Gardner Ackley, chairman of the Council of Economic Advisers (CEA), called for a tax increase in December, 1965. But Johnson, fearing that if Congress had a choice, it "would give him the war, but not the Great Society," decided to "hold back on the real estimates of the cost of the war for a year," to weaken the otherwise obvious case for a tax increase. Robert S. McNamara cleverly planned, for budgeting purposes, that the war would be over by June 30, 1967, but he kept, according to Halberstam, the real dimensions of the war secret—"secret, it turned out, even to the President's own economists."[5]

Halberstam delivered a tough indictment: Johnson had lied to Congress, the American public, and his own staff about the real costs of Vietnam. Johnson sought, instead, guns *and* butter—heavy Vietnam spending, coupled with an expansive Great Society. It was a "living lie" that in the end created "economic chaos."[6] Halberstam's account has become the conventional wisdom of the period. Other writers have repeated it,[7] and *Newsweek* cited the widely understood knowledge that during the Vietnam build-up, "Lyndon Johnson actually hid the cost of the war from Ackley, thus blunting what could have been an earlier call for a tax increase."[8]

As the documents available at the Lyndon B. Johnson Library show, however, these fateful events traveled a considerably more complex path. The documents cast great doubt on the Machiavellian image of a deceitful Lyndon Johnson. His advisers were far more uneven in their support for a tax increase than Halberstam has suggested, and Johnson's reasons for not proposing an earlier tax increase were not as simple as the guns-and-butter theory that Halberstam spins. Johnson did indeed want his butter, as the documents show, and he did fear that Congress would prefer to choose between them rather than to grant a tax increase. But in the early stages, guns and butter did not seem like incompatible choices. At the later stages of the Johnson years, the explosion of American cities into flames and the expansion of combat in Vietnam, combined with the great investment of moral and political capital into both campaigns, made retreat on either front unthinkable. Only as retreat became less possible, however, did the economic costs become clear. This was the essential irony, the pivotal tragedy, of an administration that was rocked to its foundation at the very zenith of its power.

I

Most of John F. Kennedy's cabinet, including Council of Economic Advisers Chairman Walter Heller, were in a plane over the Pacific when they heard the news of the president's assassination. The plane immediately was turned around, and on the trip back to Washington the conversation turned to the new president's grasp of economics.

The cabinet members were not sure that Johnson understood the Keynesian theory behind the proposed tax cut: lower federal taxation to stimulate private expansion.[9] "There was a great deal of apprehension" about Johnson, Heller later remembered.[10] Heller went from the plane to his office and worked all night on a memo to Johnson, in which he outlined the state of the economy and the need for a tax cut.[11]

Kennedy's Keynesian advisers in the CEA had had a very difficult time convincing the president to propose a cut in income taxes. Kennedy had come to office with a strong commitment to supporting the sagging dollar abroad, and that stance argued against easier money. He was fiscally conservative and hesitated to counter Eisenhower's old-time balanced-budget religion. Federal Reserve Board Chairman William McChesney Martin, Jr., furthermore, was preaching that the country's unemployment problem was structural, based upon shifts in the labor market, rather than cyclical, based upon the ups and downs of the economy. Extra money pumped into the economy to increase demand would put few of the unemployed back to work if they were unemployed because they lacked the skills a changing economy needed or because they lived in an economically declining region. Most of all, Kennedy was simply not convinced that the Keynesians were right.

In August, 1962, Heller finally convinced Kennedy and Treasury Secretary C. Douglas Dillon, and the president went on television to announce a $10 billion tax cut, to be proposed in January's State of the Union address. Once announced, however, the plan came under attack from liberals and conservatives alike. From the Left came complaints that the tax cut unfairly benefited the rich and would, in the long run, not stimulate economic growth. From the Right, some economists complained that the tax cut might fuel inflation or create deficits. The tax plan bogged down in the Senate and barely passed in the House in September, just two months before the assassination.[12]

On the evening of the slain president's burial, Johnson surprised his inherited economic advisers by enthusiastically embracing the tax cut.[13] But Ackley said later, "He frightened us at that first meeting": to ensure the passage of the tax cut, Johnson announced that he planned to keep the federal budget to less than $100 billion.[14] The budget ceiling, his advisers acknowledged, would help solidify conservative support for the tax cut, but it would greatly dilute its stimulative effects. For Johnson, however, the tax cut served purposes other than economic ones. It was to be a demonstration of who was in charge and of the new president's skill in dealing with Congress.[15]

Johnson quickly sealed his victory by signing the tax cut into law on February 26, 1964, just three months after the assassination.

For economic advisers who at first had been leery about the new president, the passage of the tax cut was the rite of passage into the "new economics." Johnson proved to be an eager audience for his economic advisers, and he relied on them more than Kennedy had. Economic advice was built on the "Troika," an informal group of three created during the Kennedy years and carried over into Johnson's administration. It consisted of the secretary of the Treasury (first, C. Douglas Dillon and then, after 1965, Henry Fowler); the director of the Bureau of the Budget (Kermit Gordon, until 1965; Charles L. Schultze, from 1965 to 1968; and Charles J. Zwick, for the remainder of the administration); and the chairman of the Council of Economic Advisers (Walter Heller, who was succeeded in 1965 by Gardner Ackley and in 1968 by Arthur M. Okun). The Troika prepared regular forecasts for the president and supplied him with recommendations, especially during the intensive budget season in December.

Johnson developed an especially close relationship with the CEA. For Heller, Ackley, and their colleagues on the council, the White House was a seminar room, and Johnson was their only student. As Ackley explained, "We considered this one of our main responsibilities: to try to teach him economics." And for the most part, Johnson proved "a very good student, a very interested student," according to Ackley.[16] The text for the seminar was the constant flood of memos with which the CEA deluged him. Johnson voraciously consumed them, good and bad news alike, and he carried his favorites around for days in his jacket pocket to show to those with whom he spoke. The memos were unusual in form and much different from the memos the CEA had prepared for Kennedy. They were more outline than prose, and the key phrases were underlined, so they could not be missed. "He wanted information that he didn't have to work too hard to get," Ackley later explained.[17] Johnson complimented the CEA for the memos, and he even occasionally sent a dense Treasury Department memo to the CEA and asked for an "English translation."

Johnson, the "new economics," and the new economists were riding high in the saddle. Within recent memory the economy had never been rosier. Heller bragged to Johnson that the economy was "showing new vitality and promise," with "no inflation in sight."[18] It was a triumph of economic planning, the first conclusive demonstration of the federal government's ability to frame a fiscal policy to stimulate the economy; it was also the foundation for Johnson's 1964 victory over Barry Goldwater. With the passage of Kennedy's tax cut, Johnson wrapped himself in the martyr's mantle. It marked, according to Rowland Evans and Robert Novak, the "epitome of Lyndon Johnson's early presidency."[19] As Johnson put it in his memoirs, he became a candidate who promised "imaginative fiscal and monetary policies that would eliminate the old cycles of boom and bust."[20] During the fall campaign, Goldwater, having opposed the tax cut, had precious little room for maneuvering on the economic issue. Perhaps most important, the successful passage of the tax cut was a central symbol of political success and active attack on the nation's problems, and that made Johnson a formidable presidential candidate.

The tide stayed high until June 1, 1965, when Federal Reserve Board Chairman William McChesney Martin surprised the financial community and shocked the White House with a speech suggesting "disquieting similarities between our present prosperity and the fabulous twenties."[21] Martin apparently was attempting to warn about the difficulty of keeping expansion within bounds, the need to apply properly timed monetary and fiscal medicine to economic problems, and the increasing interrelationship of the domestic and international economies. The administration's economists, however, rejected the implication that the boom in the economy might end in a 1929-style bust. The CEA staff, in fact, was concerned mainly about the possibility of slower economic growth, rising unemployment, and the possible need for more economic stimulus late in 1966. Early projections suggested that the economy might slow down and need more, not less, governmental help, perhaps through another tax cut or through the enactment of the revenue-sharing plan that Walter Heller had championed.[22]

On the same day, Lyndon Johnson requested a supplemental appropriation for Vietnam. The early months of the Vietnam build-up did not worry the CEA; in fact, Ackley suggested that more military spending might provide a much-needed stimulus. "Our economy has lots of room to absorb a defense step-up," he told Johnson on July 30. "Nobody can seriously expect that the kind of program you outlined is going to overheat the economy, strain industrial capacity, or generate a consumer buying boom." He concluded that the "overall effects are most likely to be favorable to our prosperity" and to reduce the need for a further tax cut.[23]

As the fall went on, however, Johnson's economic advisers viewed the step-up in military expenditures with growing alarm. In early September, Ackley condemned a column by Evans and Novak that suggested Vietnam spending would bring inflation in 1966,[24] but in early

November a special interagency committee warned that rising defense expenditures might produce "a significant and undesirable acceleration in the pace of overall economic activity."[25] The Federal Reserve, in fact, was so worried that on December 6 it raised the discount rate—the rate that banks pay on loans from the system—from 4 to 4.5 percent, to try to slow the economy. Johnson angrily disassociated himself from the decision and said he regretted that the board had decided to act before the administration had completed work on the new budget.[26] Administration officials had for weeks been putting pressure on the Federal Reserve to delay any action until January, when the budget picture would be clearer. Martin himself was scheduled to meet with Johnson within a few days to discuss the economic outlook. Some observers, in fact, speculated that Martin had acted preemptively to prevent Johnson from using the meeting to apply the "Johnson treatment." Johnson's economists were increasingly agreed on the need to apply the brakes, but they were not sure just how, when, or how strongly to do so. Martin had no such uncertainty; he pressed ahead.

By mid December, Ackley, as Halberstam has suggested, was vigorously arguing for a tax increase.[27] After the first few months of the war, Ackley said, "We were becoming pretty clear about what was going on."[28] On December 17, Ackley sent Johnson a memo that put the matter plainly: the economy was starting to heat up. If the budget were in the $115 billion range, "there is little question in my mind that a significant tax increase will be needed to prevent an intolerable degree of inflationary pressure." If the budget were $110 billion, "the question is more difficult," but Ackley suggested that a tax increase would probably still be needed. Johnson was concerned that even a hint of a possible tax increase not be leaked. He scrawled on Joseph Califano's cover note over Ackley's memo, "*Caution* them not to go into detail with staff & keep away from all *reporters*."[29]

Ten days later, Ackley was even more emphatic. He wrote to the president: "The only conclusion I can reach is that an increase of individual and corporate income tax rates should be planned, whatever the FY1967 budget may be (within the limits we have heard discussed). Tactically, it may only be feasible to propose higher taxes later in the year. From an economic standpoint, it needs to be done as soon as possible."[30] Johnson, in fact, was getting the same advice from many other members of his administration. Former CEA Chairman Heller, who had returned to the University of Minnesota, joined Charles Schultze, director of the Bureau of the Budget, in arguing for a tax increase.[31] Even Defense Secretary McNamara suggested the need for a tax increase and for estimating defense expenditures on the high side. Administration budget officials were considering two different estimates for the total defense budget: $57 and $60 billion. McNamara argued that the administration ought to use the higher figure to help preserve credibility on the budget.[32]

In December, 1965, no one had a clear idea of how much the Vietnam War would cost. That, of course, is characteristic of war: no one knows in advance how big any war will be. The United States' last major experience in wartime planning—Korea—had produced wildly unrealistic defense budgets. Defense planners had overestimated the cost of fighting the war: by almost 13 percent in fiscal 1953 and by more than 11 percent in fiscal 1954.[33] Johnson's economic advisers were well aware of the past record and were therefore hesitant to take too seriously the estimates for Vietnam. By the end of 1965, furthermore, actual defense spending was lagging far behind contracted obligations.[34] The rapid expansion of the war was a firm possibility, but it was a danger that lay in the future. McNamara, furthermore, had struggled for almost five years to get military spending under control. He had brought the Planning-Programming-Budgeting System to the Defense Department to try to force the military chiefs out of their old interservice rivalries. The Vietnam build-up now created great pressures from the Pentagon for all sorts of military spending under the guise of "We're in a war now." But having struggled to gain some measure of control, McNamara was reluctant to hand the generals a blank check, and he shied away from making long-term predictions of a rapid military build-up.[35]

Director Schultze of the Bureau of the Budget (BOB) therefore developed a two-pronged plan.[36] McNamara would assume that the war would be over by June 30, 1967, the end of the fiscal year. The planning assumption, Schultze said later, put "everybody on notice, although nobody in the early stages paid much attention to it, that this budget was understated simply on technical grounds, but understated by an amount nobody knew."[37] Johnson was getting advice, especially from Congressman Wilbur D. Mills, chairman of the tax-writing House Ways and Means Committee, not to put the full cost of the Vietnam War in the budget; "people will really be startled," he warned.[38] Since nobody knew how much the war would cost, the budget simply would state that fact and would warn that more requests might be needed later.

The second prong of the plan was to request a supplemental Vietnam appropriation later in 1966, when the full picture would be clearer, and at the same time to ask for the tax increase. Although

Ackley pressed urgently in December for an immediate tax increase, Treasury Secretary Fowler and BOB Director Schultze were less sure about just when a tax increase would be needed. Coupling the tax increase with the Vietnam supplemental appropriation would, Schultze thought, improve the chances for congressional passage and would help to minimize attack on the Great Society programs in the meantime. Congressman Mills, Johnson was told, "clearly showed that he had no appetite for a tax increase bill in 1966." If the issue were opened then, Mills warned, both Democratic liberals and conservative Republicans "would start tearing at the budget instead."[39]

The tax increase in 1965 was therefore a tricky political matter. Johnson estimated that he could get a tax increase to pay for a big war, but if he asked for a tax increase, the Great Society would be an inviting target for those who opposed the social programs. Johnson, furthermore, wanted only a limited war. His problem at this stage came more from hawks, who pressed for a wide war, than from doves, who desired to reduce U.S. involvement. The president thus had a dilemma: he could get a tax increase, he thought, only for a war bigger than the one he planned, and then only at the cost of his Great Society. To keep the war limited and to save the social programs from attack, Johnson decided to forestall the decision on a tax increase in late 1965.[40]

The economic case, furthermore, was tricky. It was difficult to predict just how big a problem inflation might become so long as the full scale of Vietnam was unknown. Given the Korean experience and the possibility that the war would indeed turn out to be limited, Johnson's advisers were leery about jumping too quickly toward a large tax increase, especially since the much-vaunted 4 percent "full employment" goal was nearly at hand. The "new economics" offered the possibility of relatively easy stabilization: the federal government could pump up growth through increased spending and tax cuts; tax increases could slow a booming economy. In the models, each side of the stabilization equation worked with equal ease and accuracy. In the political world, Johnson and his economic advisers overestimated how easy it would be to apply fiscal stimulus—and underestimated how difficult it would later be to apply restraint.

For the administration in late 1965, the central question was how to restrain an overheating economy without disrupting the nation's strong economic growth. Johnson's economic advisers saw the puzzle in terms of fine tuning the demand, rather than in terms of waging an all-out war against inflation.[41] The Federal Reserve's preemptive strike helped to forestall the need for immediate action. Some administration officials believed that if the Federal Reserve had not acted, there would have been a better chance for a tax increase early in 1966, but others have suggested that the result probably still would have been the same even if the Federal Reserve had been persuaded to wait. Schultze argues that the administration, especially President Johnson and Treasury Secretary Fowler, simply did not have the stomach for a tax increase at the time.[42]

The budget that Johnson finally proposed in January, 1966, was $112.8 billion, halfway between Ackley's $110 billion "probable" tax-increase level and his $115 billion "little question" level. The estimate for defense spending, $58.3 billion, was also in the middle of the $57–$60 billion range, with all estimates hinging on a projected end of the war on June 30, 1967. Johnson made clear in his budget message that the final budget would change as circumstances in Southeast Asia shifted. And to slow down the economy a bit, he proposed a $4.8 billion tax package to accelerate the collection of corporation income taxes, to change the withholding schedule for individual income taxes, and to postpone the scheduled reduction in telephone and excise taxes. Missing from the package was the major increase in corporate and individual income taxes that Ackley had recommended. The administration secretly went with Schultze's two-pronged plan, with a later tax-increase proposal to be tied to the Vietnam supplemental appropriation. The January budget won congressional support, and Congressman Mills agreed to back Johnson's small-tax-increase package.[43] The package won speedy passage in March.

Johnson's advisers were hopeful that they could beat any inflation problem before it became a crisis. "If you can finance the Vietnam war with a minimum of stimulus," Schultze wrote to the president just after Christmas 1965, "this will be an accomplishment of equal magnitude to the Great Society legislative program."[44] The decision to go with Schultze's strategy, however, laid the groundwork for charges that Johnson had lied about the cost of the war. The fiscal 1967 budget, announced in January, 1966, underestimated the eventual expenditures for defense by 16 percent, largely because Vietnam expenditures grew from $6 billion in fiscal 1966 to $20.6 billion in 1967. The administration later covered these extra costs through a supplemental appropriation, as Schultze had suggested. As the war wore on, however, the administration's budget requests came far closer to the mark. The fiscal 1968 budget underestimated the total expenditures for defense by less than 7 percent, and in 1969 the underestimate was less than 2 percent. By that time, however, the image of duplicity had already been formed.

II

The Johnson administration's hopes that it could fine tune any inflation quickly turned sour. The minor tax increase at the beginning of 1966 proved little more than a Band-Aid for the hemorrhage of military spending. Congress voted a $13.8 billion supplemental appropriation for Vietnam in the spring of 1966 and followed that with a fiscal year 1967 defense appropriation of $58 billion, the largest defense bill since 1943. Inflation, meanwhile, heated up. The consumer price index rose by 5 percent in 1966, the largest increase since the Korean War—a major shock after the relatively stable prices of the early 1960s.

Ackley and his council continued to campaign, in the early spring, for a tax increase. The CEA told the president that "a further tax increase is needed to counter inflation" because "the economy is breaking all reasonable speed limits." The council members continued: "We are not facing an explosive situation. A little inflation won't be fatal. But inflationary psychology and inflationary symptoms are taking root. If they do get firmly established, it will be hard to uproot them, and hard to resist pressure for overly-restrictive action."[45] But Johnson again backed away from the tax increase, and he ordered his staff to stop issuing any public warnings about the state of the economy and the need for a tax increase.[46]

In his memoirs, Johnson explained that he simply could not gather any support for the tax increase. His cabinet officers were opposed, and so were businessmen. At a meeting of one hundred and fifty leading business officials on March 30, 1966, Johnson asked for a show of hands: "How many of you would recommend tomorrow a tax increase to the Congress for the purpose of restraining our economy?" No one raised his hand. A similar question, posed to a group of labor leaders, produced a similar result. The House leadership, meanwhile, reported that of the twenty-five members of the House Ways and Means Committee, Johnson could expect no more than four votes for a tax increase—and Wilbur Mills, the most crucial vote, would not be among them.[47]

Halberstam ascribes more sinister motives. Johnson, he said, could get no support for a tax increase because he consciously chose not to disclose the real cost of the war and the implications of not raising taxes. Halberstam charged that members of Congress "were asked to give estimates and projections on a step as important as a tax increase based on totally erroneous information." It was "an extraordinary bit of manipulation," Halberstam wrote, and he quoted a Washington reporter who said it was the "single most irresponsible act by an American President" in the fifteen years he had been observing capital politics.[48] Halberstam suggests that a rousing call to arms, if backed by a revelation of Vietnam's true financial costs, would have created political support for a tax increase. But Johnson was firmly committed to keeping Vietnam a limited venture, and the president's soundings in December convinced him that on those grounds he could not move the Congress and, especially, Wilbur Mills to action.

Ackley warned Johnson that without a tax increase, the Federal Reserve would further tighten money.[49] For his part, Federal Reserve Board Chairman Martin left no doubt about what he would do. "The rise in prices has to be slowed down *this* year," he wrote to Treasury Secretary Fowler. If the job were not done with fiscal policy, Martin told Fowler that it would be done with monetary policy. He predicted that tighter monetary policy would mean higher interest rates, weakening of the savings-and-loan industry, harm to the municipal-bond market, and slowing of housing construction.[50]

Martin proved to be a good prophet. In the spring the Federal Reserve moved to slow the expansion, and by summer the growth in the money stock had fallen almost to zero. Interest rates moved to historic highs. Rates for prime commercial paper averaged 5.55 percent for the year, the highest by far in the postwar years and nearly twice the 1961 level. Savings and loans became overextended, and mortgage money almost dried up. Rates on state and local bonds soared, and two leading bond houses, caught with large inventories of unsold bonds, almost failed.[51] The monetary tightening helped to slow the boom, but it also produced a credit crunch, with high costs to some sectors of the economy. Johnson's Populist blood curdled at the high rates, but his advisers managed to keep him from denouncing the Federal Reserve by convincing him that some action had to be taken. The Federal Reserve, meanwhile, enjoyed the active but quiet support of the administration's economists.[52]

As Johnson's advisers began in the fall of 1966 to consider the budget for the next fiscal year, they reached the first broad-based agreement on the need for a tax increase. On September 2, 1966, eight advisers sent a joint memo to Johnson, in which they called for immediate action to reduce spending and to ask "at an appropriate time in the future" for "whatever tax measures are necessary" to pay for Vietnam.[53] Backed by, among others, Treasury Secretary Fowler, Defense Secretary McNamara, BOB Director Schultze, CEA Chairman Ackley, and presidential adviser Califano, the memo represented a remarkable meeting of the minds on a question that before had proven so difficult.

Johnson agreed, and on September 8 he sent a special economic message to Congress. He announced an immediate cut in spending of $1.5 billion and the suspension of the 7 percent investment tax credit. While he said he would not know the full budget situation until the implications of Vietnam were clearer and until Congress had completed its work on other appropriations bills, he did pledge, "This Administration is prepared to recommend whatever action is necessary to maintain stable growth and prosperity of the past five and one-half years and to pay for current expenditures out of current revenues, as we are doing."[54] Indeed, at that point, the budget was not far out of balance; the deficit for fiscal 1966, just ended, was less than $4 billion.

Having finally joined forces on the tax increase, however, Johnson's advisers began to get cold feet three months later. The Federal Reserve's tight money had at least temporarily blunted the inflation, and the Federal Reserve had begun to back off. The administration's background studies had meanwhile begun to show "persistent and pervasive softening" in the economy. Housing starts had plunged, business investment had slowed, and automobile sales had dropped. "The economy clearly does not need additional total restraint," one staff report argued; "in fact, some modest additional stimulus is in order."[55] It was easy to make an "old economics" case for a tax increase to balance the budget. If a tax increase were to be passed, however, the president's advisers feared that the slowdown in late 1966 might develop into a full-scale recession in 1967.[56]

Just as in the debate over the previous year's budget, the president's advisers were unsure about what problems they faced. Some suggested that he request from Congress the authority to invoke a stand-by tax quickly if needed.[57] Johnson's appointees to the Federal Reserve Board believed that the economy had been slowed down enough and opposed a tax increase, but Budget Director Schultze, Treasury Secretary Fowler, and the members of the Council of Economic Advisers favored a small tax increase, to go into effect no earlier than July 1, 1967.[58] The economy would be too soft during the first half of the year, and they worried that a tax increase might weaken it further. In fact, Treasury Secretary Fowler suggested that a modest deficit, spurred by increases in defense spending, might nicely complement the Federal Reserve's easier monetary policy. Later, a moderate tax increase would start to soak up some of the economic growth before it could unloose inflation. To the advisers, however, the question was a close one, and former CEA Chairman Heller, in his Christmas message to Johnson, hoped that "you will get Divine guidance on the question of a 1967 tax increase, since economic guidance gives you no very firm answer at the moment."[59]

In the next week, as the deadline for preparing the budget approached, Johnson's advisers decided that the economy would need a stimulus in the first half of 1967 and that any tax increase should wait until the second half of the year. By that point, they thought, the danger of inflation might be growing quickly enough to justify a small tax increase. "But," Fowler, Schultze, and Ackley wrote Johnson, "we need to keep the maximum degree of flexibility to back away from a tax increase—and even to release impounded spending—if the economy appears even weaker than we expect in the first half, or if prospects for a second half revival do not seem promising."[60] This led to the plan that Johnson proposed in his fiscal 1968 budget message: a 6 percent surtax on individual and corporate income taxes, effective July 1.[61] To keep flexibility, however, the administration did not send a formal proposal to Capitol Hill. That would come later, when the economic advisers had determined that the danger of recession had passed and that inflation was reigniting.

The proposal was certainly not popular with the American people. A Harris poll in February, 1967, which circulated at the White House, showed that 65 percent of those questioned opposed the surtax, while only 24 percent approved, compared with a much smaller split of 49 to 44 percent a year before. Worries about inflation had cooled off considerably from the previous year; in 1967, 68 percent thought that inflation was heading up, compared with 92 percent the year before. Because the public saw inflation as a less serious problem, the urgency for the tax increase lessened; and given the choice, 75 percent of those polled would rather cut spending than increase taxes. To at least one White House adviser, the case was clear: Johnson had waited one year too long to propose a tax increase.[62] For his part, Johnson was finally convinced of the need for a tax increase and said so in a May press conference. He exploded when one wire-service report said the administration was still not decided on the need for a tax increase. He ordered an aide to uncover the source for the story: "Find out who this is. This is not right. Wire me a report fast."[63]

In June, Johnson's economic advisers were convinced that the time had come to revive the surtax. The dip in the economy that they had sensed in the late fall of 1966 had proved to be very shallow and short-lived, and by early summer the economy was heating up again alarmingly. Budget deficits were growing to levels unprecedented except in times of a major war. Inflation had started to rise, bringing the prospect of tighter money from the Federal Reserve and a renewal of the previous year's credit crunch. There were early signs, further-more, of a serious balance-of-payments problem with foreign coun-tries. Domestic industries were expanding rapidly to fill the wartime demand, but Schultze warned Johnson that the boom could turn to bust when military spending would shrink at the end of the war.[64] But while Johnson's advisers agreed on the need for a tax increase, they could not agree on its size or timing. In frustration, Johnson scrawled on one report of differences among his aides: "For God's sake get agreement."[65]

That agreement finally came in July, on a plan to increase the earlier proposal for a 6 percent surtax to 10 percent, effective retro-actively to July 1 on corporate taxes and to September 1 for individual income taxes. Both surtaxes would expire on June 30, 1969, and would produce two years of restraint.[66] The fears of a grossly unbalanced budget and of galloping inflation finally led Johnson in July to ask Congress for the surtax, nineteen months after Ackley first had made the case for a tax increase. By then, evidence of an inflationary boom was unmistakable, and it was clear, explained Charles J. Zwick, Schultze's successor as budget director, that "you couldn't support both guns and butter without an increase in taxes."[67]

Johnson's advisers had misread the scale of the dip in the economy, and the rapid upswing had taken them by surprise. They had misjudged, by an even larger margin, just how much more dif-ficult it would be to pass a tax increase than a tax cut. The "new economics" logic of fine tuning thus developed a bias in favor of stimulus over restraint. Johnson himself finally agreed to the tax in-crease when the costs of not doing so became unmistakable. In his White House economics seminar, he understood the theory that his advisers argued, and he eagerly embraced the happy side of the Keyne-sian equation; but he hesitated in taking painful steps until the evidence was incontrovertible. By that time, as his advisers had warned, the inflationary demon had been unleashed.

III

The tax surcharge encountered immediate problems with Chair-man Wilbur Mills of the House Ways and Means Committee. He could see no signs of an economic upturn in July when the administration was reviving the plan, and as Gardner Ackley's successor as CEA Chairman, Arthur Okun, wrote later, "Congress would not act on a forecast; it wanted facts."[68] Califano warned the president, "Mills is going to be more difficult to sell this time than in the past."[69] Mills was making it clear that he did not like the tax surcharge and did not think it would pass Congress.[70] His position was simple: Johnson would have to choose between guns and butter. Mills would move toward restraint, but he preferred cutting the Great Society programs to increasing taxes.[71] To Budget Director Schultze, it was "clear that Wilbur Mills, many of the other Democrats, and all the Republicans on Ways and Means are going to try to hold us up" for bigger budget cuts.[72]

At a meeting with congressional leaders a few weeks after Johnson had submitted his proposal, Congressman Hale Boggs made the point simply to Johnson: "With Mills you can get it out of committee, and without Mills you can't."[73] Ackley meanwhile continued to warn, now in even harsher terms, about the implications of a failure to act. Without a tax bill, he wrote to Johnson on October 13, there would be "interest rates that will curl your hair, a new depression in housing, a new surge in imports" that would worsen the balance of trade and increase inflation in 1968 to almost 5 percent—with even worse to come in 1969. With a tax increase, inflation would be only about 2.5 percent, he said.[74]

Despite the warnings, Mills was unmoved. The congressional liaison staff learned that Mills was feeling neglected by Johnson. The president, Mills hinted, had not called him to the White House for consultation since the tax bill went up.[75] Despite the signals the president was getting, however, aide Larry O'Brien, Schultze, and Ackley all opposed making a bow to Mills.[76] Mills then broached his own plan, through a staff member, to get the bill moving. He would support a tax increase if the administration would agree to a $4 billion cut in expenditures, with Congress and the president sharing the responsibility for selecting the cuts.[77] The staff investigated this plan and thought they had a deal, but Mills subsequently backed away.[78]

Johnson tried to rally his forces in late October and asked Califano to get the word out: "Let's not give up yet."[79] But from many sources the president learned that Mills would not budge for the rest of the year. Congressman Carl B. Albert glumly reported, "Mills told me he would not report it out until the climate in the country is ready for it—whatever that means."[80] The president's personal relations with Mills had soured, and Mills made it plain that he would not budge unless the president agreed to spending cuts.[81] The very fact that Mills was trying to dictate spending cuts, however, enraged George H. Mahon, chairman of the House Appropriations Committee, in whose domain rested decisions on spending.[82] Johnson believed, furthermore, that Mills did not want to sully his powerful reputation by reporting the tax bill until he was sure he could get it passed. Mills used that excuse in turn to block the tax measure. He was "flim-flamming us," remembered congressional liaison J. Barefoot Sanders, Jr., later. Sanders was convinced that Mills could have passed the bill without large cuts if he had tried.[83]

Part of the bad blood, Budget Director Schultze speculated, had its roots in the administration's flip-flops on the investment tax credit. When the administration was looking for extra revenue in November, 1966, Mills backed the president in suspending the investment tax credit. A few months later, in March, 1967, Mills again backed the administration in restoring the credit when the economy dipped. "He felt he had been made to look like a fool," Schultze explained, and he was leery about going along with the economic forecasters once again—especially without the benefit of the solicitous LBJ "treatment."[84] For his part, Mills made this explanation to the Johnson Library's oral history project: "All I was ever trying to do in respect to the 10 percent surcharge was to describe the circumstances that would have to be brought to bear in order to get the 10 percent tax increase passed. The President knew what I was doing. He couldn't buy it."[85]

By early 1968, the White House had become convinced that Mills did not want a tax bill at any price. He told the congressional liaison staff that he wanted the administration to assure him of at least 175 votes on the floor before he would report the bill. The congressional liaison staff, however, could win no guarantee that if they did round up that many votes, Mills would in fact report the bill and that if he did report it, he would not then insist on extra conditions, such as a ceiling on federal spending. That put the congressional liaison staff on the spot. They counted only 110 "will support" votes and 33 "will probably support" votes among Democrats in the House, and they doubted they would ever be able to round up more than 155 votes until Mills had reported the bill. Members of Congress did not want to commit themselves blindly to a tax increase, and as the 1968 election drew closer, the prospect of voting for any tax increase became less and less attractive.[86] Treasury Secretary Fowler reported that neither Mills nor Mahon "want to block the parade," but "neither one is particularly anxious to assert the type of 'gung ho' boldness in leadership it may take" to get the bill passed.[87]

The impasse enormously frustrated Johnson. The cities were uneasy, the limited war was running beyond all expected bounds, the economy was heating up quickly, and he could not get firm action on any front. He badly wanted something that would cool the economy but would not wreck his domestic programs. Just a few days after announcing that he would not seek reelection, he said to congressional leaders: "If I were a dictator, I would say I've got to have $15 of the $24 billion in taxes we repealed [in 1964] back again. When we cut taxes, we didn't have a war and cities problem as we do now."[88] His frustration boiled over even into Vietnam strategy. He wanted some "radical new ideas," he told his staff, ideas that would lead to getting the troops out and to putting the money into economic development instead. With everybody withdrawing forces, perhaps there could be a United Nations–supervised election—and a reduction in the administration's economic problems.[89]

Administration officials began a new phase of negotiations with Mills. The administration suggested a 4:10:6 formula: $4 billion in immediate expenditure reductions, $10 billion less in further spending authority, and $6 billion less in present spending authority. Mills insisted on a 5:20 formula: $5 billion in immediate cuts and $20 billion in cuts in future obligations. Budget Bureau studies showed that the administration could cut no more than $4 billion without deeply hurting the Great Society. And even if Johnson were to accept the Mills 5:20 plan, there would be no guarantee that Mills would then accept the surtax.[90]

Califano saw the battle as "a critical turning point in your [Johnson's] Presidency," where "the importance of winning the tax fight transcends the fiscal problems." Without it, he warned on May 2, 1968, Johnson would lose all effectiveness in Congress and the executive branch, and he would have a far-harder time in leading the country. Califano urged Johnson to "give consideration to coming out fighting" and to "turn loose everything we have to take the Ways and Means Committee away from Mills."[91] At a press conference the next day, Johnson did indeed draw his guns. He said simply, "The Congress has not been that cooperative," and he singled Mills out by name. Mills's plan, Johnson hinted, "would injure the national interest instead of serving it." He then argued, "I think we are courting danger by this continued procrastination, this continued delay. Don't hold up a tax bill until you can blackmail someone into getting your own personal viewpoint over on reductions."[92]

When Mills still would not budge, the administration decided to outflank him. The constitution requires that all tax measures originate in the House, and House procedures required tax bills to originate in Mills's Ways and Means Committee. Mills's refusal to move thus had effectively blocked the bill for months. Senate leaders, however, worked with the administration to attach the surtax to a relatively innocuous House-passed bill that extended soon-to-expire excise taxes. At this point, Mills could duck the bill no longer. The Senate passed the bill on April 2, and that led to a long and tumultuous conference. Mills continued to press for higher spending cuts than the administration was willing to accept. Meanwhile, an international gold crisis increased pressure for quick action on the deficit.

The conference committee finally came to agreement near the end of June, and on June 28, thirty months after Ackley had first made the case for the surtax, Johnson, without ceremony, signed it into law. The bill set a retroactive 10 percent surcharge on individual and corporate income taxes, with the individual increase effective April 1, 1968, and the corporate increase effective January 1, 1968. Both surcharges were to be effective until July 1, 1969. In addition, the compromise required a $6 billion immediate cut in spending and a further cut of $8 billion in unspent appropriations authority. The compromise thus favored Mills in current spending cuts, but the administration was able to escape with $11 billion less in cuts for unspent appropriations authority than Mills had wanted. Furthermore, Congress, for the first time in history, set a ceiling on federal spending of $180.1 billion for fiscal 1969, compared with the president's budget request of $186.1 billion. Congress told the president how much to cut—but not where.

IV

The last major decision that Johnson faced before leaving office in January, 1969, was whether to recommend that the surtax be extended an extra year, until July 1, 1970. The Vietnam War was showing no signs of slowing down, and the president faced a large budget deficit without the extension. But President-elect Richard Nixon refused to commit himself to the extension. Califano urged Johnson, "I do not want to see you leave office with a budget that will be attacked" for "gimmickry and budget manipulation" or for "failure to maintain the momentum you have spent 5 years building in social programs."[93] Johnson agreed, and he recommended the one-year extension.

After making the decision, Johnson was in a reflective mood. In a meeting with members of the CEA staff and their families, he said to them: "If I had it to do over again I would not have changed much. I would have made the same decision to recommend a guns-and-butter budget to the Congress, and I still would have ignored the counsel of those who called for a breathing spell in the enactment of new legislation."[94] Those decisions turned out to be some of the most fateful in modern economic history. They helped to unloose a rampant inflation that proved unexpectedly difficult to quell, an inflation that persisted, to the consternation of economic theorists, even in the midst of recessions and high unemployment.

The roots of these decisions were far more complicated than the argument that Johnson lied to protect both Vietnam and the Great Society. White House economists underestimated the degree to which Vietnam was fueling the economy in late 1965, and they overestimated the slowdown that occurred in late 1966 and early 1967. The federal deficit grew rapidly, from $3.8 billion in fiscal 1966 to $8.7 billion in 1967 and $25.2 billion in 1968. Growth in spending for Vietnam—a $14.5 billion increase in 1967 and a $6.3 billion increase in 1968—added greatly to the deficit, but increases in Great Society programs and the slowdown in the economy significantly caused it to increase as well. The Federal Reserve rode to the rescue in 1966, with tight money that in the short run kept inflation from getting completely out of hand, but the system's stop-and-go policies had serious effects on some sectors of the economy, made the economy more unpredictable, and only worsened the basic disease. The success of the "new economics" during the early years of the Johnson presidency had been bright. The tax cut demonstrated that government could indeed deliver a well-timed stimulus, and the "full employment" goal of 4 percent was palpably close. But the future proved more difficult to predict than the president's economists had hoped. Once the future was clear, it became far more difficult to apply restraint than stimulus, and once the surtax had been enacted, governmental economists had overestimated the slowing effect that it would produce.[95]

Johnson himself was quite naturally leery of embracing the harsh medicine that went with bad news until the implications were obvious. But even after those implications were painfully apparent, one of the last of the congressional barons, Wilbur Mills, remained intransigent. Only by outflanking the chairman was Johnson finally able to win congressional passage of the tax increase. For a president who had come to the job with an unquestioned reputation for skill in dealing with Congress and who had demonstrated his skill by winning a tax cut within weeks of taking office, the irony was painful.

The irony is part of the essential tragedy of Lyndon Johnson and his administration. He unquestionably had a deep philosophical commitment to federal action, both for peace in Vietnam and for the needs of the poor.[96] Once committed, he felt inescapably bound to the goals. Bill Moyers tells a revealing story. Moyers once asked Johnson, "If you could talk to anybody, just sit there with our shoes off and talk, who would you like to talk to?" Johnson replied, "I'd like to talk to Toynbee." "Why?" Moyers asked. "He could help me understand what I'm up against in Vietnam. It's that God damn slate that you find when you walk into this office. You know, it wasn't written by Kennedy, and it wasn't written by Eisenhower, it was written by history. And I just don't understand it." As Moyers reflected later: Johnson "fought that war because he felt that history had decided we should. Well, we know that history is what men make it."[97] For Johnson, destiny and confusion among his advisers led him into an economic trap that he felt he could not escape from.

The biggest irony of all was that the tax increase proved to be too little and too late to rein in inflation. The Federal Reserve, in a hopeful reaction to Congress's passage of the surcharge, eased back on the money supply in mid 1968 as it waited for the increase to take hold. The surcharge, however, created barely a ripple in the economy, and by the end of 1968 the Federal Reserve reluctantly concluded that the surcharge was a dud. After several cycles of ease and restraint, the Federal Reserve once again stepped on the brakes to slow the economy and thus further worsened the stop-and-go monetary policy that had existed behind the scenes since 1966.

By this time, the seeds of fundamental economic instability had been planted. War-induced inflation, accompanied by the expansion of social programs and left unchecked by a tax increase, led consumers to begin to expect inflation to continue. The longer it remained, the harder it proved to uproot, and inflation became brutally persistent. Complicating matters further was the growth of unemployment, first to uncomfortable and, later, to crisis levels. This cruel combination, which was christened stagflation, was the ultimate rebuff to the Keynesian economists who surrounded Johnson. Inflation and unemployment were supposed to be trade-offs, and Keynesian theory simply could not explain how the two could grow simultaneously. The unexplainable happened nonetheless, and the result was a decade of instability that spilled over into international crises as well. Meanwhile, the federal government had its last balanced budget in fiscal 1969 before beginning seemingly endless years of deficits. The attempts by Johnson and his advisers to manage the economy foundered on economic uncertainty and political reality as they unintentionally helped to steer the nation onto economic shoals.

Lyndon Johnson proved to be an able student in the economics seminar that his advisers ran for him. He was a quick study, but he found it hard to embrace the full implications of his lessons, especially when the lessons were unclear. He found it difficult to deal with the uncertainty of economic predictions, to jump before the evidence was irrefutable. Johnson was a man of considerable subtlety in public policy. He attempted to fight a limited war when it would have been easier to fight a large one; he battled for the Great Society, even in the face of a widening war, when many members of Congress gladly would have cut the social programs. He was a president caught in his dreams, unable to control his destiny, and in the end he was destroyed by this conflict.

Notes

1. Otto Eckstein, "The Economics of the 1960's: A Backward Look," *Public Interest* 19 (Spring, 1970): 88.

2. Herbert Stein, *The Fiscal Revolution in America* (Chicago: University of Chicago Press, 1969).

3. Richard L. Schott interview with Bill Moyers, June 20, 1978, pp. 38–39. Professor Schott is a faculty member at the Lyndon Baines Johnson School of Public Affairs, University of Texas.

4. David Halberstam, "How the Economy Went Haywire," *Atlantic Monthly*, Sept., 1972, pp. 56–60, and *The Best and the Brightest* (New York: Random House, 1972).

5. Halberstam, "How the Economy Went Haywire," pp. 56–58.

6. Ibid., p. 56.

7. See, e.g., Matthew J. Golden, "The 'No-Tax Decision' of 1966," in U.S. Commission on the Organization of the Government for the Conduct of Foreign Policy, vol. 3, app. H (Washington, D.C.: U.S. Government Printing Office, June, 1975), pp. 185–95.

8. *Newsweek*, Nov. 6, 1979, p. 43.

9. William Manchester, *The Death of a President* (New York: Harper & Row, 1967), p. 360.

10. Walter Heller oral history, Lyndon Baines Johnson Library (hereafter cited as LBJL), tape 1, p. 13. All subsequent oral histories and documents, unless otherwise noted, come from the Johnson Library.

11. Heller to Johnson, memo, Nov. 23, 1963, Council of Economic Advisers Administrative History, vol. 2, pt. 1.

12. For an account of Kennedy's struggles with the tax cut see Allen J. Matusow, *The Unraveling of America: A History of Liberalism in the 1960s* (New York: Harper & Row, 1984), pp. 30–59.

13. Rowland Evans and Robert Novak, *Lyndon B. Johnson: The Exercise of Power* (New York: New American Library, 1966), p. 309.

14. Later, in fact, Ackley proposed a $97.9 billion budget, even lower than the $98 billion budget that the House Republicans were seeking. For a discussion see James L. Sundquist, *Politics and Policy: The Eisenhower, Kennedy, and Johnson Years* (Washington, D.C.: Brookings Institution, 1968), p. 52.

15. Secretary of the Treasury Douglas Dillon urged the president to take this move for similar reasons (see Dillon to Johnson, memo, Nov. 25, 1963, WHCF EX FI 11-4).

16. Gardner Ackley oral history, tape 2, p. 12. For similar views see Walter W. Heller, *New Dimensions of Political Economy* (New York: W. W. Norton, 1967), p. 29; and Arthur Okun oral history, tape 11, p. 10.

17. Ackley oral history, tape 1, p. 12.

18. Heller to Johnson, memo, June 2, 1964, WHCF EX FI 11-4.

19. Evans and Novak, *Lyndon B. Johnson*, p. 376.

20. Lyndon Baines Johnson, *The Vantage Point: Perspectives of the Presidency, 1963–1969* (New York: Holt, Rinehart & Winston, 1971), p. 103.

21. *New York Times*, June 2, 1965, p. 1.

22. Susan J. Lepper and Frank W. Schiff to the Council of Economic Advisers, memo, June 28, 1965, WHCF CF FG 11-3.

23. Ackley to Johnson, memo, July 30, 1965, CEA Administrative History, vol. 2, pt. 1.

24. Ackley to Johnson, memo, Sept. 2, 1965, WHCF EX FI 11.

25. Paul A. Volcker, Charles J. Zwick, Daniel H. Brill, and Arthur M. Okun to Fowler, Schultze, Martin, and Ackley, memo, Nov. 6, 1965, CEA Administrative History, vol. 2, pt. 1.

26. Presidential statement, Dec. 5, 1965, WHCF EX FI 6.

27. Halberstam says that the CEA sent Johnson a memo arguing for a tax increase on Dec. 10, 1965 (see "How the Economy Went Haywire," p. 57). A thorough search of the Johnson Library and of Ackley's papers at the University of Michigan's Bentley Library, however, shows no such memo.

28. Ackley oral history, tape 11, p. 2.

29. Ackley to Johnson, memo, Dec. 17, 1965, WHCF EX FI 4 (emphasis in the original). Johnson refers to this memo in his memoirs (see *Vantage Point*, p. 440).

30. Ackley to Johnson, memo, Dec. 27, 1965, WHCF CF FI 4.

31. Heller to Johnson, memo, Dec. 22, 1965, WHCF CF FI 11-4.

32. Joseph Califano to Johnson, telex, Dec. 23, 1965, WHCF EX FG 110; see also Walter Heller oral history, tape 2, p. 44. Some have suggested that McNamara opposed the tax increase (see Golden, " 'No-Tax Decision,' " p. 190).

33. Hayes Redmon to Bill Moyers, memo, Dec. 4, 1965, WHCF EX FI 4.

34. "Federal Fiscal Policy in the 1960's," *Federal Reserve Bulletin* 54 (Sept., 1968): 709.

35. Charles L. Schultze oral history, tape 2, p. 8.

36. Schultze to Johnson, memo, Dec. 27, 1965, WHCF CF FI 4.

37. Schultze oral history, tape 2, p. 8.

38. Larry Levinson to Johnson, telex, Dec. 29, 1965, WHCF CF FI 4.

39. Ibid.

40. Johnson tells the story in his memoirs (see *Vantage Point*, p. 325).

41. See, e.g., Schultze oral history, tape 2, p. 3.

42. Okun oral history, tape 1, pp 23–25; Schultze oral history, tape 2, p. 6.

43. Henry H. Wilson, Jr., to Johnson, memo, Jan. 10, 1966, WHCF CF LE/FI 11.

44. Schultze to Johnson, memo, Dec. 27, 1965, WHCF CF FI 4.

45. Ackley, Okun, and James S. Duesenberry to Johnson, memo, Mar. 12, 1966, WHCF CF FI 11. Johnson acknowledges this memo in his memoirs (see *Vantage Point*, p. 444).

46. Robert A. Kintner to Fowler, Connor, Wirtz, Freeman, and Ackley, memo, June 29, 1966, WHCF EX FI II-2.

47. Johnson, *Vantage Point*, p. 444.

48. Halberstam, "How the Economy Went Haywire," p. 59.

49. Ackley to Johnson, memo, May 10, 1966, WHCF EX FI 11.

50. Martin to Fowler, memo, June 6, 1966, WHCF CF FI II-4.

51. G. L. Bach, *Making Monetary and Fiscal Policy* (Washington, D.C.: Brookings Institution, 1971), pp. 126–28.

52. In his memoirs, Johnson acknowledged, "The major burden of slowing the inflation was left to monetary policy in the form of higher interest rates" (see *Vantage Point*, p. 445).

53. Fowler et al. to Johnson, memo, Sept. 2, 1966, WHCF EX FI 11.

54. *Public Papers of the Presidents of the United States: Lyndon B. Johnson, 1966*, vol. 2, p. 444.

55. Robert A. Wallace, Zwick, and Okun to Fowler, Schultze, and Ackley, memo, Dec. 12, 1966, CEA Administrative History, vol. 2, pt. 1. The memo was part of the regular Troika-II exercise, where the second-level officials from the Treasury Department, the Bureau of the Budget, and the Council of Economic Advisers prepared a forecast for their principals.

56. Califano to Johnson, memo, Dec. 8, 1966, WHCF CF BE 5-4.

57. Francis M. Bator to Johnson, memo, Dec. 21, 1966, WHCF EX FI 11-4.

58. Califano to Johnson, memo, and Fowler to Johnson, memo, Dec. 23, 1966, and Fowler, Schultze, and Ackley to Johnson, memo, Dec. 30, 1966—all in WHCF CF FI 11-4.

59. Heller to Johnson, memo, Dec. 23, 1966, WHCF EX FI 11.

60. Fowler, Schultze, and Ackley to Johnson, memo, Dec. 30, 1966, CEA Administrative History, vol. 2, pt. 1; see also Califano to Johnson, telex, Dec. 31, 1966, WHCF CF BE 5-4.

61. Califano to Johnson, memo, Jan. 4, 1967, WHCF EX FI 11. A surtax is a tax on a tax; taxpayers would calculate their tax liability and then would add another 6 percent.

62. Fred Panzer to Johnson, memo, Feb. 24, 1967, WHCF EX FI 11-4.

63. Note on a memo from Jim Jones to Johnson, Dec. 5, 1967, WHCF EX FI 11-4.

64. Schultze to Johnson, memo, July 11, 1967, WHCF EX FI 11-4.

65. Califano to Johnson, June 12, 1967, WHCF EX FI 11-4.

66. Fowler, Wirtze, Trowbridge, McNamara, Schultze, Ackley, and Califano to Johnson, memo, July 22, 1967, WHCF EX FI 11.

67. Charles J. Zwick oral history, tape 11, p. 4.

68. Arthur M. Okun, *The Political Economy of Prosperity* (Washington, D.C.: Brookings Institution, 1970), p. 86.

69. Califano to Johnson, memo, July 19, 1967, WHCF EX FI 11-4.

70. Surrey to Fowler, memo, July 2, 1967, WHCF CF FI 11-4.

71. Barefoot Sanders to Johnson, memo, Sept. 13, 1967, WHCF EX FI 11-4.

72. Schultze to Johnson, memo, Sept. 16, 1967, WHCF EX LE/FI 11-4.

73. Jones to Johnson, notes from Sept. 19, 1967, Congressional Leadership Meeting, Meeting Notes file, box 2.

74. Ackley to Johnson, memo, Oct. 13, 1967, WHCF EX FI 11-4.

75. White House notes, however, show that Mills met at the White House with the president and with Treasury Secretary Fowler on August 3 and that he joined congressional leaders at a September 9 breakfast meeting with the president (see Stan Ross to Califano, memo, May 7, 1968, WHCF EX FI).

76. Califano to Johnson, memo, Oct. 5, 1967, WHCF EX FI 4/FG.

77. Schultze to Johnson, memo, Oct. 19, 1967, and Larry O'Brien to Johnson, memo, Oct. 17, 1967—both in WHCF EX LE/FI 11-4.

78. Okun oral history, tape 2, p. 21.

79. Johnson's note on UPI dispatch, Oct. 30, 1967, WHCF EX LE/FI 11-4.

80. Jones to Johnson, notes on Oct. 31, 1967, Congressional Democratic Leadership Meeting, Meeting Notes file, box 2; see also Califano to Johnson, memo, Nov. 11, 1967, and Sanders to Johnson, memo, Nov. 28, 1967—both in WHCF EX FI 11-4.

81. Barefoot Sanders oral history, tape 2, p. 44.

82. Johnson, *Vantage Point*, p. 445.

83. Sanders oral history, tape 2, pp. 41–44; see also Johnson, *Vantage Point*, p. 445.

84. Schultze oral history, tape 2, p. 20.

85. Wilbur Mills oral history, p. 14.

86. Sanders to Johnson, memo, Feb. 29, 1968, and Joseph M. Barr to Johnson, memo, Apr. 22, 1968—both in WHCF EX LE/FI 11-4.

87. Fowler to Johnson, memo, Mar. 2, 1968, WHCF CF LE/FI 11/4.

88. Notes on Congressional Leadership Breakfast, Apr. 2, 1968, Meeting Notes file, box 2.

89. Memo from Jim Jones, Apr. 19, 1968, WHCF EX SP.

90. Sanders to Johnson, memo, Apr. 27, 1968, WHCF EX LE/FI 11-4.

91. Califano to Johnson, memo, May 2, 1968, WHCF EX LE/FI 11-4.

92. *Public Papers . . . 1968*, pp. 223–25.

93. Califano to Johnson, memo, Jan. 6, 1969, WHCF EX FI 11.

94. Johnson, *Vantage Point*, p. 342.

95. Charles E. McClure, Jr., "Fiscal Failure: Lessons of the Sixties," in Phillip Cagan et al., *Economic Policy and Inflation in the Sixties* (Washington, D.C.: American Enterprise Institute, 1972), p. 11.

96. See George C. Herring, "The War in Vietnam," and Mark I. Gelfand, "The War on Poverty"—both in *Exploring the Johnson Years*, ed. Robert A. Divine (Austin: University of Texas Press, 1981), pp. 27–62 and 126–54.

97. Schott interview with Moyers, June 20, 1978, pp. 39–40.

A Bibliographical Note

The Johnson Library's holdings on economic policy constitute one of the finest parts of the collection, but they have been relatively little explored. The subject has escaped the closures for security or privacy reasons that afflict other parts of the papers. Johnson's economic advisers, furthermore, ran a seminar through the memos that they wrote for the president, so there is an unusually rich record of debates, arguments, and decisions.

In addition, the oral histories from the economic policy makers are valuable. The library's oral-history project has interviewed all of the main actors, and many of the histories are very helpful in interpreting the memos, in confirming perceptions, and in suggesting arguments that are not otherwise available. In addition, the library contains a "Meeting Notes File," which contains notes on meetings in which the president participated. These notes contain unusually frank comments not available elsewhere. Put together, all of these sources support the accuracy of Johnson's memoir, which is itself an important document for studying these questions.

This essay touches on only a few of the vastly important economic problems with which the Johnson administration dealt. Other relatively unresearched issues on which the library contains rich holdings include the role of Johnson's Council of Economic Advisers, congressional strategy on economic policy, and the budgetary process—especially the Planning-Programming-Budgeting system that Johnson extended throughout the government.

4 | Foreign Aid and the Balance-of-Payments Problem: Vietnam and Johnson's Foreign Economic Policy

Burton I. Kaufman

WHEN VICE-PRESIDENT LYNDON JOHNSON was suddenly elevated to the White House after the assassination of President John F. Kennedy on November 22, 1963, he was faced with a series of problems—and opportunities—in the area of foreign economic policy. The most important of these were maintaining at least the present level of foreign aid against growing congressional opposition and resolving the nagging balance-of-payments deficit. Until about 1966 the president enjoyed strong congressional support in dealing with these problems. But the United States' growing involvement in Vietnam changed all that.

The war affected the administration's foreign economic policies in at least two ways. First, it exacerbated the balance-of-payments problem, thereby helping to weaken the dollar in international money markets and to undermine the international monetary system, based as it was on the stability of the dollar. Second, by helping to turn a once friendly into an increasingly hostile Congress, this country's growing involvement in the conflict also undermined the administration's effectiveness on Capitol Hill and made it difficult for the White House to get its high-priority items, including its spending proposals for foreign aid, through the House and Senate without major cuts and revisions. Indeed, foreign aid became the focus of congressional misgivings and discontent over the war and over U.S. foreign policy in general, and the huge cuts that the program sustained were directly attributable to Congress' displeasure with the administration's escalation of the war after 1965.

I

Initiatives that had begun under Kennedy and, in some cases, under President Dwight D. Eisenhower before him set the agenda of the new administration after Johnson entered the White House in 1963. Basic to that agenda was maintaining or even increasing the size of the nation's foreign-aid program. This promised to be difficult, for foreign aid had never been particularly popular, either among the American public or on Capitol Hill. Dating back to the Truman Doctrine of 1947 and the Marshall Plan of 1948, the aid program had moved gradually from European reconstruction to defensive alliances and, finally, during Eisenhower's administration, to the economic development of Third World countries.[1] President Kennedy had called for an even greater emphasis on economic aid to Third World nations, and soon after taking office, he had asked Congress to replace the Mutual Security Act, by which foreign aid had been administered for the previous ten years, with new legislation that would emphasize an expanded program of development loans. Congress responded by authorizing $7.2 billion for such loans over a five-year period. This allowed Kennedy to streamline the entire foreign-aid program and to establish, in November, 1961, the Agency for International Development (AID), which combined into one agency most of the nation's technical- and economic-assistance programs overseas.

However, the House and Senate rejected Kennedy's request for a five-year appropriation, insisting that the funds be appropriated annually as they had always been. Furthermore, Congress cut heavily into the administration's requests for foreign aid, questioning the management and effectiveness of foreign aid, arguing that too much emphasis was being placed on military aid, and raising doubts about the United States' ability to fund the program. In fact, by the time Kennedy was killed in 1963, congressional opposition to foreign aid had reached a new high, and Congress had cut the president's recommendations for fiscal 1964 by a record 34 percent, a problem that his successor would have to face almost immediately after assuming office.[2]

The new president shared many of the same concerns that Congress did about the foreign-aid program. Indeed, in a number of respects, Johnson was more in sympathy with the program's critics than with its defenders. As majority leader in the Senate for most of Eisenhower's eight years in office, Johnson had almost always helped to push the president's foreign-aid requests through Congress.[3] Having taught Mexican-American students as a young man and then having represented in Congress a state that had a large Spanish-speaking population, he had also long regarded himself as an expert in Latin American affairs. As president he would display a particular interest in the Alliance for Progress, which had been established in 1961 to stimulate economic recovery and development in Latin America.[4] In addition, he had a real interest in eliminating hunger and in providing adequate nourishment world-wide, which he would make clear throughout his administration.[5]

On the other hand, many of Johnson's own views on the foreign-aid program were narrowly circumscribed. As a congressman and a senator, he had not displayed any particular interest in world affairs, and to the extent that he had considered such issues as foreign aid, he had been concerned not so much with their long-term economic or social benefits to other nations as with their costs and with the political return to the United States (and to himself). Even after he had been in the Oval Office for more than a year, he had said to a group of congressmen, "One of the troubles with the aid program is that you fellows place all the incompetent people you know in aid jobs"; he added, "I know, because I used to do it myself." In other words, as president, Johnson was not against foreign aid; far from it; but he did have doubts about the cost effectiveness and the administrative efficiency of the program, concerns that were sometimes more important to him than the program itself. Furthermore, he expected some form of measurable political return for America's munificence, if nothing more than evidence of political gratitude on the part of the recipient towards its benefactor.[6]

Other considerations also heavily influenced Johnson's attitude on foreign aid and, for that matter, on most foreign economic issues. In the first place, while he loyally supported Kennedy's aid program, with its increased emphasis on development assistance, just as he had supported most of Eisenhower's requests for aid, Johnson never felt comfortable with Kennedy's approach to the Third World. Johnson believed even more strongly than Kennedy had in regional programs of mutual self-help, such as the Alliance for Progress, for Latin America, and similar programs for Asia and Africa. He was also convinced that the world's other industrialized nations had to assume more of the responsibility for the Third World, and he placed far more emphasis than Kennedy had on the importance of private investment in underdeveloped countries. In this respect, Johnson's approach to economic development was a throwback to the early years of the Eisenhower administration, when Eisenhower had tried to substitute a program of expanded trade and private investment for foreign aid.[7] Perhaps as important, Johnson rarely failed to consider the domestic political consequences of his foreign economic programs. Just as he expected a political benefit to the United States from the assistance that it provided to other countries, he was hesitant to undertake any initiative that might either weaken him politically or undermine the office that he represented. Conversely, he was willing to expend great effort and to take considerable risks in order to maintain presidential integrity.

The limits of Johnson's commitment to foreign aid and his abiding concern with political considerations was clearly evident in his conflict with Congress over Kennedy's aid program for 1964. To be sure, after taking office, Johnson stated his determination to restore some of the large cuts that had already been made in the separate authorization bills passed by the House and the Senate. He even made an unexpected evening visit to Capitol Hill to meet with House Speaker John W. McCormack's informal "Board of Education" session of congressional leaders to press for the full authorization, and Johnson warned Otto Passman of Louisiana, who led the fight against foreign aid in the Appropriations Committee, that if he (Johnson) did not get the full $3.6 billion, he would carry the battle to the House floor, where he would whip Passman.[8]

The president was far more concerned with Kennedy's tax bill and his civil-rights measure, however, than he was with the foreign-aid legislation. Thus, Johnson never carried through with his threat to the Louisiana congressman. Even with respect to the aid program, Johnson was worried more about an amendment to the appropriations legislation that had nothing to do with foreign assistance than with the aid program itself. Just before Kennedy was killed, Republican Senator Karl E. Mundt of South Dakota attached to the measure a rider, which would have prohibited the Export-Import Bank from guaranteeing loans to finance trade with any Communist countries. Johnson regarded Mundt's amendment and other similar ones as a challenge to his office and as a test of his new authority as president. Therefore, he decided to take whatever steps were necessary to defeat the proposals. The vote on the amendment was set for November 26, the day of President Kennedy's funeral. Johnson later commented: "We could not afford to lose a vote like that, after only four days in office. If those legislators had tasted blood then, they would have run over us like a steamroller when they returned in January, when much more than foreign aid would depend on their actions."[9]

By using his considerable powers of persuasion and by displaying all the political acumen that had made him such an effective majority leader when he was in the Senate, the new president was able to defeat Mundt's amendment and similar efforts. From the White House, Johnson stayed on the phone, contacting his supporters to keep them in line. At the same time he invoked Kennedy's memory to win over undecided or uncommitted members of the House and the Senate. Towards the end of the fight, when the House balked at a conference report that excluded restrictions that the House had recently passed, he called the members of the House, many of whom had already left Washington for the Christmas holidays, back to town for another vote. On the next day, December 23, he invited the congressmen to the White House for a reception, where he stood on a chair in the State Dining Room to press his case. In an unusual 7:00 A.M. session less than twenty-four hours later, the House agreed to a second conference report, which allowed the president to authorize export guarantees if he found them to be in the national interest.[10]

As a number of newspapers later noted, Johnson's decisive actions during his first few weeks in office, including his successful fight against credit restrictions on East-West trade, quickly established his reputation as a strong and dynamic leader. But the new president left his first bout with Congress over foreign aid convinced that dramatic changes would have to be made in how the aid program was presented to Congress if additional cuts were to be avoided. Believing that there was a great deal of waste and mismanagement in the aid program and having real reservations about its benefits for the United States, the new president even considered splitting up the Agency for International Development in order to make the foreign-aid program more palatable to Congress.

Eventually, Johnson decided against this, having been advised by congressional leaders that too many changes had already been made in the administration of the program.[11] Instead, Johnson adopted another tactic. Believing that previous cuts had seriously eroded the prestige of the presidency, he decided to present Congress with a "pre-shrunk" request for 1965, which would make it extremely difficult for the House and the Senate to reduce it still further. At the same time, he would make clear to the House and the Senate that he was placing more emphasis on self-help by recipient nations and that he intended to rely more on private investment to assist in the economic development of Third World nations, even making such investments eligible for a special tax credit.[12]

Accordingly, in his message to Congress in March, Johnson asked for only $3.52 billion in foreign aid, or approximately $1 billion less than what Kennedy had asked for a year earlier. "The funds I am requesting," Johnson remarked, "will be concentrated where they will produce the best results, and speed the transition from United States assistance to self-support wherever possible."[13] During the ensuing legislative process, administration leaders and congressional supporters pushed the point that the request for aid represented a "harder figure" than any of the other proposals in recent years. They also continued to emphasize the program's increased emphasis on self-support and private investment.[14]

In all, Johnson encountered relatively little difficulty in pushing his program through Congress and in getting most of what he had sought. There continued to be the usual objections to foreign aid that had been raised since at least Eisenhower's administration. Significantly, Johnson's request in May for $125 million in additional economic and military assistance for South Vietnam troubled some congressmen who were already worried about the worsening crisis in Southeast Asia. Compared to a year earlier, however, the congressional debate over foreign aid in 1964 was muted. For the first time in the nineteen-year history of the foreign-aid program, the House Foreign Affairs Committee approved the president's full requests for funding, including the additional aid for Vietnam. Furthermore, the final appropriation of $3.25 billion was only $267 million, or 7.6 percent, less than the original request, the lowest percentage cut in the entire history of the aid program. Johnson's strategy of presenting Congress with an already scaled-down program, his usual attention to every detail of the legislative process, and the death in May of the chairman of the House Appropriations Committee, Clarence Cannon of Missouri, who had supported past efforts to trim foreign aid—all accounted for getting the program through Congress relatively unscathed.[15]

By the time that Johnson signed the foreign-aid legislation into law in October, he was also having to pay more and more attention to the balance-of-payments deficit. This, too, was a problem that he had inherited from the Eisenhower and Kennedy administrations. In fact, because of a precipitous drop in U.S. holdings of gold—from $24 billion in 1954 to about $18.7 billion in 1959, as a result of the payments deficit—Eisenhower had been forced to adopt many of the same policies that Johnson would later employ. These included the tying of aid to the fostering of trade, a cutting back in military expenditures overseas (a major item in the deficit), and the discouraging of Americans from investing abroad, except in Third World countries where U.S. capital was still considered to be essential to economic development.[16]

Nevertheless, the balance of payments had continued to deteriorate even after Kennedy had become president. As large amounts of gold continued to leave the United States, the dollar came under speculative attack. In order to reestablish confidence in the dollar, to offset speculative surges, and to put an end to the heavy losses in the nation's gold stock, the Kennedy administration had created a series of new financial tools and had obtained an agreement among the finance ministers and the central bankers of the ten leading industrial countries (the so-called Group of Ten) to make available $6 billion in supplementary resources to the International Monetary Fund (IMF) for lending to any one of the ten. But while these measures stopped the hemorrhaging of America's gold holdings and the gold outflow for 1961 and 1962 slowed by half from what it had been in 1960,[17] the balance of payments, on which the stability of the dollar ultimately rested, continued to worsen.

In an effort to deal with this continuing problem, Kennedy had announced in July, 1963, a comprehensive balance-of-payments program, the major feature of which was an interest-equalization tax, designed to stem the flow of U.S. capital abroad by increasing the cost to foreign borrowers of raising money in the United States. The program also provided for a further tying of foreign aid to U.S. exports, a further reduction in overseas military costs, and a decision to seek a $500 million standby credit from the IMF. But before the program could be fully implemented, Kennedy had been killed, and it was left to Johnson to deal with the whole thorny problem of the balance of payments.[18]

From the time that he had taken office, the payments deficit had affected almost every aspect of Johnson's foreign economic program. Because of the unfavorable balance of payments, for example, the president had directed, in December, 1963, that maximum use be made of dollar credits rather than local currencies for the purchase of agricultural goods that were being sold under PL 480, or the Food for Peace program.[19] Similarly, the administration had increased the tying of AID grants and loans to American procurement as part of its program to reduce federal expenditures abroad. For the same reason, it had ordered significant cuts in overseas military spending and in the number of government personnel who were serving abroad. Finally, it had proposed a 50 percent increase in the quotas of the IMF as a way of bolstering the dollar and the much weaker pound.[20]

In fact, finding ways to achieve both additional financing for the U.S. deficit and increasing international liquidity were the main thrusts of Johnson's international monetary policy, just as they had been for Kennedy.[21] But the Europeans—especially the French, Dutch, and Belgians—opposed a significant enlargement of the IMF (which provided deficit nations with short-term balance-of-payments loans) because the fund operated under the existing gold-dollar system, which, they believed, allowed Washington to pay its debts by speeding up its printing presses. President Charles de Gaulle of France, especially, wanted to dethrone the dollar as a reserve currency and to force greater discipline on the U.S. economy, which he considered to be profligate.[22] Instead of a 50 percent increase in the IMF quotas, therefore, the Europeans agreed in August to only an overall increase of 25 percent, an action that White House aide Francis Bator and National Security Adviser McGeorge Bundy termed "more mouse than elephant."[23]

Nevertheless, the administration's overall scorecard for dealing with the balance-of-payments deficit during its first year in office was encouraging. The liquid deficit for 1964 was pegged at $2.4 billion, down 28 percent from 1963 and down 39 percent from the annual average for the years 1958 through 1960.[24] Gold losses were even more encouraging, being 60 percent less than the previous year and almost 90 percent less than the annual average for 1958 through 1960.[25] To be sure, the United States was still not out of the woods. Indeed, figures for the last quarter of 1964 showed a worsening of the payments deficit, so that at the end of January, a cabinet committee on the balance of payments met at the White House to review possible additional measures for holding down the dollar outflow from the United States. For the most part, however, the mood of the meeting was sanguine. Although there was by now consensus that additional measures were called for, most participants at the meeting did not regard the situation as critical. "There is danger in too small and too weak a program," Chairman Gardner Ackley of the Council of Economic Advisers (CEA) thus told the president. "But *there is also danger in too strong and restrictive a program*" (Ackley's italics). Consequently, the committee recommended only a program of carefully monitored voluntary restraints on direct investments and short-term loans abroad, a program that McGeorge Bundy referred to as one of "moral suasion."[26]

On February 10, President Johnson presented the proposal to Congress. Although he asked the House and the Senate to renew and extend existing legislation, including the 1964 Interest Equalization Tax, the president made clear that the heart of his program was a voluntary program of credit restriction. Assuring Congress that the state of the dollar throughout the world was "strong—far stronger than three or four years ago"—and that the dollar remained "as good as gold, freely convertible at $35 an ounce," he said his recommendations were "designed to serve our balance-of-payments objectives without imposing direct controls on American business abroad." "*We seek to preserve the freedom of the market place*," he concluded (Johnson's italics). Publicly, the administration refused to estimate the impact that the program would have on the payments deficit. But privately, administration officials anticipated cutting the deficit in half, from about $3 billion in 1964 to approximately $1.5 billion for 1965.[27]

One proposal for dealing with the balance-of-payments problem that the White House decided not to adopt was tightening credit and raising interest rates as a way of discouraging imports and of attracting foreign capital. Although considerable discussion took place over this issue, the administration concluded that the domestic economy was still not sufficiently robust to withstand such a tight money policy.[28] Powerful groups, including organized labor, also spoke out against tightening credit, which George Meany, president of the American Federation of Labor (AFL), told Johnson would be "a dangerous measure in an economy of persistent unemployment and rapid increases in both productivity and labor."[29]

In Europe, reaction to the president's balance-of-payments program was mixed at best. On the one hand, there was satisfaction that the United States was concentrating on limiting the outflow of capital, and there was a sense that the bank part of the program would probably work. On the other hand, there were serious doubts about the administration's ability to curtail corporate outflows by voluntary means, and there was much regret that in its program, the White House did not include provisions for tightening domestic credit.[30] The attitude in the United States was also mixed, as some businessmen expressed puzzlement as to what exactly they were expected to do, while others made clear that they could not curtail foreign spending projects that were already under way. For the most part, however, the general feeling within the business community was one of giving the program a chance to see what it would accomplish.[31]

Congress felt much the same way. In hearings before the Senate Banking and Currency Committee that began in March, Treasury Secretary Douglas Dillon and other administration officials spelled out the administration's case for restricting the flow of capital abroad. A number of economists and academicians also testified before the committee, debating among themselves whether the balance-of-payments deficit represented a "crisis" or a "near crisis," an argument that mystified some senators.[32] On the whole, however, the administration had an easy time in Congress. By the end of September the House and Senate had passed virtually unchanged the entire package of legislation that Johnson had requested.[33]

Indeed, 1965 marked the height of achievement insofar as Johnson's foreign economic policy was concerned. Not only did Congress give the president almost everything that he wanted with respect to his balance-of-payments program, but the payments deficit itself declined to $1.3 billion, the smallest deficit since 1957 and less than half the $2.8 billion figure for 1964. This was enough to convince administration officials that the problem was under control.[34] Almost as important, Johnson succeeded in getting his foreign-aid request of $3.38 billion through the House and the Senate pretty much intact, just as he had a year earlier. The final appropriation of $3.2 billion represented a cut of just 6.9 percent, the smallest on record, smaller even than the 7.6 percent reduction a year earlier.[35] A major debate did take place over the future and structure of foreign aid, which taxed relations between the White House and Chairman Fulbright of the Senate Foreign Relations Committee, who wanted to separate economic from military assistance and who favored a multiyear authorization for foreign aid.[36] The differences between Fulbright and the administration, which did not want to stir the already-murky waters of foreign aid, might have served as a warning of the difficulty that the president would soon face in the Senate.[37] But together with the payments legislation that Congress has already approved, the passage of the aid legislation for 1965 added to the already existing image of Johnson as being the most effective president since Franklin Roosevelt. The year 1965 had indeed been a very good one for President Johnson.

II

It was the last such year, however. As a result of the Vietnam War, matters changed dramatically during the next year and stayed that way for the remainder of Johnson's administration. The improvement in the balance of payments that had taken place in 1965 proved to be transitory, not intrinsic. Although there were complex reasons for this, having to do largely with excess demand and weak fiscal policies, a major factor—as the administration realized but failed to do anything about—was the cost of the Vietnam War, which further inflated an already overheated economy, creating import demand, cutting into export growth, and causing an outflow of gold and dollars that threatened the very stability of the dollar, and indeed, the international monetary system.[38] But the balance-of-payments deficit was not the only casualty of the Vietnam War; the White House's foreign-aid program became a victim as well. For opponents of the war, particularly in the Senate, opposition to foreign aid became a way of striking back at the White House where it was particularly vulnerable while presenting their own case to the American public. As a result, the debates over foreign aid, beginning in 1966, became increasingly acerbic, and the cuts in the program became more and more severe.

It would be unfair to blame the Vietnam War entirely for the nation's balance-of-payments problem. As we have already seen, the payments deficit was one that President Johnson had inherited from Presidents Eisenhower and Kennedy. Furthermore, as early as 1965, a number of administration officials had begun to express concern about Johnson's program for dealing with the payments deficit, both before and after Congress had acted on the program and before the war could have much effect on the nation's economy. For the most part, however, the recommendation of these economic experts was merely to ask for stand-by controls on foreign credits should the president deem them necessary.[39]

More important, the administration chose to ignore the connection between the Vietnam War and the nation's balance of payments even though it was well aware that such a connection existed. It did not act to counter the impact that the war had on the payments deficit, through a combination of fiscal and monetary policy, because (1) it did not think the payments deficit posed any major threat to the dollar and (2) it was committed until too late to a "guns and butter policy." As a result, the conflict in Southeast Asia continued to exacerbate the nation's balance-of-payments problem, thereby weakening the dollar and ultimately undermining the international monetary structure, which was based on the dollar.

Although the cost of the Vietnam War in terms of the nation's balance of payments cannot be measured precisely, it certainly was substantial. Several respected economists have put the annual costs at $3.6 billion from 1964 to 1967. Of this amount, they attribute $1.6 billion to increases in direct military spending abroad and $2 billion to the additional costs of inflation. If these figures are even approximately correct, then a major portion of the payments deficit during these years was due to the war in Vietnam. As Robert Shaffer, a senior economist with the Bank of America thus commented in a report to the Senate Foreign Relations Committee in 1970, "The war in Southeast Asia cannot take the blame for the whole of our inflationary and balance of payments problems, but it is obvious that it must share a large part of them."[40]

Furthermore, administration officials were fully aware of the impact that the war was having on the balance of payments. As early as the end of November, when the military build-up in Vietnam was still in its initial stages, a specially appointed cabinet committee commented on the connection between the war and the deficit. Forecasting an overall deficit of $1.4 billion for 1966, it attributed a good part of the increase to a growth of $290 million in Defense Department spending overseas, accountable "entirely to our intensified effort in Southeast Asia." "A further $200 million increase in expenditures may occur next year and worsen the projected deficit by that amount," the committee also stated. However, the committee recommended that the president merely tighten the existing voluntary program.[41]

The committee's forecast of a $1.4 billion deficit in payments for 1966 proved to be remarkably accurate. The actual figure of $1.42 billion represented an increase of only $123 million over the deficit for 1965, which was still only about half the $2.8-billion figure for 1964. Nevertheless, what concerned public officials both in the United States and abroad, both within the administration and on Capitol Hill, was the fact that there was any deterioration at all. Although the cabinet committee had accurately estimated the size of the payments deficit, other administration officials had predicted at the beginning of the year that the balance of payments would move into equilibrium, which was defined by the administration as a deficit or surplus no greater than $250 million. Not only were they proven wrong, but by the end of 1966 the deficit was growing, not contracting. Moreover, the gains that the voluntary program had achieved were being more than offset by the costs of the war in Vietnam.

That the balance-of-payments program was not working as well as the administration had hoped was revealed by a report the Department of Commerce issued early in 1966, a report that showed that the country's major corporations planned to spend a record $8.8 billion in plants and equipment overseas during the year. Also, preliminary estimates indicated that the nation's trade balance would decline significantly over the year, thereby exacerbating the deficit. Indeed, figures on the balance of payments that were released in May showed a seasonally adjusted first-quarter deficit in payments of $582 million.[42]

The White House was clearly worried by these latest figures. But precisely because it attributed the deficit to the military build-up in Vietnam rather than to any basic weakness in its own economic policies, the administration concluded that no radical change was called for in its balance-of-payments program. At a press conference on May 18, Treasury Secretary Henry Fowler thus blamed the war in Southeast Asia for the deficit in two ways. Not only did the war involve direct military outlays abroad, he said, but by heating up the economy, it also raised prices and adversely affected the nation's balance of trade. As a result, instead of an anticipated improvement from the previous year's $4.8 billion trade surplus, first-quarter figures showed the surplus dropping to an annual rate of $4.4 billion for 1966. *"We suggest that careful analysis will support the proposition that, absent the Vietnam build-up, the United States might have moved substantially closer to equilibrium in its balance of payments,"* the treasury secretary concluded (Fowler's italics).[43]

What Fowler was saying, in other words, was that the American economy and the American dollar were basically sound. The balance-of-payments deficit could and would be controlled. In the absence of the conflict in Southeast Asia, the United States might already have approached equilibrium. As for the dollar, whatever weakness was attributed to it was more the result of its heavy responsibilities as a reserve currency than of any other factor, including the need to pay for the overseas costs of the war. By sloughing off the economic impact of the Vietnam War in this way and by concluding that the international monetary system was structurally stable, the administration was ignoring the additional stresses and strains that the war was placing on the nation's balance of payments. As a result, the dollar was further weakened in international money markets, and the world's entire monetary structure was placed in jeopardy.

In fact, the administration always remained far more concerned about increasing international liquidity than about the impact that the war was exerting on the nation's balance of payments. If by creating a new reserve currency the dollar could be relieved of some of its international responsibilities, the White House was confident that it could handle the nation's payments deficit. In June, 1965, therefore, President Johnson instructed Treasury Secretary Henry Fowler to establish a special study group on international monetary reform to look into the matter of a substitute for the dollar. An advisory committee, known as the Dillon Committee after its chairman, former Treasury Secretary C. Douglas Dillon, was also formed.

On the recommendation of the study group and the Dillon Committee, Secretary Fowler issued a call on July 10 for an international conference to consider the creation of a new reserve asset in the IMF, which would be based upon a system of "special drawing rights." A number of different versions of this system were already in existence at the time Fowler asked for an international meeting. Although the precise details still had to be worked out, essentially the concept being developed in Washington was to have an asset that, like gold, could be used to buy foreign currencies and to settle balance-of-payments deficits without having to rely on the credit facilities of the IMF.[44]

In August, Fowler and Undersecretary of State George Ball visited all the major West European capitals to push for the convening of a conference on international liquidity, which, they argued, would eliminate the need for new monetary gold or increased holdings of dollars. No mention was ever made of the economic consequences of the Vietnam War.[45] Indeed, the administration presented its case for a new reserve asset on the basis of an insufficiency of gold to keep pace with the rapid growth of world trade, rather than on the United States' payments deficit and a corresponding weakness in the dollar. In explaining the rationale for a system of "special drawing rights," President Johnson later remarked: "By supplementing gold and dollars, the 'special drawing rights' system would relieve pressure on both."[46]

Just as the Europeans had earlier expressed doubts about the administration's balance-of-payments program, so now they expressed reservations about its plan for a new reserve asset. With the notable exception of France, which was still concerned mainly with reducing or ending the special status of the dollar, the Europeans were not so much against a new asset per se; but they preferred an asset that was somehow linked to gold. Most certainly they did not want the United States—or England—to escape honoring their international obligations by paying their deficits with "funny money" instead of with hard currencies. Reporting on a series of sessions that the Group of Ten held in Paris at the end of January, Treasury Secretary Fowler thus informed the president that the meetings "revealed a wide *area of agreement* on international monetary reform, but a *very sticky disagreement on the relation between gold and the new reserve unit*" (Fowler's italics). Fowler concluded that "the Continentals are not going to be easily budged from their determination to hitch the new unit to gold and to keep it in a secondary position to gold."[47]

Fowler was right. The Group of Ten held a series of meetings throughout 1966 and well into 1967. It agreed that a new reserve currency was needed, but it failed to agree either on the form of that new currency or on whether it should simply increase existing IMF drawing rights. The deadlock was not broken until the end of April, when the United States agreed that the European members of the Common Market would have veto power over the manufacture of the new asset by increasing their quotas under the weighted voting procedures of the IMF. Even then, there was a further delay until September before agreement was reached in principle on the establishment of the new asset, to be known as Special Drawing Rights (SDRs), and many details of the system were still not resolved.[48] The result was that when an attack against the British pound began in November, which would spread to the dollar and threaten the entire international monetary structure, the administration was forced, in President Johnson's words, "to deal with it by using the tools at hand."[49]

The assault on the British pound had not been unexpected in Washington. Great Britain's balance of payments was chronically far worse than that of the United States, and its inability to inspire confidence in its long-term economic future had led to recurring speculation against sterling since 1961. In 1964 the United States had taken the lead in arranging a $3 billion package of credits from the Group of Ten members plus Austria. This massive support turned the speculative outflow into an inflow and thus saved the pound. In 1965, Undersecretary of State George Ball personally negotiated an additional $925-million package of credits from the United States and the European central banks. By mid 1966 the British were able to announce that they had repaid all of their short-term debts to foreign banks, although they still owed the United States about $500 million. Already the trade gap had begun to widen ominously again, however; and once more the pound came under heavy pressure, in part because the Vietnam War was helping to drive interest rates up in the United States, thereby attracting capital away from London. The British responded with a tough economic policy at home and with heavy borrowing abroad, which included almost a doubling of their credit (or swap) line with the United States, from $700 million to $1.35 billion. The program worked well through the first quarter of 1967. Towards the end of 1966, Great Britain even enjoyed a surplus in its balance of payments.[50]

Then the British were hard hit again by a disappointing amount of exports, by rising interest rates abroad, and, finally, by the Arab-Israeli war of June, 1967. The conflict led to the closing of the Suez Canal, substantial withdrawals of sterling, and increased costs for imports, largely for petroleum. In a last-ditch effort to hold the sterling rate by drawing funds back to Great Britain, London increased the discount rate sharply. The United States tried to help by making selective market purchases of sterling. But this time the speculative pressures were too great. Britain began to lose reserves at a rate of $250 million a day. Finally, on November 18, 1967, London announced to Washington that it was devaluing the pound from $2.80 to $2.40. Those who had gambled on a devaluation of sterling and had cashed their pounds in for gold had won their bet.[51]

The situation that the United States was now facing became perfectly clear. "Now the dollar is in the front line," Treasury Secretary

Fowler remarked rather imprudently but truthfully after news of the devaluation was officially announced in London. Washington was fully aware that the price of gold would come under great upward pressure in the case of a British devaluation, as speculators turned to their next likely candidate for devaluation, the already-weakened dollar. *"The gold market has been under strong demand pressure during most of 1966 and 1967, and little relief appears in sight,"* Secretary Fowler thus informed President Johnson a few days before sterling was devalued (Fowler's italics). If sterling fell, Fowler said, there would be great monetary unrest. Perhaps the only solution to the crisis would be a rise in the price of gold.[52]

The White House was determined, however, to keep the dollar as "good as gold"—that is, to keep the dollar convertible at the exchange rate of $35 an ounce. To do otherwise, to effectively devalue the dollar by increasing the price of gold, would have had far-reaching consequences, not the least of which would be to drive up the overseas expenses of United States defense commitments, including the cost of the war in Vietnam. It would also make imports for American consumers more expensive, something that the administration was anxious to avoid.

Estimating that losses would be as high as $2 or $3 billion a day (compared to Britain's highest daily loss of $1.3 billion), the administration thus turned to the gold pool, which had been established in London during Kennedy's administration in order to prevent undue speculation in gold and to channel gold to central banks in an orderly fashion.[53] The strategy was risky, for it was far from certain that the pool would go along with the United States in holding down the price of gold.[54]

As it was, in the week after the devaluation, the pool was called on to support the gold market to the extent of $580 million in gold, with the United States supplying 60 percent of the gold.[55] Furthermore, the European members of the pool were becoming more and more concerned about the losses that they were sustaining. As demand for gold continued to grow, some erosion of European support became evident. By the end of December, losses in the gold pool reached more than $1.5 billion. Exacerbating the crisis were two additional developments. First, preliminary figures indicated that the U.S. balance of payments would deteriorate very badly during the fourth quarter of 1967. When these figures were made public, concern about the dollar was almost certain to be translated into additional speculative demand for gold. Second, U.S. losses of gold were rapidly bringing American gold reserves close to the amount necessary in order to meet the legal requirements that gold be held to cover 25 percent of the domestic issue of notes, or about $10 billion. The Federal Reserve Board could waive this requirement, but this was hardly understood in European markets; in any case, the gold-cover requirement had a bad psychological effect on the gold market, because it suggested that the United States would soon be unable to meet its commitment to keep the dollar convertible.[56]

To meet the immediate crisis, the president outlined, on New Year's Day, a new and much-tougher balance-of-payments program. Forecasting a payments deficit of $3.5 to $4 billion, the president stated that the United States could not "tolerate a deficit that could threaten the stability of the international monetary system—of which the U.S. dollar is the bulwark." As the centerpiece of his program, he announced a series of mandatory controls over private investments abroad. He also authorized the Federal Reserve Board to tighten its program restraining foreign lending by banks, and he announced a series of steps that were designed to lower government spending overseas, curtail unnecessary U.S. travel abroad, and increase the U.S. trade surplus. Such a program, he said, would "keep the dollar strong. It will fulfill our responsibilities to the American people and to the free world." Two weeks later, in his State of the Union message, the president asked Congress to remove the legal requirement for a 25 percent gold cover on issues of notes, remarking that this would free up more gold in defense of the dollar.[57]

Reaction abroad to the president's balance-of-payments message was highly favorable, and for a few months, this had a tranquilizing effect on the speculative fever. But doubts about the president's ability to get his program through Congress contributed to a build-up of pressures against the dollar once more. In Washington, various proposals were considered to deal with this latest chapter in the gold crisis, including a recommendation by the Dillon Committee to close the gold pool, adopting in place of the pool a two-price system that would keep the official price for gold—or the price at which official transactions would take place—at $35 an ounce while letting the private market set its own limits.[58]

This was the policy that the administration adopted. The resumption of heavy speculation in gold in early March made it abundantly clear that the United States would have to take new steps to protect the $35 price of gold. In the first week of March the pool had to put $300 million of gold into the market. In four days beginning on March 11, the pool lost approximately $1 billion. By the end of the week, speculative fever had gotten out of control. To make matters worse, the members of the pool, except for Germany, announced their intention to replace their losses by drawing gold from the United States. In response, Secretary of State Dean Rusk informed all diplomatic posts on March 15 that the London gold market was to be closed that day and that the United States had invited the central bankers of Europe to an emergency meeting in Washington to discuss the situation.[59]

At the meeting, which convened on the sixteenth, Chairman William McChesney Martin of the Federal Reserve Board announced flatly that the United States had ruled out any increase in the official price of gold. He also made it clear that either agreement had to be reached on some plan based on the $35 price or a new system would have to be established in which the dollar would no longer be convertible. With really little choice between going along with the United States or risking total chaos, the central bankers agreed to a two-tier system, pledging neither to sell nor, for the time being, to buy gold in the private market, thereby giving up potential profits but leaving speculators with the problem of unloading their gold at prices that might fall below $35 an ounce. Soon after the announcement of the two-tier system, the price of gold in the private market retreated back towards $35 an ounce.

For the moment, then, the gold crisis was over, and the dollar remained convertible at $35 an ounce. Ironically, a near revolution in France in 1968, led by rioting students and workers who were protesting a rise in unemployment and a slowdown in the growth of the economy, had the incidental consequence of strengthening the dollar while undermining the French franc. Meanwhile, the machinery had been put in place that would finally, in 1970, result in the issuing of a new reserve asset, the SDRs.

In reviewing the critical months from November, 1967, when the British first announced that they were going to devalue the pound, until March, 1968, when the two-tier gold system was established, President Johnson was thus able to claim that a "historic turning point" had been reached in terms of the international monetary system: "The world's leading bankers were telling the speculators that henceforth the banks would be looking to the new international currency, not to gold, to enlarge monetary reserves. They were committed to building the international economy on the basis of intensive partnership."[60]

This was hardly the case, however. These critical months had disclosed just how fractured and fragmented the international monetary system really was. Paradoxically, they had also underscored just how interrelated the world economy was, just how dependent it had become on the shaky dollar, and just how much the stability of the dollar rested ultimately on a resolution of the United States' balance-of-payments difficulties. Here lay the crux of the problem for the White House; here also lay the ultimate dilemma for its entire foreign economic program. Because, as administration officials had always realized, in the absence of a settlement of the Vietnam War or of steps to deal with a basic war-related cause of the payments problem—war-generated inflation—the chances of a settlement of the payments deficit were greatly diminished. Yet the president continued to be committed to carrying on the conflict in Southeast Asia, and he opposed the type of tax increase that might have cooled off the domestic economy.

In fairness to Johnson, in his State of the Union address of January 10, 1967, he did propose a 6 percent surcharge on income taxes, which was later raised to 10 percent. This was really a case of too little, too late, however; for by the time Congress had approved the measure in 1968, the payments deficit had become chronic, and the dollar was under speculative siege. Besides, until the gold crisis at the end of 1967, the heart of the administration's balance-of-payments program continued to be voluntary controls on foreign investments and credit. Only after the crisis had mounted did the White House move to a more comprehensive program that included mandatory controls.

Furthermore, by 1968 the war had so undermined the president's support in Congress that most of his legislative proposals for dealing with the balance-of-payments problem were defeated on Capitol Hill. The president did get Congress finally to pass his tax surcharge, which had been rejected a year earlier; and the House and the Senate also agreed to lift the 25 percent gold cover against Federal Reserve notes, which the president wanted. But they rejected his proposals to tax Americans who were traveling abroad, and they defeated the Trade Expansion bill of 1968, which was designed to increase exports by a further liberalization of world trade. They also failed to act on a third administration proposal, which was aimed at attracting foreign visitors to the United States by waiving visa requirements in certain cases.[61]

III

The Vietnam War loomed large, however, not only over the balance-of-payments program but also over Johnson's foreign-aid program. Many members on Capitol Hill, particularly in the Senate, expressed their discontent over the war and over the administration's handling of foreign policy by voting against the program, by severely cutting the president's spending recommendations, and by rejecting his proposals for major changes in the program, including multiyear authorizations and the separation of economic- from military-assistance bills.

The White House, in order to get its foreign-aid bill through Congress in 1965, had agreed to conduct a review of the entire aid program. As a result of the review, which was conducted during the fall of 1965, the president forwarded to Congress in January a $3.39-billion foreign-aid bill, which was the smallest in the history of the program, but one that was also substantially different from his two earlier proposals in terms of assumptions and objectives. As in the case of his earlier requests for aid, Johnson continued to place great emphasis on the self-help aspects of economic assistance; indeed, he now made self-help and regional cooperation the core of his program.[62]

At the same time, however, the president proposed separating the military-aid and the economic-aid programs by introducing two separate bills, and he requested five-year authorizations for each program. He also spoke more eloquently than ever before about the need to attack the root causes of world misery and poverty, to address the problems of disease and overpopulation, and, above all, to deal with the problems of world hunger, which he referred to as "a catastrophe for all of us." In order to eliminate hunger and to make the developing countries self-sufficient in food, he proposed a broad program of food aid and agricultural assistance, which he labeled his Food for Work program.[63] In effect, by asking to separate economic from military aid and by seeking a multiyear authorization for the aid program, Johnson was responding to Fulbright and to the other senators who had long pushed for such legislation. By his eloquent appeal to rid the Third World of disease, overpopulation, and hunger, Johnson may also have hoped for additional support in the upper chamber from senators who had long been concerned with the social plight of the underdeveloped countries. This did not happen, however; for by the time that Congress took up the foreign-aid program, the war in Vietnam had become the Senate's overriding concern.

At just what time the Senate began to turn against Johnson in regard to Vietnam is difficult to say. Certainly even in 1966, the president's conduct of the war was still enjoying considerable support in the upper chamber, perhaps majority support. But stung by the rapid escalation of the war and by the apparent unwillingness of the administration to negotiate a settlement of the conflict on terms that North Vietnam could accept, the Senate Foreign Relations Committee vented its anger by attacking Johnson's foreign-aid request for 1966 in nationally televised hearings that were dominated by the topic of Vietnam. Roles became totally reversed in the debate over foreign aid. Now the administration led the fight for multiyear authorization of the aid program, while committee chairman Fulbright, who one year earlier had pushed for this measure, chose to attack the administration's aid program because it did not place enough emphasis on multilateral aid and because it would aid such dictatorial regimes as the former Diem government in South Vietnam, which, Fulbright held, had led to "full scale war."[64]

Despite a personal appeal from Secretary of State Dean Rusk for a five-year authorization bill,[65] the committee reported out a bill that limited the foreign-aid program to a one-year authorization. Although the committee did go along with the administration in reporting out separate bills for economic and military aid, it also cut the president's economic-aid request by slightly under $100 million and his military-aid request by $25 million, not in themselves major reductions but ones that did reflect its change of attitude from a year earlier, when it had cut the president's original request by $28 million. In sending the measure to the floor of the Senate, the committee made clear just how much it had been influenced by its discontent over the Vietnam War, a war, it said, that "casts a very long shadow" and that had led many members of the committee to "feel that the United States is overcommitted, or in danger of becoming overcommitted, in the world at large."[66] Even after the measure had reached the full Senate, the war continued to dominate the debate as Fulbright, who had agreed to manage the legislation, nevertheless voted for a series of restrictive amendments and cuts in his committee's own bill.[67]

As a result, the total authorization for economic and military assistance was cut by nearly $500 million from what the president had requested. These reductions were salvaged in the House, where support for the war was much greater.[68] Even in the lower chamber, however, the Vietnam War was a major concern. Although many members of the House were reluctant to voice their opinions in an election year and therefore supported the authorization measure that came out of the Foreign Affairs Committee, the committee itself recognized the growing opposition to the aid program because of the war when it stated in its report on the aid legislation, "Much of the criticism of foreign aid reflects dissatisfaction with the world situation or with aspects of U.S. foreign policy which the foreign assistance program has been used to implement."[69]

Furthermore, in the ensuing appropriations process, the aid program was sharply cut back to $2.9 billion, almost $450 million less than what the administration had originally requested and $567 million, or 16.3 percent, less than what Congress had authorized—the largest percentage cut since 1964 and the first time since 1958 that the aid program had been funded under $3 billion. Trying to explain the rationale for these reductions, Senator Thomas Dodd of Connecticut pointed to a "neo-isolationism which threatens the entire structure of our foreign policy." He then added that "whatever their motivation . . . it is difficult to escape the impression that [these neo-isolationists] are using the foreign aid program . . . as an instrument of pressure in an effort to compel the Administration to revise its Viet Nam policy."[70]

Dodd's observation applied even more to the 1967 fight over foreign aid. Anticipating a struggle, Johnson had established a special task force on foreign aid in October, under AID's administrator William S. Gaud, to recommend improvements in the program and to consider "the steps necessary to create a stronger public and congressional constituency for the program." The task force made a series of recommendations, which emphasized particularly the importance of popular participation and self-help in all phases of the development process,[71] themes that Johnson had underscored in his annual message to Congress, in which he asked for a $3.2-billion foreign-aid package. Stressing also the importance of regional development programs, the president told the House and the Senate that his program represented the "minimum contribution to mutual security and international development which we can safely make."[72]

Congress had not bought that argument a year earlier, however, and it did not buy it in 1967. Indeed, congressional support for foreign aid dropped to an all-time low when the House and the Senate adopted a series of restrictive amendments that were aimed at curbing the president's authority to conduct foreign policy. Both directly and indirectly, the war in Vietnam once more had determined the outcome of the debate. In the House the issue was not so much the war itself as it was the need for fiscal restraint. But even this was tied into the costs of the war. A conservative coalition of Republicans and southern Democrats, who had greatly influenced the House's action on other administration-sponsored legislation, argued that vast cuts were needed in foreign aid so as to reduce the nation's mounting deficit. They were joined by a number of northern liberals, who were convinced that given the escalating costs of the conflict in Southeast Asia, cutting foreign aid was the only way to save at least some of the domestic programs of the faltering Great Society.[73]

In the Senate the link between opposition to the foreign-aid program and opposition to the war was even more direct, as Fulbright and a group of other Democratic senators continued to use the debate over foreign aid as a vehicle for attacking the White House's conduct of the war. Over the summer and fall of 1966, relations between the White House and the chairman of the Senate Foreign Relations Committee had deteriorated from bad to worse, as Johnson and Fulbright had clashed over such issues as sales of arms to the Mideast, which the senator blamed for initiating an escalation in the Middle East arms race and which the president defended as necessary in light of a massive Soviet arms build-up in the region, including the sale of MIG-21s to Iraq.[74] They also came to loggerheads over Johnson's decision to increase the number of countries that were receiving development loans and technical assistance under the foreign-aid programs. Fulbright accused the president of violating the intentions of Congress, which had placed restrictions on the number of countries that could receive such aid. Johnson responded that Congress had given him the authority to exceed the statutory limits when he deemed that it was in the national interest to do so.[75]

Although both of these questions came up in the 1967 debate over foreign aid, it was the war in Southeast Asia which, more than any other issue, shaped the discourse and determined the dialogue that took place. Using the same metaphor as it had a year earlier, the Foreign Relations Committee described the "shadow of Vietnam" as hanging even "far longer and darker" over foreign aid than it had a year earlier.[76] Similarly, in responding to Secretary of State Rusk, who had just finished urging the Foreign Relations Committee to support the foreign-aid program as a way of bringing about a more peaceful world, Chairman Fulbright commented: "Perhaps I do not view it in the right perspective. But when you talk about building a peace, while at the same moment we are waging an ever-increasing war, it leaves one with a sense of schizophrenia."[77]

Consequently, the Senate and the House cut the president's request for 1968 by nearly $1 billion, or from $3.12 billion to $2.19 billion. This was $408 million less than the $2.7 billion appropriation for 1956, hitherto the smallest appropriation in the history of the foreign-aid program. Moreover, they restricted the president's authority over foreign aid in a number of ways, including the ban on selling arms on credit to Third World countries after 1968 and the revocation of the president's discretion to waive the ceiling on the number of nations that would be eligible to receive development loans, which Congress had set at twenty. In sum, Congress delivered a crushing blow to the president's foreign-aid program, which reflected clearly its displeasure with the administration's policy in Southeast Asia.[78]

Matters became even worse for the White House in 1968, as the House and the Senate again ripped into the administration's requests for foreign aid, approving a bill that, for the second year in a row, established a record low in funding. In fact, the battle over foreign aid in 1968 was almost a repeat of the conflict between the White House and Congress a year earlier. Once more the president made the smallest aid request, $2.9 billion, in the history of the program, repeating the now-familiar themes about the program's stress on self-help and on multilateral and regional programs of economic development but giving special attention to the need for agricultural growth and population planning in Third World nations in order to win their "war against hunger."[79] As in 1967, however, the war in Vietnam dominated every aspect of the legislative process. In the hearings before the Senate Foreign Relations Committee, which again were televised nationally, Secretary Rusk was forced to devote virtually all of his testimony to a defense of the administration's policy in Southeast Asia, as Chairman Fulbright set the tone of the hearings on opening day by commenting that it was "not possible to talk about foreign aid, or indeed any problem of this country's foreign relations without discussing the war in Vietnam."[80] In fact, Rusk had agreed to appear in open session before the committee only because the administration believed the alternative would be no aid bill at all, which would enable the press to report that the White House had "sacrificed foreign aid" for Vietnam.[81]

Rusk's appearance before the Foreign Relations Committee, however, did the administration scarcely any good, as the committee in July reported out a bill adding an additional $48 million to the $968 million in cuts that the House had already made on the president's request. In sending the measure to the floor of the Senate, which approved the committee's recommendations virtually unchanged, the committee remarked that it had "acted on the foreign aid bill this year against a background of growing concern over the international posture of the United States and over the problems which the American people face at home." The committee added that "over both the foreign and domestic crises hang the fiscal and balance-of-payments crises . . . which fundamentally result from the overcommitment both at home and abroad."[82]

Indeed, the reductions in appropriations that were finally approved by the House and by the Senate in October were, in terms of percentages, the largest ever. The $1.76-billion measure that was sent to the president was $1.16 billion, or 39.7 percent less, than the $2.92 Johnson had originally requested. Furthermore, the heaviest cuts were made in precisely those development programs, such as the Alliance for Progress, that the president had emphasized in his February message to Congress. Also, Congress had placed further restrictions on the president's authority to dispense foreign aid, including the ban on such assistance to nations that were already trading with North Vietnam. It would be too much to say that opposition to the war in Vietnam was the only reason for Congress' hostility to Johnson's foreign-aid program. Clearly, all the concerns that Congress had been expressing for years about the program, as well as new worries about the balance-of-payments deficit, were evident in this latest debate over foreign aid. But certainly the Vietnam conflict was the central issue in 1968, even more than it had been in 1967.

IV

In a real sense, then, President Johnson's foreign-aid and balance-of-payments programs were casualties of the Vietnam War. One can legitimately ask, "So what? What was at stake here?" After all, the critics of foreign aid had long contended that such assistance to Third World countries (as opposed to Marshall Plan aid to Europe) had been money down the drain, failing either to bring about economic development in the Third World or to make friends for the United States or even to prevent hunger and starvation in places such as Africa or certain parts of Asia. Even President Johnson had had serious reservations about the effectiveness of foreign aid, and there is plenty of evidence to support the position of those who advocated cutting the aid program or eliminating it entirely. As for the impact of the Vietnam War on the nation's balance of payments and, by extension, on the international monetary system, one can also legitimately wonder whether, in the long run, much could have been done to redress the balance of payments or even whether the existing gold-dollar monetary system was defensible or worth defending. After all, it seems perfectly clear in the middle of the 1980s, with record-level payments deficits being recorded almost every quarter, that the United States' balance-of-payments problems are so generic that no single action taken by any president in the 1960s could have stayed the red ink that has flowed for more than a quarter of a century in America's international accounts, much less could have prevented the system of floating exchanges, which replaced fixed rates in 1971 and with which the world has been successfully conducting international business ever since.

Whether or not the foreign-aid program has successfully achieved even a small part of the many goals ascribed to it over the last forty years, however, the fact remains that it was *the* central feature of U.S. foreign economic policy from the 1940s through at least the 1960s. Furthermore, as the United States became increasingly concerned with developments in the Third World, beginning sometime in the 1950s, the foreign-aid program became integral to the nation's overall foreign policy and remained so throughout the 1960s. One only has to point to one of the better-known parts of that program, the Alliance for Progress, to illustrate this point. Moreover, whether or not the program has been successful in achieving its goals, it has had a number of important institutional spin-offs, such as the Inter-American Development Bank (IADB), for Latin America, and the International Development Association (IDA), a soft-lending agency of the World Bank, which the United States helped to establish at the end of the 1950s in order to promote Third World economic development and which in the 1980s is assuming an important role in refinancing the huge international debts of Third World countries. Such achievements as these are not to be scoffed at lightly.[83]

As for the balance-of-payments problem, even if the payments deficit appears in the 1980s to be rooted in fundamental structural changes in the world economy over the last twenty-five years, most notably competition from Japan and other developed or developing nations, the fact remains that in the 1960s the Vietnam War exacerbated an already-serious payments problem, that this weakened the dollar, and that ultimately the weakened dollar undermined the existing international monetary structure. Furthermore, the administration understood perfectly well the interrelationship between the payments deficit and the Vietnam War, but it chose to ignore this fact, because it was satisfied that the dollar was basically sound, it was unprepared to risk the political flack that any economic tightening as a result of the war might create, and it was most certainly unwilling to reconsider its military commitment in Vietnam. So, like its foreign-aid program, its balance-of-payments program fell victim to the war in Southeast Asia.

Although this chapter has emphasized only these two programs, they were by no means the only foreign economic issues that concerned the president during his five years in office. There were a number of other problems, inherited from the previous administration, with which Johnson also had to deal as president. These included the P.L. 480, or "Food for Peace," program; the Kennedy Round of tariff negotiations; the establishment of the Asian Development Bank; quotas on oil imports; increased funding for the Export-Import Bank; and the expansion of East-West trade. But while all of these matters received considerable attention during Johnson's administration, none was regarded by the White House as being more important than the questions of aid and the balance-of-payments deficit, and many of them shared the common denominator with aid and the payments deficit of being affected in a way that was contrary to the administration's policies because of the war.

To take just one example, in Johnson's well-known speech at Johns Hopkins University on April 7, 1965, in which the president offered to enter into peace talks with North Vietnam, he also held out the prospect of a massive billion-dollar economic-development program for Southeast Asia. As part of the program, in December the United States would join with thirty-two other nations in signing a charter for the establishment of the Asian Development Bank. And in his foreign-aid message of February 9, 1967, Johnson indicated that he would ask Congress for $200 million as the United States' contribution to a special trust fund to be administered by the bank. Even before he had submitted his proposal to Congress, however, he had been advised by Treasury Secretary Fowler that it was likely to receive a hostile reception because of the war and because of the United States' huge financial commitments in Southeast Asia.[84] In September, the president did submit a request to Congress in which he asked for $200 million for the bank, but the atmosphere in Congress was so hostile that the president delayed forwarding the proposal for a week, and once the request was sent, it never made its way out of committee.[85] In 1968, Johnson again asked for congressional approval of a $200-million U.S. contribution to the bank's special trust fund; but the results were the same as they had been a year earlier. The bill died in committee after the Foreign Relations Committee rejected an amendment to the legislation providing that no more than $25 million should be appropriated for the bank in any single year until the Vietnam conflict was ended.[86] In terms of Johnson's foreign economic policy, then, the war in Vietnam had the same cancerous effect as it had on other aspects of the administration's foreign and domestic policies, destroying what had been the most promising—and popular—administration since the New Deal and turning it into a dying patient over whose early demise few tears were shed.

Notes

1. Burton I. Kaufman, *Trade and Aid: Eisenhower's Foreign Economic Policy, 1953-1961* (Baltimore, Md.: Johns Hopkins University Press, 1982), pp. 104-8, 206-9; Robert A. Pastor, *Congress and the Politics of U.S. Foreign Economic Policy, 1929-1976* (Berkeley: University of California Press, 1980), pp. 256-71.

2. Pastor, *Congress*, pp. 268-72.

3. Kaufman, *Trade and Aid*, pp. 109, 140, 173, 205.

4. Walter LaFeber, "Latin American Policy," in *Exploring the Johnson Years*, ed. Robert A. Divine (Austin: University of Texas Press, 1981) (reprinted as *The Johnson Years, Volume One: Foreign Policy, the Great Society, and the White House* [Lawrence: University Press of Kansas, 1987]), pp. 63-64.

5. Vaughn Davis Bornet, *The Presidency of Lyndon B. Johnson* (Lawrence: University Press of Kansas, 1983), p. 163; Walt Whitman Rostow, *Diffusion of Power* (New York: Macmillan, 1972), p. 423.

6. Philip Geyelin, *Lyndon B. Johnson and the World* (New York: Praeger, 1966), p. 33.

7. Ibid., pp. 12-33, 37-39.

8. R. A. Dungan to the President, Dec. 13, 1963, White House central files (hereafter cited WHCF), box 16, folder FG2/Eisenhower, Johnson Papers; *Congressional Quarterly Almanac* 19 (1963): 289-92; *Time*, Dec. 6, 1963, p. 23. Unless otherwise specified, all files are in the Johnson Papers at the Johnson Library in Austin, Texas.

9. Lyndon Baines Johnson, *The Vantage Point: Perspectives of the Presidency, 1963-1969* (New York: Holt, Rinehart & Winston, 1971), p. 39.

10. Johnson to Mike Mansfield, Dec. 19, 1963, WHCF, box 24, folder FO3-2; Johnson, *Vantage Point*, pp. 39-40.

11. Memorandum for the President, Feb. 4, 1964, "Congressional Views on Foreign Aid Program," attached to memorandum for the President, Feb. 4, 1964, WHCF, box 21, folder FO3-2.

12. Memorandum for Ralph Dungan from David Bell, n.d., attached to memorandum for the President, Feb. 4, 1964, ibid.

13. *Public Papers of the Presidents of the United States: Lyndon B. Johnson, 1963-1964* (Washington, D.C.: Government Printing Office, 1965), pp. 393-98 (hereafter cited as *Public Papers*).

14. Memorandum for the President from McGeorge Bundy, "The Administration's Argument on Its AID Presentation," National Security file, aides files, McGeorge Bundy files, box 1.

15. After trying unsuccessfully to make sharp cuts in the appropriations bill, Otto Passman told reporters, it was "ridiculous that the President . . . would play politics to the extent he has with this bill" (*Congressional Quarterly Almanac* 20 [1964]: 67-68); and ibid., pp. 296-315. See also Memorandum for the President, May 8, 1964, WHCF, box 22, folder FO3-2.

16. Kaufman, *Trade and Aid*, pp. 176–96.

17. Memorandum for the President from Douglas Dillon, Dec. 2, 1963, and attachment, WHCF, box 49, folder FO4-1; Arthur M. Schlesinger, Jr., *A Thousand Days: John F. Kennedy in the White House* (Boston: Houghton Mifflin, 1965), pp. 544–48.

18. Memorandum for the President from Douglas Dillon, Dec. 2, 1963, and attachment, WHCF, box 49, folder FO4-1; and Schlesinger, *Thousand Days*, pp. 544–48. See also U.S. Congress, Joint Economic Committee, *The United States Balance of Payments: Statements . . . on the Brookings Institution Study "The United States Balance of Payments in 1968,"* 88th Cong., 1st sess. (1963), esp. pp. 67–70, 116–19, 341–54.

19. Memorandum for David Hume from Richard Reuter, Jan. 2, 1964, and attachments, WHCF, box 24, folder FO3-2.

20. Memorandum for the President, May 27, 1964, WHCF, box 49, folder 4-1.

21. Fred C. Bergsten, *The Dilemmas of the Dollar: The Economics and Politics of the United States International Monetary Policy* (New York: New York University Press, 1975), pp. 83–84.

22. Memorandum for the President from Walter Heller, Aug. 5, 1964, WHCF, box 32, folder FO 4.

23. Memorandum for the President, Aug. 10, 1964, NSC file, aides files, McGeorge Bundy files, box 2.

24. The figures used in this essay are based on the liquidity balance, which includes short-term claims against the United States, rather than the basic balance, which measures long-term flows and was generally more favorable to the United States.

25. Memorandum for the President from Ackley, Dec. 10, 1964, WHCF, box 32, folder FO4-1, and memorandum for the President from McGeorge Bundy, Jan. 22, 1965, NSC file, aides files, McGeorge Bundy files.

26. Memorandum for the President from Ackley, Feb. 1, 1965, WHCF, box 32, folder FO4-1, and memorandum for the President from Bundy, Feb. 1, 1965, NSC file, aides files, McGeorge Bundy files.

27. *Public Papers, 1965*, pp. 170–77; memorandum for the President from Ackley, Feb. 10, 1965, WHCF, box 32, folder FO 4.

28. Memorandum for the President from Ackley, Feb. 9, 1965, WHCF, box 49, folder FO4-1.

29. Meany to Johnson, Feb. 8, 1965, WHCF, box 32, folder FO 4.

30. Memorandum for the President: European Press Reaction, Feb. 19, 1965, and memorandum for the President, Feb. 27, 1965, office files of Bill Moyers, box 5, folder "Balance of Payments."

31. See, e.g., Walter F. Carey, president of the U.S. Chamber of Commerce, to Johnson, Feb. 19, 1965, attached to Johnson to Carey, Mar. 1, 1965, WHCF, box 32, folder FO 4.

32. U.S. Congress, Senate, Committee on Banking and Currency, *Hearings: Balance of Payments*, 89th Cong., 1st sess., pp. 4–51, 436.

33. *Congressional Quarterly Almanac* 21 (1965): 864–76.

34. "Report of the President from the Cabinet Committee on Balance of Payments," n.d., White House confidential file, box 49, folder FO4-1; *Congressional Quarterly Almanac* 21 (1965): 866.

35. *Congressional Quarterly Almanac* 21 (1965): 422.

36. U.S. Congress, Senate, Committee on Foreign Relations, *Senate Report 170*, 89th Cong., 2d sess.

37. Memorandum for the President, Apr. 14, 1965, NSC file, aides files, McGeorge Bundy files, box 3; "The Agency for International Development: An Administrative History, 1963-1968," pp. 70-71, ibid.

38. Robert Warren Stevens, *Vain Hopes, Grim Realities: The Economic Consequences of the Vietnam War* (New York: New Viewpoints, 1976); see also U.S. Congress, Senate, Committee on Foreign Relations, *Hearings: Impact of the War in Southeast Asia on the U.S. Economy*, 91st Cong., 2d sess.

39. Memorandum for the President from Henry Fowler, Oct. 12, 1965, White House confidential file, box 38, folder FO-627.

40. Stevens, *Vain Hopes*, pp. 105-8; U.S. Congress, Senate, Committee on Foreign Relations, *Hearings: Impact*, p. 30.

41. Memorandum for the President from Fowler, Nov. 26, 1965, and memorandum for the President from Francis M. Bator, Nov. 29, 1965, White House confidential file, boxes 45 and 49, folder FO 4.

42. Memorandum for the President from Ackley, Mar. 26, 1966, and memorandum for the President from Fowler, May 16, 1966, White House confidential file, box 49, folder FO4-1.

43. Memorandum for the President, May 10 and 16, 1966, White House confidential file, box 49, folder FO4-1.

44. Robert Solomon, *The International Monetary System, 1945-1981* (New York: Harper & Row, 1982), pp. 128-29; and Martin Mayer, *The Fate of the Dollar* (New York: Times Books, 1980), pp. 156-59.

45. "The Department of State during the Administration of President Lyndon B. Johnson," vol. 1, pt. 8, chap. 9, Johnson Papers.

46. Johnson, *Vantage Point*, pp. 314-15.

47. Memorandum for the President, Feb. 5, 1966, WHCF, box 23, folder FO4-1; see also Mayer, *Fate of the Dollar*, pp. 157-58; Solomon, *International Monetary System*, pp. 130-31.

48. Mayer, *Fate of the Dollar*, pp. 158-59.

49. Johnson, *Vantage Point*, p. 315. On this same point see also memorandum for the President from Fowler, Sept. 11, 1967, White House confidential file, box 50, folder FO4-1.

50. "The Department of State during the Administration of President Lyndon B. Johnson," vol. 1, pt. 8, chap. 9; memorandum for the President, Oct. 19, 1967, NSC file, NSC history, box 54, folder—Balance of Payments Program.

51. Memorandum for the President from W. W. Rostow, Oct. 19, 1967, NSC file, NSC history, box 54, folder—Balance of Payments Program.

52. Memorandum for the President, Nov. 13, 1967, ibid., box 53.

53. Memorandum of conversation, Nov. 24, 1967, ibid., box 53, folder—The Gold Crisis.

54. Ibid.

55. To the President from Rostow, Nov. 22, 1967, ibid.

56. "The Gold Crisis," folder—Gold Crisis, bk. 1, ibid.

57. *Public Papers*, 1968/69, pp. 8-13, 33.

58. "The Gold Crisis," NSC file, NSC history, box 53, folder—Gold Crisis, bk. 1.

59. Ibid.

60. Johnson, *Vantage Point*, p. 319.

61. *Congressional Quarterly Almanac* 24 (1968): 717–34.

62. Memorandum for the President, Sept. 23, 1965, NSC files, aides files, McGeorge Bundy files, box 5.

63. *Public Papers*, 1966, pp. 117–26.

64. U.S. Congress, Senate, Committee on Foreign Relations, *Hearings: Foreign Assistance Act of 1966*, 89th Cong., 2d sess., 1966, pp. 12, 104–8.

65. Memorandum for the President, May 26, 1966, White House confidential file, box 49, folder FO3-2-1; memorandum for the President, May 27, 1966, WHCF, box 23, EX, folder FO3-2.

66. U.S. Congress, Senate, Committee on Foreign Relations, *Senate Report 1359*, 89th Cong., 2d sess., p. 4.

67. *Congressional Quarterly Almanac* 22 (1966): 409–15.

68. Ibid., pp. 402–6, 415–18.

69. U.S. Congress, House, Committee on Foreign Affairs, *House Report 165*, 89th Cong., 2d sess., pp. 4–5.

70. *Congressional Quarterly Almanac* 22 (1966): 418–23.

71. Memorandum for William S. Gaud from Joseph A. Califano, Oct. 5, 1966, and various task-force reports, Task Force, box 19, folder—Foreign Aid.

72. *Public Papers*, 1967, pp. 164–72.

73. *Congressional Quarterly Almanac* 23 (1967): 690–92.

74. Walt Rostow to Fulbright, Nov. 11, 1966, WHCF, box 48, folder 3-2.

75. Johnson to Fulbright, Feb. 15, 1967, WHCF, box 24, folder FO3-2.

76. U.S. Congress, Senate Committee on Foreign Relations, *Senate Report 499*, 90th Cong., 1st sess., pp. 2–12.

77. U.S. Congress, Senate, Committee on Foreign Relations, *Hearings: Foreign Assistance Act of 1967*, 90th Cong., 1st sess., p. 167.

78. *Congressional Quarterly Almanac* 23 (1967): 679–83, 698–99; see also memorandum for the President, Aug. 17, 1967, WHCF, box 24, folder FO3-2.

79. *Public Papers*, 1968/69, pp. 199–208; U.S. Congress, House, Foreign Affairs Committee, *Hearings: Foreign Assistance Act of 1968*, 90th Cong., 2d sess., pp. 17–25.

80. *Congressional Quarterly Almanac* 24 (1968): 427.

81. Harry McPherson to the President, Feb. 26, 1968, White House confidential file, box 24, folder FO3-2.

82. U.S. Congress, Senate, Committee on Foreign Relations, *Senate Report 1479*, 90th Cong., 2d sess., p. 3.

83. Kaufman, *Trade and Aid*, pp. 133–75, 197–211.

84. Memorandum for the President, Sept. 12, 1967, WHCF, box 19, folder IT 80; see also Joe Califano to the President, Sept. 12, 1967, ibid.

85. Joe Califano to the President, Sept. 20, 1967, ibid.

86. *Congressional Quarterly Almanac* 24 (1968): 547. On the importance that some members of the administration attached to the bank see also Eugene Black to the President, Jan. 3, 1968, WHCF, box 19, folder IT 80.

Part 2 | Protecting the Environment

5 | Lyndon Johnson and Environmental Policy

Martin V. Melosi

IN QUANTITATIVE MEASURES ALONE the Johnson administration's "New Conservation" deserves more attention than it has yet received. No less than nine task forces directly addressed environmental problems (see list 1, Appendix). Between 1963 and 1968 the president signed into law almost three hundred conservation and beautification measures, which were supported by more than $12 billion in authorized funds. This represented more environmental measures than had been passed during the preceding 187 years. The legislation spanned issues from land policy to water pollution and from wilderness areas to urban open space (see list 2, Appendix). Thirty-five areas were authorized for addition to the National Park Service.[1]

Given the scale of legislative action and heightened national interest in the environment during the 1960s, it is surprising that the record of the Johnson administration remains diffuse—if not obscure. Admittedly, the field of Environmental History is quite new and its limits are still being defined. Yet, few historians have looked beyond the popular environmental signposts of the 1960s—such as Rachel L. Carson's *Silent Spring* (1962), the Santa Barbara oil spill (1969), the National Environmental Policy Act (1969)—to identify and evaluate the "New Conservation." Several questions, barely explored, require careful attention: How does the conservation and beautification record of the Johnson administration fit into the evolution of the modern environmental movement? Was the New Conservation really new? What was the role of President Johnson in establishing environmental policy between 1963 and 1968? An assessment of documents in the LBJ Library—and some speculations based on the existing literature—can begin to answer these questions.

From Conservationism to the Modern Environmental Movement

The variety and extent of the conservation and beautification programs of the Johnson presidency demonstrate a commitment to the environment that is on a par with any administration before or since. While not providing the leadership on every issue, the Johnson administration's wide-ranging activity supports the claim that the 1960s constituted a transitional period from an old-style conservationism, concerned primarily with the utilization of natural resources, to a modern environmentalism, emphasizing quality-of-life issues and environmental protection.

The "old" conservation, initiated in the Progressive Era, was an effort to conserve, preserve, manage, or protect the nation's resources. As business reform was meant to bring order to the American economy of the late nineteenth and early twentieth centuries, so conservation was meant to rationalize the use of natural resources. What came to be known as "the conservation movement" in the United States had its intellectual antecedents in eighteenth-century Europe and its American origins in the early nineteenth century.

By the late nineteenth century, several milestones had marked the coming of the movement, including the publication of George Perkins Marsh's *Man and Nature* (1864), the development of the "national park" idea, the establishment of the U.S. Geological Survey (1879), and the founding of John Muir's Sierra Club (1892). By the turn of the century the conservation movement had achieved national status, especially with the presidency of Theodore Roosevelt.

Public policy on resource questions after 1900 was guided by those who wished to prevent waste through efficient use—or resource conservationists—as opposed to those who were more interested in saving what remained of the wilderness—or preservationists. Some historians, such as J. Leonard Bates, thought that the conservationists of the Progressive Era were combatting the greed and wastefulness of the business world. Others, especially Samuel P. Hays, perceived that professionals and scientists from the East, acting from within the federal bureaucracy, were employing centralized policy-making powers to curtail the waste of resources and to establish programs of "wise use" in the West. This meant that western interests were often at loggerheads with federal conservationists, since the former wanted local control and the ability to exploit the resources for their own economic ends.[2]

The New Deal built on the legacy of the Progressive Era. Franklin Roosevelt brought into office a strong personal interest in conservation, and he surrounded himself with men of similar thought, such as Harold L. Ickes, Henry A. Wallace, Henry Morgenthau, Jr., and Hugh Hammond Bennett.[3] But of more importance, the massive problems of the Great Depression—especially related to the dust bowl in the West and to economic strife in the South—helped to steer the New Deal government toward federal solutions to pressing environmental problems. The soil-conservation program emphasized the efficient use and management of soil resources to preserve agricultural lands. A concern for grazing lands in the West led to the Taylor Grazing Act (1934). Reforestation programs, aided by the establishment of the Civilian Conservation Corps (CCC), complemented soil conservation. In addition, the New Deal government conducted several resource-development projects, led the drive to develop the nation's wildlands and rivers, and participated in a program of scientific game management.

The Tennessee Valley Authority (TVA) is probably the best known of the resource-development activities. It was the most sophisticated application of the multiple-use concept that had yet been devised. TVA was a multipurpose river project that involved flood control, the production of fertilizer, soil conservation, reforestation, the construction of inland waterways, the promotion of regional economic growth, and the generation of hydroelectric power. As part of the New Deal recovery program, TVA was also meant to serve as a source of unemployment relief in the South.

While the various conservation programs of the New Deal were not organized through a coherent environmental policy, there was little doubt that they perpetuated federal leadership in the management of the nation's resources. However, for several years after the New Deal, conservation policy on the national level failed to grow much beyond the narrow interest in resource management. The publication of Rachel Carson's *Silent Spring* in 1962 is often cited as the beginning of the modern environmental movement. Although Carson's attack on pesticides was significant, a single event did not give rise to such a diverse movement. The modern environmental movement in the United States arose during the 1960s, but its roots were embedded in the past, especially in resource conservation, preservationism, naturalism, antipollution, and public-health campaigns both in the United States and in Europe.

The recent origins of the movement are to be found in post–World War II natural-environment issues, such as outdoor recreation, wildlands, and open space; in concerns over environmental pollution; and in the maturing of ecological sciences. It is also linked to the "sixties" generation. Cynics have argued that political and economic elites either sponsored or supported environmental activities as a way of distracting protesters from antiwar, antipoverty, or civil-rights activities. However, the political and social turmoil of the 1960s presented an opportunity for raising questions about environmental protection, and it provided willing supporters, especially among idealistic teens and young adults.

The environmental movement was rooted in more than youthful idealism. While drawing its major support from the middle and upper-middle classes, politically it functioned as a coalition that cut across class lines and varying interests.[4] Older preservation groups, such as the Sierra Club (1892) and the National Audubon Society (1905), were experiencing a revival of interest by the late 1960s and early 1970s. More recent organizations that had corporate backing, such as Resources for the Future (early 1950s) and Laurance Rockefeller's Conservation Foundation (mid 1960s), promoted the efficient utilization of resources. Legal remedies received attention from the Environmental Defense Fund (1967) and the Natural Resources Defense Council (1970).

Into the 1970s, aggressive and often militant protest and citizen action were carried out by groups such as Friends of the Earth (splintered off from the Sierra Club), Zero Population Growth, the National Wildlife Federation, and Ecology Action. Also individuals, such as biologists Rachel Carson and Barry Commoner, popularized and promoted the study of ecology. Beyond the borders of North America, "Green parties" and "ecoactivists" inaugurated their own versions of environmental protest.

Modern environmentalists generally shared an appreciation of the fragility of ecological balances, a notion of the intrinsic value of nature, a personal concern for health and fitness, and a commitment to self-reliance. They by no means espoused uniform political views or reform tactics. Some accepted governmental intervention as a way either to allocate resources or to preserve wildlands and natural habitats. Others were suspicious of any large institution as the protector of the environment. Some believed that the existing political and social structure was capable of balancing environmental protection and economic productivity. Still others blamed capitalism for promoting uncontrolled economic growth, materialism, the squandering of resources, and even the coopting of the environmental movement for capitalism's own ends.[5]

While the modern environmental movement gained national attention quite dramatically during the late 1960s and the early 1970s, we have only impressionistic notions of its roots, nature, scope, and achievements. Samuel P. Hays is attempting to provide a synthesis for the modern environmental movement in much the same way that he attempted to define and explain the conservation movement of the Progressive Era. Hays's long-awaited book on modern environmental politics is nearing completion, but glimpses of his synthesis have already appeared in several article-length studies. Hays supports the notion that the early to mid 1960s were significant in the development of the modern environmental movement. He sees three distinct stages in the evolution of environmental action: the initial thrust, between 1957 and 1965, which emphasized natural environmental values in outdoor recreation, wildlands, and open space; the growing interest in "ecology," between 1965 and 1972, which focused on antipollution and environmental protection; and the period after 1972, which brought to public attention such issues as toxic chemicals, energy, and the possibilities of social, economic, and political decentralization.

While one might quibble with the precise chronological breakdown of the modern environmental era, Hays points to the significant shift from conservation to environmentalism during the 1960s, a shift that reinforces a growing belief among scholars that the National Environmental Policy Act of 1969 (NEPA) was as much a culmination as a new starting point for governmental interest in environmentalism. In this context the Johnson administration must be viewed as a transitional force in the evolution from old-style conservationism to modern environmentalism.[6]

The Johnson Administration in the Environmental Era

In a 1968 memorandum that summed up the conservation achievements of the Johnson administration, Secretary of the Interior Stewart L. Udall stated:

> A general conclusion—quite inescapable—is that Presidential leadership has changed the outlook of the nation with regard to conservation and has added vital "new dimensions." No longer is peripheral action—the "saving" of a forest, a park, a refuge for wildlife—isolated from the mainstream. The total environment is now the concern, and the new conservation makes man, himself, its subject. The quality of life is now the perspective and purpose of the new conservation.[7]

From his vantage point at the end of the Johnson presidency, Udall casts the administration in a visionary role—an advance agent of modern environmentalism. However, the very name New Conservation suggests a looking backward as well as a looking ahead. While environmental activity was vigorous, some programs were merely extensions of Progressive Era or New Deal resource management; others focused more clearly on antipollution and other quality-of-life issues.

In some cases the administration was a leader; in some, a follower; in others, a usurper. Despite Udall's claim, the New Conservation was not a coherent, consistent program.

This is not to say that the New Conservation was mere illusion or simply public relations. As a transitional concept it blended the governmental traditions of the past while reacting to contemporary environmental issues that were emanating from several sources—both inside and outside the government. An examination of the holdings of the Johnson Library suggests that the promotion of the New Conservation by Secretary Udall and others guided the president and several of his advisers toward a more sophisticated, holistic perspective on the environment. However, because the presidential papers essentially provide a "view from the top," they also reveal the perspective of national leaders who were taking credit for pioneering programs and policies that were as much the result of mounting grass-roots sentiment and congressional actions as of executive leadership. However, before we can set limits on the Johnson administration's achievements in establishing environmental policies and programs, we must try to determine what forces shaped the New Conservation within the government. A brief look at key individuals and groups who were close to the president is in order.

The Legacy of JFK

As with other issues, it is difficult to determine exactly what impact a completed term by John F. Kennedy would have had on environmental policies and legislation. It seems clear, however, that the Kennedy presidency provided the most-immediate momentum for the New Conservation of the Johnson years. Kennedy was the first president since Franklin D. Roosevelt to take any direct initiative on environmental policy. During the 1960 presidential campaign, Kennedy authorized the Natural Resources Advisory Committee. One of his first special messages to Congress, in February, 1961, dealt with the development and conservation of natural resources. In May, 1962, he called the White House Conference on Conservation, which went beyond the old "wise-use" issues to examine questions dealing with the deteriorating quality of the environment.

While Kennedy's congressional record on the environment was anemic, he brought a new mind set to the presidency which led naturally into an elaboration of environmental policy on many fronts. Most significantly, he rejected the notion that environmental issues were state and local responsibilities. His predecessor, Dwight D. Eisenhower, had believed that the federal role in conservation and antipollution could be extended, but only if additional federal funding was not involved. James L. Sundquist has noted: "The major contribution of John F. Kennedy to national thinking about the outdoor environment was, perhaps, an open mind about the budget."[8] The exercise of federal authority, backed by a commitment to more federal funding, was the underpinning for Kennedy's environmental policy. It was the Johnson administration, however, that took action on those impulses.[9]

Lady Bird

The terms *natural beauty* and *beautification* permeated the conservation rhetoric of the Johnson administration. In a speech to the 1964 graduating class of the University of Michigan, President Johnson asserted: "We have always prided ourselves on being not only America the strong and America the free, but America the beautiful."[10] Indeed, one of the working groups that developed the Great Society programs was on "natural beauty." And most significantly, in May, 1965, the White House Conference on Natural Beauty met in Washington, D.C., and produced its report, "Beauty for America."[11]

Lady Bird Johnson was the person who was most responsible for the president's heightened aesthetic sense. In response to the 1965 State of the Union address, she stated: "I liked the accent on education, on medical research, and on preserving this nation's beauty— the preservation of the beauty of America along the highways, in the cities, in National Parks—'the green legacy for tomorrow.' I hope we can do something about that in our four years here."[12] Between 1965 and 1968 she actively sought to make "natural beauty" a key national issue.

Casual observers of the Johnson administration's environmental record have difficulty in seeing beyond what they believe to have been the superficial commitment to environmentalism that was expressed in the drive for natural beauty. To the severest critics, the beautification projects of the First Lady were little more than aesthetic frivolities. This kind of criticism underestimates the influence that Lady Bird had on her husband and the catalytic role that she played in raising environmental issues to national attention. The concern for beautification may not have taken environmental issues much beyond traditional conservation, but it did reinforce the commitment that grass-root organizations and the Kennedy administration brought to the issues.

A memo from Matthew Nimetz to Joseph Califano noted that an article in the December, 1967, issue of *Sports Illustrated* was "critical of the Federal effort [on the environment] to date: it says we concentrate too much on 'natural beauty' and too little on more fundamental problems."[13] Whether that is a fair assertion is another question, but it is a testament to the influence of the First Lady that the drive for beautification carried such significance. Lady Bird's campaign against billboards, her plea for urban beautification, and her support for preserving natural beauty kept environmental issues before the American people and on the agenda of the president. Secretary Udall wrote to the president that "the leadership of the First Lady and her nation-wide crusade for beautification has been a vital part of [the] attempt to re-educate the country."[14] While the president was prone to refer to the beautification program as "Lady Bird's business," her activities brought to Washington a key ingredient necessary in order to launch an effective environmental program.[15]

Stewart L. Udall

Within the administration, no one wielded more influence over conservation policy than did Secretary of the Interior Udall, the first Arizonan to be selected for the cabinet. Udall had interrupted his college studies to work for two years as a Mormon missionary; then he had served in World War II; and ultimately he had practiced law in Tucson with his brother, Morris. Beginning in 1954, Stewart Udall had served his first of his three terms as a United States congressman. On the Committee on Interior and Insular Affairs, he was recognized as a member of the "conservation bloc." In 1959 a House fight over a labor bill brought him into contact with Senator John F. Kennedy. Udall's delivery of Arizona's votes at the 1960 Democratic National Convention, according to Douglas H. Strong, "won Kennedy's gratitude and Lyndon B. Johnson's respect for his [Udall's] political skill." It also won Udall the secretaryship of the Department of the Interior, a position that he held from 1961 through 1969.[16]

Prone to impulsive statements and lacking strong administrative ability, Udall made a slow start as secretary of the interior. In time, this dedicated conservationist and dedicated liberal made his presence felt in the Kennedy and Johnson administrations. For most of his tenure, he maintained a good working relationship with both presidents, keeping environmental issues constantly before them. He found LBJ to be "very receptive" to new programs and policies, but Udall also believed that the successes that were achieved during the Johnson years would probably have come also if Kennedy had served his full term.[17]

Udall played an important role as cheerleader in both administrations, persuading Kennedy to send a conservation message to Congress, the first such in decades; encouraging Lady Bird to stress beautification and conservation programs; and reminding LBJ of the importance of the New Conservation. Beyond that role, Udall was a central advocate of expanded programs in numerous areas, including outdoor recreation, the national park system, and antipollution.[18]

Udall embodied the faith that the federal government could lead the country in the conservation battle. This was not to be symbolic leadership but was to be a commitment to fund new programs and to invest in environmental protection. In Udall's words and actions could be seen the transformation of old-style conservationism into modern environmentalism. He was among the first government officials to defend the conclusions of Rachel Carson's *Silent Spring*. His perspective on the role of the Interior Department also reflected a change in direction. Rather than administering the department as a loosely knit group of bureaus and agencies that promoted resource development and protected western interests, he saw the department's mission as serving national environmental needs. He was not without inconsistencies, however. When issues of water development and scenic conservation clashed, Udall tended to take the traditional pose of the westerner, so he supported water development.[19]

In *The Quiet Crisis* (1963), Udall stated his philosophy in clear terms:

> America today stands poised on a pinnacle of wealth and power, yet we live in a land of vanishing beauty, of increasing ugliness, of shrinking open space, and of an overall environment that is diminished daily by pollution and noise and blight.
> This, in brief, is the quiet conservation crisis of the 1960's.[20]

Udall's rhetoric showed many of the signs of the modern environmental movement—namely, a relatively broad ecological perspective, a concern for quality-of-life issues, and a commitment to environmental protection. However, his preoccupation with traditional conservation issues—such as land policy, national parks, reclamation, and resource management—marked him as a transitional figure in the history of American environmentalism more than as a pioneer of a new ethic.[21]

President Lyndon B. Johnson

The Kennedy legacy, Lady Bird, and Stewart Udall—all helped to create the New Conservation as well as to shape Lyndon Johnson's own environmental views. But other factors—less direct but equally obvious—also influenced the president. In a 1973 *Audubon Magazine* editorial, for example, one of Johnson's admirers wrote: "The man from the Texas hill country had a deep love for the land, and his efforts to preserve and restore it not only laid the foundation for the environmental crusade of the 1970s, but enriched the quality of life for all Americans."[22] By implication, at least, Johnson emerges from these lines as the modern equivalent of Franklin Roosevelt—as he liked to be reminded by his aides and advisers. Udall stated in an oral interview that Johnson "thought about the land a lot the way Roosevelt did. Roosevelt was his idol and you could come up with a good idea and say, 'This is good for the land and good for the people,' he bought it."[23] The comparison with FDR the conservationist—which crops up repeatedly in the literature—gave Johnson yet-another important link to his revered political past as a Roosevelt liberal. If for no other reason, Johnson could give broad support to the New Conservation as perpetuating the goals of the New Deal.

Yet Johnson had a broader vision for America than the New Deal—namely, the Great Society. By happy coincidence, rising grassroots interest in quality-of-life issues tapped the spirit of the Great Society that President Johnson envisioned. In his speech at the University of Michigan he claimed that the Great Society was "a place where the city of man serves not only the needs of the body and the demands of commerce but the desire for beauty and the hunger for community. . . . It is a place where men are more concerned with the quality of their goals than the quantity of their goods."[24] In a letter of thanks to a member of the Task Force on Natural Resources (1964), Johnson noted the need for "imaginative programs of resource development," and he added: "In the years immediately ahead we have, I believe, an unparalleled opportunity to take some major steps forward toward creating the Great Society. You and your colleagues on the Natural Resources Task Force have made a major contribution toward that goal."[25]

The impulse for a federal solution to social problems, which was deeply embedded in the Great Society, was firmly connected to the environmental programs of the Johnson years. The noted environmentalist Lynton K. Caldwell argued, in *Environment: A Challenge for Modern Society* (1970):

> Lyndon B. Johnson . . . anticipated the environmental quality issue in his Great Society address, on May 22, 1964, which spoke directly to the values of the post–World War II generation that would shortly determine the direction of American politics.

His espousal of natural beauty and environmental quality surprised and gratified conservationists, who had not looked for this type of commitment from a professional politician from western Texas. The depth of the Johnson commitment was open to question. But regardless of the President's sincerity, the fact that he had publicly identified himself with the environmental issue strengthened its position in American political life.[26]

Caldwell's cynicism about Johnson's sincerity in promoting the New Conservation is not completely unwarranted. The president's Great Society idealism was clearly tempered by his political pragmatism. Geographer Richard A. Cooley has argued that in supporting programs in conservation and natural beauty, Johnson "knew a political issue when he saw one."[27] And Caldwell, assessing the Democrats' stance on environmental issues during the 1964 presidential campaign, asserted that candidate Johnson stayed clear of potentially dangerous environmental-quality issues—pollution, urban sprawl, public transportation—by associating with "the more easily managed expression 'natural beauty.' "[28] On the other side, John P. Crevelli accepts LBJ's environmentalism as sincere: "There is no other conclusion to make than that Johnson believed in his words."[29] Also, as a strong advocate of "more is better," Johnson took great pride in the "sheer bulk" of legislation during his administration.[30]

Johnson certainly took advantage of the growing environmental spirit of the times. And there is little doubt that as a professional politician, he sensed the value of the New Conservation to his larger Great Society goals. However, the influence of FDR and the New Deal, the Kennedy legacy, Lady Bird, and Stewart Udall cannot be ignored if we are to have a complete picture of Johnson's commitment to environmentalism. A reasonable conclusion is that Lyndon Johnson— through a variety of influences—supported the New Conservation as an integral part of his Great Society. In this way, he helped to place environmental issues in a larger political context. To be sure, there were limits to his environmentalism; these are manifest in political constraints and partisan considerations, in distractions from myriad social programs, and in his preoccupation with the Vietnam War.

In order to better understand the breadth and depth of the New Conservation, we must look beyond presidential leadership to the bureaucratic structure that devised the executive environmental policy and to the legislative activity that produced new environmental laws.

Key Departments and Agencies

The New Conservation was not simply the province of a small group of individuals—not even the president. To what extent the Johnson administration was committed to a new direction in environmental policies and programs depended, in part at least, on the interaction of key departments and agencies. Even after the establishment of the Environmental Protection Agency during the Nixon administration, environmental programs were diffused throughout the federal bureaucracy, with no central clearing house for the establishment of policy. This suggests that U.S. environmental policy has been and still remains fragmented, reflecting the collective interests and actions of governmental agencies and of Congress.

At least since the New Deal, there have been several attempts to consolidate federal environmental programs into a single department in order to offset the fragmentation of environmental policy. A favorable political climate during the 1960s led congressional leaders and officials in the Johnson administration to seek such a consolidation. In 1964 the President's Task Force on Government Organization, which was chaired by Donald K. Price, recommended that five new executive departments be created, including a Department of Natural Resources (DNR). One option suggested the merging of the Departments of Interior and of Agriculture, with nonresource programs going to other departments. The other option was that the Department of Agriculture be retained but that the Forest Service and the Soil Conservation Service be transferred to the Department of the Interior. With either option, the task force recommended that some water-resource functions of the Federal Power Commission and of the Army Corps of Engineers be moved to the new Department of Natural Resources. Little came of these plans.

In 1965, Senator Frank E. Moss of Utah again proposed that natural-resource agencies be reorganized into a DNR. The Corps of Engineers, perpetually an opponent of reorganization, fought the Moss bill. The corps favored the status quo as a way of protecting its monopoly over dozens of public-works projects. In addition, the Bureau of the Budget argued against giving to the new department the coordination and planning functions that Congress had assigned to the Water Resources Council through the Water Resources Planning Act of 1965.

In 1967 the President's Task Force on Government Organization, chaired by Ben Heineman, called for an even larger Department of Natural Resources and Development, which would include the Corps of (Civil) Engineers and the Departments of the Interior, Housing and

Urban Development, Transportation, and Agriculture. By this time, the fate of such attempts at reorganization was preordained.[31]

The very reason for the attempted mergers is why they never occurred—namely, the vested interests of the departments and agencies. The development of programs has most often taken priority over making comprehensive environmental policy, since programs can be controlled by the agencies, whereas policy cannot be. Secretary Udall favored a Department of Natural Resources for the obvious reason that the Department of the Interior stood to gain the most from such an arrangement. But he, too, recognized the difficulties posed by interagency rivalry. In a memorandum to Joseph Califano, Udall stated his belief that the Johnson administration could "succeed where the others failed" if the president would formulate a "sound plan," if congressional realities were kept in mind, and if the Cabinet would observe "team discipline."[32] But Udall had to depend upon the president to initiate the action that would create the DNR. And Johnson was too much the politician to be caught up in such a web.

Even relatively small-scale change in the environmental apparatus created serious internal tensions. In 1966, Udall attempted to secure the transfer of water-pollution programs from HEW to Interior. Originally, Udall sought the transfer of air-pollution programs as well, but he trimmed down his request. Key adviser Joseph Califano initially cautioned the president not to rush into a decision to authorize the transfer: "The political feasibility of such action at a time when HEW is considering an Assistant Secretary for Environment is highly questionable." However, he eventually supported Udall's stance, arguing that most of the outside experts on the task force agreed with the move since the president had initiated his program "to attack water pollution on a river basin basis."[33]

HEW Secretary John W. Gardner was predictably strenuous in his opposition, arguing that since Interior had close working relations with the oil and mining industries—which were major industrial polluters—that the department had "a built-in conflict of interest." Senator Edmund S. Muskie of Maine, one of the leading congressional environmentalists, pointed to the impropriety of dismantling and transferring the new Water Pollution Control Administration—established under HEW's control in 1965—before it had been fully established and was operational. He also pointed out that Interior was western oriented, while the most serious pollution problems were in the East. And he warned about the potential political fallout from such an untimely move, namely, fuel for the Republicans' claim of "Administration confusion," and criticism from state and local officials.[34]

Udall, however, prevailed in this miniwar. Clearly, Interior feared the repercussions from having both Interior and HEW set standards for water quality, rather than having HEW maintain control of the Water Pollution Control Administration. Dual responsibility would mean having Interior set the standards on river-basin plans and having HEW set the standards on all other rivers. Also, enforcement might become inconsistent. Most significantly, dual responsibility would pit HEW and Interior against each other in relations with Congress and the president. Udall's advisers asked: "If we were starting from scratch today would we create a Corps of Engineers and a Bureau of Reclamation?"[35]

The dispute over the Water Pollution Control Administration points to the need for a better understanding of the internal workings of executive agencies—such as Interior, Agriculture, HEW, the Federal Power Commission (FPC), and TVA—that are responsible for environmental programs.[36] Interdepartmental or interagency rivalries also help to demonstrate why national environmental policy remained fragmented and particularist in the wake of a more holistic perspective on the environment that was coming from outside the government during the 1960s.

It is unfair, however, to assume that the relative influence of governmental agencies that are concerned with the environment remained static. Stewart Udall's expertise and his close working relationship with the president gave Interior much leverage over its cabinet rivals. The Public Health Service, which traditionally had played an important role in antipollution, was being raided by other agencies. A case in point is the transfer of its water-pollution programs to HEW and then to Interior. The most significant shift in influence over environmental policy during the Johnson years was the rise of the Office of Science and Technology (OST), which played an increasingly important role in advising the president on issues of environmental quality. In many ways, OST functioned like the Council on Environmental Quality (CEQ), which was established along with the Environmental Protection Agency (EPA) in 1970. The CEQ proved to be a relatively weak advisory body, but it was the only government agency designed to oversee energy and environmental issues.

OST provided an overview of energy and environmental issues, but it was more aggressive in asserting itself than was the CEQ. In 1957, President Dwight Eisenhower had created the post of special assistant to the president for science and technology as a response to the launching of Sputnik. In 1962, President Kennedy had established the Office of Science and Technology, with the special assistant retaining primacy in matters concerning national-security policy, intelligence, arms control, and other international initiatives. In addition, the Office of Director of Defense Research and Engineering was created, to reduce the work load in the area of military problems.[37]

Under the leadership of Director Donald F. Hornig, OST began to broaden its responsibilities to include problems of health and the environment. Precedent for such a move went back as far as 1959, when the President's Science Advisory Committee intervened to study a public scare over tainted cranberries on the eve of the holiday season.[38] Little by little, Hornig brought OST into most major environmental issues that the Johnson administration was facing. OST participated in several environmental task forces; director Hornig chaired both the 1966 Task Force on Natural Resource Studies and the 1968 Task Force on the Quality of the Environment.

Hornig noted in an oral interview that OST's range of activities was dictated by "the sense of significance, either by what matters to the President at any given time or perhaps more important—is to try to anticipate for him what is going to matter."[39] Without the heavy programmatic commitment of other agencies that had interests in the environment—and the limits that go with it—OST could range over many issues without significant constraint. Of particular importance was the role of OST in promoting the coordination of and the providing of data on the scientific and technical programs relating to pollution abatement.[40]

Despite its flexibility in addressing environmental issues, OST was wary about attempts to weaken its power. Senator Gaylord Nelson of Wisconsin introduced a bill in July, 1965, to designate Interior as the primary agency for ecological research. But OST opposed the bill and, through a delay in its own study of research programs, helped to table it. When he reintroduced his bill, Senator Nelson proposed to locate a council on environmental quality in the office of the president. Again, OST successfully headed off such a plan.[41]

While OST kept potential rivals at bay in the Johnson administration, the establishment of the EPA and the CEQ during the Nixon years had diminished its influence over environmental matters. Without enforcement functions and without its own programs to manage, OST never was likely to emerge as an omnibus agency like a department of natural resources. OST's de facto role in coordinating environmental policy was formalized with the CEQ, thus offering an important precedent but with the same limits. EPA assumed primary responsibility for enforcing antipollution laws, but it rarely demonstrated a capacity for providing a policy overview. Vested interests that were based upon a broad distribution of programs throughout the federal bureaucracy worked against a coordinated environmental policy—or at least against interagency cooperation. Yet during the Johnson years, OST—and Interior—broadened the efforts of the executive branch in addressing environmental quality as a national issue.

Major Environmental Issues, 1963–68

The Johnson administration's support for and development of environmental legislation was vigorous, but it was not clearly focused nor well coordinated. The vigor grew out of a response to (1) the leadership of Stewart Udall, Lady Bird, and others within the administration; (2) grass-roots enthusiasm for many quality-of-life issues; and (3) the actions of congressional leaders, such as Senators Muskie, Nelson, and Henry M. Jackson (Washington), Congressman Wayne Aspinall (Indiana), and others. The lack of focus and coordination stemmed from the complexity and scope of the issues, the relative newness of "environmentalism" as opposed to "conservationism," and the nature of the federal bureaucracy.

The overarching goal of the administration—if there was one—was to wed concern over the environment to the larger goals of the Great Society. This meant either identifying with continuing congressional efforts at environmental reform or writing new legislation. New proposals came primarily from special task forces—nine in all—which focused on recreation, natural resources, natural beauty, environmental pollution, and energy.[42] In large measure, the early task forces focused on traditional issues of conservation—the wilderness, water resources, wildlife—but increasingly the studies emphasized pollution problems and the urban environment. By and large, the administration's proposals on conservation enhanced the existing programs rather than redirecting them. However, the antipollution measures were more far-reaching, while the conceptual emphasis on the urban environment was very innovative.

Wilderness, Parks, and Public Lands

The rhetoric of "natural beauty" tended to camouflage the administration's emphasis on traditional conservation programs during the early Johnson years. Especially through Udall's leadership, the administration concentrated on extending the national park system and the public-lands program rather than on reevaluating the basic tenets of conservation. In response to the 1964 Task Force on the Preservation of Natural Beauty, Interior noted that the report failed to discuss the Wilderness Act and various proposals in regard to national parks.[43] But the 1966 Task Force on Natural Resource Studies devoted considerable attention to the administration's plan to expand the national park system, to develop a national trails system, and to extend the national forest system. A Bureau of the Budget memorandum explained why there was such a shift of emphasis: "The Task Force has not really functioned as a Task Force. Secretary Udall requested suggestions from each of the agencies involved. . . . The report, therefore, reflects Secretary Udall's views, with very little consideration of priorities as reflected in the responsibilities of other agencies of the Government."[44]

Udall was at his persuasive best in promoting traditional conservation programs, despite the grumblings of some officials who wanted the environmental agenda to expand more rapidly. Given the momentous impact of the Wilderness Act in 1964, however, the administration could hardly begin to set environmental policy without taking into account the important upsurge of interest in land and water conservation.

The passage of the Wilderness Act in 1964 was a conservation landmark. The act set aside four wilderness areas totaling 9.1 million acres in the national forests. It also included a provision whereby large roadless tracts in national parks, monuments, and wildlife refuges could be added to the designated wilderness areas. According to historian Roderick Nash, the concept of a wilderness system "marked an innovation in the history of the American preservation movement. It expressed . . . a determination to take the offensive. Previous friends of the wilderness had been largely concerned with *defending* it against various forms of development."[45]

The legislative battle over the wilderness had raged for nine years. The drive for wilderness legislation had begun in 1955, when Howard Zahniser, executive director of the Wilderness Society, had proposed it in a speech before a conference in Washington of the American Planning and Civic Association. The actions of the Wilderness Society, the Sierra Club and other groups, brought the idea of wilderness preservation to congressional attention. And while the 1964 act fell short of the preservationists' goals, a permanent wilderness system was created at last.[46] Although the Johnson administration did not initiate the Wilderness Act, it did incorporate the legislation into its general conservation program. Public-land-management agencies, including the Forest Service, preferred managerial discretion rather than legislative decree to set land policy. Secretary Udall and other administration leaders, however, did not resist the new momentum; they promoted additional mandates for wildlands and scenic and recreational programs.

The Outdoor Recreation Resources Review Commission (ORRRC)—a study commission established by Congress—made several recommendations which led to new actions. For example, the Land and Water Conservation Fund Act of 1964 was passed in direct response to the ORRRC's recommendations. This act provided funds for the acquisition of lands within the national forests, which was the first major opportunity to add land to the system during the post–World War II era. In 1968 the Wild and Scenic Rivers Act and the National Trail System Act followed. The North Cascades (in Washington), the Canyonlands (in Utah), and the Redwoods (in California) were added to the national park system, and Guadalupe Mountains (in Texas) was authorized. In addition, new categories of federal land administration were created—national seashores, lakeshores, and recreational areas.[47]

The accomplishments of the early to mid 1960s were not achieved in a vacuum; environmental groups and the federal courts also played a vital role.[48] But the vigor with which the administration pursued the elaboration of the wilderness and national parks systems, especially through Udall's relentless leadership, graphically demonstrates the extension of federal power in land- and water-use programs. These programs also fit the spirit of the Great Society and firmly grounded the "New Conservation" in traditional conservation causes.

Of course, considerations of practical politics determined the extent to which the president supported his Interior secretary's conservation goals. John P. Crevelli has raised some important questions about the politics of wilderness preservation during the Johnson years in his article in *Prologue*, "The Final Act of the Greatest Conservation President." In this case study about an eleventh-hour attempt in 1968 to greatly increase the nation's parklands, Crevelli discusses why Johnson settled for an additional three hundred thousand acres rather than an anticipated seven million acres. Political reality persuaded the president to accept a small victory rather than a great defeat. In the final days of his presidency, with the Vietnam War and countless domestic programs consuming his time and with his power slipping away, Johnson was fearful of asking for too much and, in the end, getting nothing. "His ego," Crevelli concluded, "would not permit a final defeat at the hands of the Congress over which he had been master for so many years on most domestic affairs."[49]

A personal consequence of Johnson's decision was an abrupt end to the strong professional and personal relationship between LBJ and Udall. In settling for three hundred thousand acres, the Sonora Desert reserve had been omitted. This large parcel was located in Udall's own congressional district in Arizona. The Interior secretary believed that Johnson had omitted the parcel to show him "who was boss," not an uncommon LBJ trait. It is more likely, however, that this decision was based on the president's belief in the "art of the possible."[50]

Water Resources

Water resources were an important component in the New Conservation. Again, the scale of activity was more impressive than the innovation in approach. A possible exception was the Wild and Scenic Rivers Act of 1968, a companion measure to the Wilderness Act, which created a system of wild rivers. Within the administration, it was perceived to be as historic as the wilderness bill. In 1965, President Johnson had suggested, in his message to Congress on natural beauty, that it was time to identify and preserve "free flowing stretches of our great scenic rivers before growth and development make the beauty of the unspoiled waterway only a memory."[51] A bill was prepared, which passed the Senate but died in a House committee. Again in 1967, Johnson had repeated his plea for scenic rivers, and the Ninetieth Congress obliged by passing a compromise bill. In all, in the Eighty-ninth and Ninetieth Congresses, seventeen bills had been introduced dealing with scenic and recreational rivers.[52]

The National Wild and Scenic Rivers Act established a river system that was composed of segments of eight rivers, made provision for additions to the system, and encouraged state participation in the preservation of scenic rivers. While the establishment of public recreational areas was not new and while the practice of federal condemnation authority to acquire areas for public purposes was not new either, the law raised controversies over the "public good" versus private property rights and over development versus nondevelopment. These issues were made intense because some of the rivers ran outside of federal lands through populated areas in the East, rather than through public lands in the West. Coming at the end of the Johnson presidency, the Wild and Scenic Rivers Act showed many of the signs of a more aggressive environmentalism that would surface during the 1970s.[53]

President Johnson's interest in the new law, as well as in other water projects, was strong and sincere. Udall has recalled:

He always had a lot of insight on water problems and this grew out of the New Deal period and the dams that were being built in his own congressional district. He had an intimacy with water projects. He knew how they functioned and this, of course, was something that President Kennedy did not have and it was something that worked to my advantage.[54]

While the Johnson administration may not have seriously challenged the status quo with its various water projects, it did promote a wide array of programs. The president gave support to the International Hydrological Decade, a world-wide effort to advance knowledge about water issues. Desalination programs were discussed extensively. Governmental officials gave the proper attention to water-development projects, which were important political links between Washington and the state governments.[55] They also generally supported the authority of the Army Corps of Engineers and the Bureau of Reclamation in building dams and reservoirs, constructing canals, and promoting flood control. However, growing criticism of the agencies for their narrow cost-benefit approach to the development of water projects led, in part at least, to the Federal Water Project Recreation Act of 1965. The act gave local governments a greater role in planning and financing federal water projects and, most importantly, gave legislative recognition to the idea that recreation and wildlife were "benefits" that were equal to economic and other utilitarian wants and needs.[56]

As with other components of the New Conservation, setting water-resources policy was understood to be primarily a federal responsibility. In 1965, President Johnson authorized officials in the Bureau of the Budget to recommend that Congress establish a national water commission to review long-term requirements for water and how the requirements should be achieved. A memorandum to Joe Califano from the Bureau of the Budget noted that "the long range water problems in the Southwest are no more acute—and probably less acute—than those in the Great Lakes and the New York–New England areas."[57]

Some water issues were recognized but were not successfully acted upon during the Johnson years. For example, in the mid 1960s, coastal wetlands began to attract attention because of their recreational potential, but also because of their environmental significance in preserving wildlife and in acting as natural flood reservoirs and pollution-treatment systems. The 1966 Task Force on Resources and Recreation recommended that the Interior Department study estuarine areas and called for the department to "protect and preserve in their natural condition" estuarine areas that were considered to be valuable for sport and commercial fishing, wildlife conservation, outdoor recreation, scenic beauty, and scientific study. It also called for permits to be issued by Interior before anyone could dredge or fill in a navigable estuarine area, and it recommended that there be stricter control of the army's projects in regard to shore-erosion control, dredging, filling, or beach protection.

However, a bill that was introduced in the Ninetieth Congress to institute the permit system was badly diluted. As finally passed, the act only authorized $250,000 for fiscal years 1969 and 1970 for the purpose of conducting a study and an inventory of estuaries. But funds were never appropriated. In addition, Congress reduced the authorization of other funds for a study of estuarine pollution to be made by the Federal Water Pollution Control Administration. As a result of federal inaction and growing public interest, some states—such as Massachusetts, Maryland, and Florida—took the lead during the late 1960s and the early 1970s in passing laws to protect coastal wetlands, while others—such as New York, Michigan, and Wisconsin—developed programs to protect inland wetlands.[58]

Wildlife

Historian Thomas Dunlap has argued that the movement for the protection of endangered species has gone through two phases. The first began during the early 1960s with a broad interest in protecting wildlife. The second phase emerged with the passage of the Endangered Species Act in 1973 and with the more difficult task of administering a practical program. "Legal protection for endangered species," Dunlap has stated, "began casually." The Land and Water Conservation Act of 1964 established a fund to support federal and state outdoor recreational and wildlife work, which was broadly defined. The Endangered Species Act of 1966—the first act of its kind—was not designed to expand the scope of federal power. It did not define endangered species effectively, and it did not clarify the problem of cooperation with the states in developing a plan of action. The secretary of the Interior was authorized to buy land, but he could not regulate the taking of endangered species.[59]

During the 1960s the federal government made some gestures to protect species from extinction, but a practical program still lay in the future. Secretary Udall was the major administration force behind wildlife protection. In fact, Udall's last act as secretary of the Interior was to sign a final order creating two wildlife refuges. However, he was unable to get the kind of attention from the president on this matter that he had on water projects. The three-hundred-thousand-acre "parting gift to future generations," which Johnson agreed to during the final hours of his administration, would aid wildlife conservation, but it was not part of a broad plan of wildlife conservation.[60] Clearly, a changing public attitude toward nature during the postwar years and the efforts of environmental groups at the grass roots influenced the writing of future wildlife legislation to a greater extent than did the efforts of the Johnson administration.[61]

Pollution Control

In the area of pollution control, the New Conservation demonstrated a close association with the modern environmental movement. Several issues and events stimulated the interest in antipollution measures. Rachel Carson's assault on pesticides is a good example of the shift from traditional conservation to a focus on human well-being. The concern over the destruction of wildlife habitats helped to stimulate an interest in the functioning of ecological systems. Environmental groups drew attention to the exploitation of natural resources. The strip mining of coal attracted considerable debate. The commercial viability of nuclear power raised questions about radiation, the siting of plants, and reactor safety. The ubiquity of air pollution—especially in the form of smog and coal smoke—moved policy makers toward clean-air standards. And oil spills, jet-engine noise, and various industrial pollutants brought into high relief the contradictions of the drive for economic growth and the wish for an improved quality of life.[62]

President Johnson set a dramatic tone about pollution in several of his public statements in the mid 1960s. For example:

> Ours is a nation of affluence. But the technology that has permitted our affluence spews out vast quantities of wastes and spent products that pollute our air, poison our waters, and even impair our ability to feed ourselves. At the same time, we have crowded together into dense metropolitan areas where concentration of wastes intensifies the problem.
>
> Pollution now is one of the most pervasive problems of our society.[63]

In principle, at least, antipollution was an integral part of the Great Society.

The administration's general approach to antipollution was consistent with the other components of its environmental policy—to confront what were perceived as national issues through the broader exercise of federal authority. The 1964 Task Force on Environmental Pollution outlined an extensive program concerning "The Federal Responsibility for Pollution." A list of fourteen guidelines for policy was presented, including federal initiative on interstate compacts or other regional plans to combat pollution; international cooperation to abate pollution in river basins, air sheds, and water zones; the development and management of economic incentives to reduce pollution; the implementation of new technical expertise to solve problems; improved monitoring systems; and better public-information programs.[64]

Whether the administration could translate its broad interest in antipollution into tangible policy was another question. While an appreciation for the functioning of ecological systems helped to identify a growing list of pollutants, legislators and administration officials responded to discrete problems instead of dealing with pollution in a holistic manner. This was the most obvious—but not necessarily the most effective—way to confront pollution problems, especially since no single agency in the federal government had the overall responsibility for pollution control at the time.

Air pollution emerged as a national problem because of the criticism of coal burning by utilities and other industrial users and also because of the rising concern over smog. Through the encouragement of health officials and academics, HEW had sponsored the first National Conference on Air Pollution in 1958. The tone of the conference was cooperation between industry and government to reduce air pollution, but it attracted few people from the coal industry and few conservationists. By the time of the third Conference on Air Pollution in 1966, both coal and environmental interests were well represented. During the mid 1960s a relatively innocuous law—the Clean Air Act of 1955—underwent several revisions that were potentially injurious to the coal and electric-utility industries. The 1967 act changed the emphasis from air pollution as a local problem to air pollution as a national problem, but one that required cooperation between industry and government. In the broadest sense, this revision brought industry into the policy-formation phase of air-pollution legislation, resulting in a Clean Air Act that many felt was "coal's law."[65]

A relatively new source of air pollution—automobile emissions—posed different problems. Los Angeles, the "smog capital of America" during the 1950s, became a living laboratory for studying massive doses of auto emissions. It became apparent during the 1960s that smog was a national problem, requiring the attention of the federal government. While California led the way in emissions control, federal law slowly moved toward a recognition of the problem. The 1963 Clean Air Act for the first time gave the federal government limited enforcement power over interstate pollution. The 1965 amendment to that act recognized the need to control motor-vehicle pollution on a national scale, and it empowered HEW to establish and enforce air-pollution standards for new motor vehicles. The 1967 Air Quality Act was the first piece of federal legislation that was designed to control lead emissions. But the automobile and oil industries continually resisted tougher standards; and while the public paid homage to clean air, it resented carrying the burden of responsibility through higher costs and reduced automobile performance.[66]

There had been considerable support for some type of federal standards both in Congress and in the executive branch. But what kind of standards? Senator Muskie—"Mr. Pollution Control"—generally opposed fixed standards on emissions, fearing that they would be "minimal rather than uniform." The administration ignored Muskie's opposition, supporting national emission standards for major industrial sources of pollution. In addition, the administration's plan gave authority to regional commissions—to be staffed and financed by the federal government—to set standards for their particular regions. Muskie continued to voice opposition, and he presented his own version of the proposed bill. The compromise version, which became the 1967 law, included many of the administration's original recommendations, including a regional orientation for setting standards. However, Muskie is credited with having shaped the standard-setting procedures by placing direct responsibility both on the states and on the federal government. While the act was the first to attempt to control lead emissions from automobiles, it mandated ambient air-quality standards for coal-burning industries. In the case of the latter, at least, the coal industry and its allies believed that they had achieved the lesser of two evils by avoiding national emissions standards.[67]

For his part, President Johnson had a difficult time in not playing politics with air-pollution legislation. Throughout the maneuverings over the bill, he was reluctant to come down hard against the automobile and coal industries, holding out hope that cooperation between the government and business could help to solve the problem. When HEW initially presented a proposal to the White House in 1965 calling for enforceable federal standards on automobile exhaust, the president queried whether the industry had been consulted. The proposal was dropped and ignored for several months. Muskie's persistence, criticism in the press, and the general momentum of the antipollution movement forced LBJ to accept a more stringent approach to standards for automobile emissions—or at least to avoid public debate over the matter.[68] A scribbled response to a suggestion that the president support the formation of a nonprofit corporation headed by business leaders to fight air pollution was telling: "Keep this away from W.H. [the White House]."[69]

Water-pollution control—including sewage treatment and oil pollution—had equal standing during the Johnson years with air-pollution control. Leadership came especially from Senator Muskie, chairman of the Senate Subcommittee on Air and Water Pollution. During the early 1960s, congressional leaders were ready to accelerate the pace of pollution-control legislation and to increase the federal role in water-pollution control. Before 1948, legal authority to control water pollution resided almost exclusively on the local level or in the states. But between the late 1940s and 1965, water-pollution control was mired in controversy over federal enforcement powers and financial assistance for the construction of waste-treatment plants.

In 1963, with a Democratically controlled Senate and a pervasive spirit of federal leadership in social programs, Muskie introduced significant amendments to the 1961 water-pollution-control act, including water-quality standards and the transfer of administrative authority from the Public Health Service to the new Federal Water Pollution Control Administration (FWPCA) within HEW. When it was finally passed in 1965, the Water Quality Act made significant headway in controlling some forms of water pollution.

The 1966 Clean Water Restoration Act was an important addition, growing out of a tortuous compromise between the executive branch and Congress. The administration was concerned about Senator Muskie's proposal for a huge increase in grant authorization for treatment facilities, and it was wary of granting strong pollution-control authority to the states. Therefore, the administration plan called for water-pollution control on a regional basis. Muskie disliked this approach because it placed less emphasis on the states' water-quality standards which he had fought for in the 1965 legislation. Because Congress resisted the idea of regional plans, favoring instead public-works programs that would be controlled by their constituencies, Muskie's version won out. While a veto was considered, the president wanted some form of water-pollution control, so he signed the bill.[70]

By the last two years of the Johnson administration, interest in water-pollution control expanded to include interest in oil pollution. The sinking of the huge tanker *Torrey Canyon* in March, 1967, helped to dramatize the need for updating federal legislation in regard to oil pollution. In 1967 the Senate passed a bill that dealt with oil pollution and acid mine drainage, and in 1968 it approved a second measure, which included sections on vessel and thermal pollution. However, lack of action in the House and other delays pushed consideration of the bills until after the Santa Barbara oil-spill disaster in 1969. This left the unfair impression that the Johnson administration had neglected a form of pollution that was linked to the president's home state. Beyond legislative action, the administration had begun to consider multiagency contingency plans for responding to oil-spill emergencies. Yet, in view of the later Santa Barbara spill, hindsight suggests that the administration had not done enough to avoid an oil-pollution disaster.[71]

Undersecretary of the Interior David S. Black attempted to explain to an administration critic about mineral development on the Outer Continental Shelf:

> In essence, we were confronted with the difficult task of achieving a balance among several factors: the right of all the people of the United States to receive the benefit of public resource development, the needs of consumers in the petroleum-short West Coast region, and the legitimate interest of the local community in preserving its natural environment.[72]

While the Johnson administration and Congress cannot be credited with having made sweeping progress in pollution control during much of the 1960s, they did address an array of pollution problems that had been given short shrift for many years. Air and water pollution received the lion's share of attention, but there was a growing interest in oil pollution, noise pollution, sight pollution (through the beautification program), and, to a much lesser degree, strip mining and nuclear radiation. A forum for discussing these crucial environmental interests had been established on the federal level. And while government leaders did not initiate the debate over pollution, they responded to it more vigorously than had their predecessors in office.[73]

The Urban Environment

Through an array of social programs, including beautification, the Johnson administration had demonstrated its interest in urban problems and the quality of city life. A concern about the urban environment not only grew out of the general environmental impulses of the decade; it also stemmed from the revival of interest in growth management. Planners and policy makers debated issues such as urban growth, development, national planning, environmental protection, and population management. While federal officials did not formalize a comprehensive policy of growth management for cities, they did institute individual programs.[74]

The general interest in outdoor recreation had its urban aspect during the early 1960s. During the Kennedy administration, the Housing Act of 1961 had included a $50-million fund for urban open space. In 1965, Congress had added $310 million for the development of parks and for urban beautification. Between 1962 and 1972, the program, which was administered by the Urban Renewal Administration, granted $442 million to more than one thousand units of government, which led to the purchase of 348,000 acres. Urban-oriented parks also expanded the purposes of the national park system. The establishment of the Cape Cod National Seashore in 1961 had begun a trend which carried forward into the Johnson years with such areas as the Fire Island National Seashore (1964).[75]

The Johnson administration gave particular attention to the delivery of sanitary services. As discussed earlier, the funding of sewage treatment was an important feature of water legislation. The administration also made strides in dealing with solid wastes. In a special message on the conservation and restoration of natural beauty, President Johnson called for "better solutions to the disposal of solid waste" and recommended federal legislation to assist state governments in developing comprehensive disposal programs and to provide funds for research and development. Soon after this call to action, Congress passed the Solid Waste Disposal Act of 1965. This act recognized the ever-mounting volume and changing character of refuse, as well as the inability of current methods to deal with the problem. Not satisfied with the act alone, Johnson, with the advice of his Scientific Advisory Committee, directed that a special study be made of the national problem of solid waste. This resulted in the 1968 National Survey of Community Solid Waste Practices. It was the first truly national study of its kind in the twentieth century.[76]

The Johnson administration moved beyond the natural habitat with its historic-preservation program. The first major commitment of the federal government in the area came with the National Historic Preservation Act of 1966. This law broadened previous legislation, such as the Historic Sites Act of 1935, which had authorized the National Park Service to survey and acquire sites. The 1966 legislation authorized the secretary of the Interior to establish the National Register of Historic Places, which includes structures, sites, districts, and cultural resources of significance to the American heritage. Listing on the register was a prerequisite to the acquiring of federal matching grants for the acquisition or preservation and for federal tax benefits.[77]

The Johnson administration's venture into the urban environment was the most imaginative and innovative aspect of the New Conservation, because it brought several new federal programs to the cities. While individual components of the urban programs stressed well-known concerns—namely, air and water pollution, recreational space, land use, waste disposal, and historic preservation—taken as a whole, they reflected a fresh recognition of the "urban environment." By elevating local issues to national prominence, cities no longer had to take a back seat to the wilderness as vital environmental challenges. The natural environment and the built environment were being fused in the national consciousness, possibly for the first time.

The Johnson Administration and the Environment

There is little doubt that the events of the early and mid 1960s—inside and outside of government—set the stage for the passage of NEPA and the blossoming of the modern environmental movement. Did the Johnson administration play a major role in these events? Lynton Caldwell has suggested that the "White House support for environmental-quality efforts was ambiguous." While the president convened a conference on natural beauty, he also signed legislation that resulted in the running of overhead powerlines through Woodside, California, even though the community was willing to put them underground. The secretary of the army continued to issue fill permits in San Francisco Bay, despite rising protests. And the White House remained neutral in environmental battles over the Florida Everglades and the Indiana Dunes. Even in cases where action that favored environmental causes was taken, "White House follow-up showed neither direction nor vigor." Part of the reason, Caldwell has argued, was Johnson's increasing preoccupation with the deepening conflict in Vietnam and with the growing civil disorder at home. Caldwell has concluded: "The Johnson administration, notably through the efforts of Secretary of the Interior Stewart L. Udall, had taken a large step forward toward a national policy for the environment. But it had stopped short of the threshold. The locus of environmental policy making shifted to the Congress."[78]

Caldwell's assessment is persuasive in several ways, but it is incomplete. The administration often demonstrated a lack of consistency in support of environmental issues. The president certainly grew more preoccupied with the domestic and international crises that were stymieing the Great Society. Congress did play a vital role in establishing new environmental laws. Yet, if we consider what came before the 1960s rather than what came afterwards, a slightly different perspective on the administration emerges.

It would be unfair to suggest that the New Conservation was the governmental expression of modern environmentalism, for it was not. Nevertheless, it was clearly an important transitional step between old-style resource conservation and the more recent emphasis on environmental quality and environmental protection. The effort to make conservation and natural beauty important political issues, rather than peripheral interests, separated the Johnson administration from most of its predecessors. In breadth of coverage, certainly, the New Conservation was new: urban environmentalism and antipollution acquired parity with wilderness preservation and land and water conservation. Several environmental issues that had formerly been regarded as local concerns achieved national status, including air pollution, sewage treatment, historic preservation, and waste disposal.

The Johnson administration cannot be credited with initiating the major environmental causes of the time, but it cannot be considered superfluous and certainly not obstructionist. Within the administration the commitment to environmental programs was built upon three major factors. First, key advisers within the administration—especially Stewart Udall and Lady Bird Johnson—acted as conduits between the emerging environmental movement and the White House. Some issues were filtered or modified by these intermediaries, but the administration was not cut off from the outside world, nor did it make decisions in a vacuum. Second, the tradition of federal involvement in the social welfare of Americans, which is consciously linked to the New Deal and which achieved broader expression in the Great Society, gave environmental programs a legitimate claim to administration support. And third, executive leadership was provided by a politically opportunistic president who happened to appreciate the broad outlines of environmentalism, if not the details of it.

There were limits, to be sure, in the New Conservation. The focus on federal responsibility or federal remedies to environmental problems—"creative federalism," as Udall called it—often paid little heed to more specific local, state, or regional issues. In some cases, political compromises restrained the environmental goals that were being expressed by those outside of government; in other cases, the federal government coopted ideas and programs in an attempt to set national policy. But we must be careful not to view the Johnson administration's—or any administration's—commitment to national remedies as an accomplished fact. The diffusion of environmental programs within the bureaucracy, the lack of a clear institutional focal point for structuring environmental policy, the myriad conflicting goals and vested interests that are represented in the executive, judicial and legislative branches of government—all worked against a cohesive national policy in regard to the environment.

The Johnson administration's New Conservation was broad, sometimes bold, and often controversial. To some, it went too far; to many environmentalists, it did not go far enough. If its place in history is not yet well established, it is because we as yet do not know what to make of a president who led us simultaneously into Vietnam and into the Great Society. We barely have a feel for the institutional mechanisms within the federal bureaucracy and Congress that shape environmental laws and carry them out. And we still know all too little about the modern environmental movement and its potential repercussions. If the study of the New Conservation has yet to provide many answers, it raises many gnawing questions about the state of environmental affairs in the United States.

Notes

1. "An Interim Conservation Report to the President from Secretary of the Interior Stewart L. Udall," July 26, 1968; memo, Harry J. Hogan to Udall, July 26, 1968; memo "The 50 most significant beautification measures signed into law by President Lyndon B. Johnson through July 22, 1968," July 25, 1968; "Beautification and Conservation Measures," office files of W. De Vier Pierson, box 11; memo, W. De Vier Pierson to the President, Aug. 9, 1968, Ex NR, box 6; memo, Udall to Joseph A. Califano, Jr., Feb. 23, 1966, White House central files (hereafter cited as WHCF), Ex NR, box 5, Johnson Library. All files, unless otherwise specified, are in the Johnson Library.

2. J. Leonard Bates, "Fulfilling American Democracy: The Conservation Movement, 1907 to 1921," *Mississippi Valley Historical Review* 44 (June, 1957): 29–57; Samuel P. Hays, *Conservation and the Gospel of Efficiency: The Progressive Conservation Movement, 1890–1920* (Cambridge, Mass.: Harvard University Press, 1959); see also James L. Penick, Jr., *Progressive Politics and Conservation: The Ballinger-Pinchot Affair* (Chicago: University of Chicago Press, 1968); Lewis L. Gould, ed., *The Progressive Era* (Syracuse, N.Y.: Syracuse University Press, 1974).

3. Joseph M. Petulla, *American Environmental History: The Exploitation and Conservation of Natural Resources* (San Francisco, Calif.: Boyd & Fraser, 1977), p. 318.

4. Richard N. L. Andrews, "Class Politics or Democratic Reform: Environmentalism and American Political Institutions," *Natural Resources Journal* 20 (Apr., 1980): 221–41. For a contrasting view see William Tucker, *Progress and Privilege: America in the Age of Environmentalism* (New York: Doubleday, 1982).

5. Some of the recent studies on the environmental movement include Walter A. Rosenbaum, *The Politics of Environmental Concern* (New York: Praeger, 1973); Petulla, *American Environmental History*, and *American Environmentalism: Values, Tactics, Priorities* (College Station: Texas A&M University Press, 1980); Allan Schnaiberg, *The Environment: From Surplus to Scarcity* (New York: Oxford University Press, 1980); Carroll W. Pursell, Jr., ed., *From Conservation to Ecology: The Development of Environmental Concern* (New York: Crowell, 1973); Roderick Nash, ed., *The American Environment: Readings in the History of Conservation*, 2d ed. (Reading, Mass.: Addison-Wesley, 1976); Odom Fanning, *Man and His Environment: Citizen Action* (New York: Harper & Row, 1975); Ian G. Barbour, *Technology, Environment, and Human Values* (New York: Praeger, 1980); Phillip O. Foss, *Politics and Ecology* (Belmont, Calif.: Duxbury Press, 1972); William Ophuls, *Ecology and the Politics of Scarcity: Prologue to a Political Theory of the Steady State* (San Francisco, Calif.: W. H. Freeman, 1977); Mancur Olson and Hans H. Landsberg, eds., *The No-Growth Society* (New York: Norton, 1973); Barry Commoner, *The Closing Circle: Nature, Man and Technology* (New York: Bantam, 1971); Donald Fleming, "Roots of the New Conservation Movement," *Perspectives in American History* 6 (1972): 7–91.

6. Samuel P. Hays, "From Conservation to Environment: Environmental Politics in the United States since World War II," *Environmental Review* 6 (Fall, 1982): 24–27; see also Hays, "The Structure of Environmental Politics since World War II," *Journal of Social History* (Summer, 1981): 533–37, 719–38, and "Three Decades of Environmental Politics: The Historical Context" (paper delivered at the Conference on the Evolution of American Environmental Politics, June, 1984, the Wilson Center, Washington, D.C.).

7. Memo, Stewart L. Udall to the President, Oct. 17, 1968. WHCF, Ex NR, box 6; see also memo, Udall to the President, Dec. 13, 1965, ibid.; Udall to Robert B. White, Nov. 11, 1965, WHCF, NR 4, box 12.

8. James L. Sundquist, *Politics and Policy: The Eisenhower, Kennedy, and Johnson Years* (Washington, D.C.: Brookings Institution, 1968), p. 345.

9. Ibid., pp. 345–61; Richard A. Cooley, "Introduction," in *Congress and the Environment*, ed. Richard A. Cooley and Geoffrey Wandersforde-Smith (Seattle: University of Washington Press, 1970), pp. xiii–xiv, 28; Frank E. Smith, ed., *Land and Water, 1900–1970* (New York: Harper & Row, 1971), pp. 683–715; see also *Public Papers of the Presidents, 1961–1963*; Arthur M. Schlesinger, Jr., *A Thousand Days* (Greenwich, Conn.: Fawcett, 1965), p. 363.

10. Quoted in Sundquist, *Politics and Policy*, p. 362.

11. For background on the conference see WHCF, NR, boxes 2 to 4.

12. Lady Bird Johnson, *A White House Diary* (New York: Holt, Rinehart & Winston, 1970), p. 215.

13. Memo, Matthew Nimetz to Califano, Dec. 11, 1967, Office Files of James Gaither, box 196.

14. Memo, Udall to the President, Oct. 17, 1968, WHCF, Ex NR, box 6.

15. Vaughn Davis Bornet, *The Presidency of Lyndon B. Johnson* (Lawrence: University Press of Kansas, 1983), pp. 136, 139. For a thorough discussion of Lady Bird's role in beautification see Lewis L. Gould's essay on the First Lady, below.

16. Douglas H. Strong, *The Conservationists* (Menlo Park, Calif.: Addison-Wesley, 1971), p. 168; see also Strong, "The Rise of American Esthetic Conservation: Muir, Mather, and Udall," *National Parks Magazine* 44 (1970): 5–9.

17. Transcript, Stewart Udall oral history interview, 1969, by Joe B. Frantz, tape 1, pp. 32–36.

18. Strong, *Conservationists*, pp. 170–74; Bornet, *Presidency of Lyndon B. Johnson*, pp. 27, 137–46.

19. See Peter Wild, *Pioneer Conservationists of Western America* (Missoula, Mont.: Mountain Press, 1979), pp. 180–81; Barbara Le Unes, "Stewart Lee Udall," in *Encyclopedia of American Forest and Conservation History*, ed. Richard C. Davis, vol. 2 (New York: Macmillan, 1983), pp. 665–66; Cooley, "Introduction," p. xiv; see also Barbara Le Unes, "The Conservation Philosophy of Stewart L. Udall, 1961–1968" (Ph.D. diss., Texas A & M University, 1977).

20. Stewart L. Udall, *The Quiet Crisis* (New York: Holt, Rinehart & Winston, 1963), p. viii. Before leaving office, Udall wrote *1976: Agenda for Tomorrow* (New York: Harcourt Brace & World, 1968).

21. Despite his crucial role in the evolution of American environmentalism, there is no full-length biography available at this time, and only a few article-length studies. WHCF, NR and FG 145 (Department of the Interior) contain the richest correspondence on Udall's role in establishing conservation policies and programs. Also useful are the administrative history of the Department of the Interior and the Records of the Executive Departments, Department of the Interior, Office of the Secretary, microfilm rolls 1–21 and boxes 1–5, 82, in the Johnson Library. To complement these sources see the Stewart Udall Papers at the University of Arizona.

22. Cynthia Wilson, "Lyndon Johnson, Conservationist," *Audubon* 75 (Mar., 1973): 122.

23. Transcript, Udall oral history interview, 1969, tape 1, p. 32.

24. Quoted in Sundquist, *Politics and Policy*, p. 362.

25. Johnson to Ray K. Linsley, Dec. 15, 1964, EX FG 11-9, box 121B.

26. Lynton K. Caldwell, *Environment: A Challenge for Modern Society* (Garden City, N.Y.: Natural History Press, 1970), p. 54.

27. Cooley and Wandesforde-Smith, eds., *Congress and the Environment*, p. xiv.

28. Caldwell, *Environment*, p. 53.

29. John P. Crevelli, "The Final Act of the Greatest Conservation President," *Prologue* 12 (Winter, 1980): 174.

30. Ibid., p. 190.

31. John C. Whitaker, *Striking a Balance: Environment and Natural Resources Policy in the Nixon-Ford Years* (Washington, D.C.: American Enterprise Institute for Public Policy Research, 1976), pp. 58–60; see also Geof-

frey Wandesforde-Smith, "National Policy for the Environment," in *Congress and the Environment*, pp. 210–11.

32. Memo, Udall to Califano, Dec. 27, 1965, WHCF, Ex NR, box 4; see also transcript, Udall oral history interview, tape 1, p. 34.

33. Memo, Califano to the President, Sept. 8, 1965; Udall to the President, Sept. 2, 1965, HE 8-1, box 22; memo, Califano to the President, Aug. 31, 1966, FG 145; memo, Califano to the President, Jan. 14, 1966; memo, Charles L. Schultze to the President, Jan. 11, 1966, FG 165, box 250; memo, Califano to the President, Feb. 14, 1966, LE/NR, box 142—all in WHCF.

34. Memo, John W. Gardner to Califano, Dec. 27, 1965; letter, Edmund S. Muskie to Udall, Feb. 7, 1966; Califano to the President, Feb. 18, 1966, FG 165, box 250—all in WHCF.

35. Edward Weinberg and Henry P. Caulfield, Jr., to Udall, Feb. 4, 1966, HE 8, box 24; memo, Califano to the President, Feb. 14, 1966; memo, Udall to Califano, Feb. 14, 1966, LE/NR, box 142; memo, Donald Hornig to Califano, Jan. 25, 1966, FG 11, box 122—all in WHCF. According to J. Clarence Davies III and Barbara S. Davies, in *The Politics of Pollution*, 2d ed. (Indianapolis, Ind.: Pegasus, 1975), p. 34: "Early in 1966 the newly created Federal Water Pollution Control Administration was transferred from HEW to the Department of Interior. The latter was much less committed to working through the states than HEW had been. Furthermore, the Democratic administration was less convinced of the value of a strong state role in pollution control than was the Congress."

36. The Johnson Library holds administrative histories for the FPC, HEW, TVA, and Interior, among others. However, these histories are largely uncritical narratives. The supporting documents are more useful. See also subject files for FG, WHCF, for individual agencies, bureaus, and commissions.

37. See the administrative history of OST and the oral interview with Donald Hornig; see also memo, Ivan L. Bennett, Jr., to Califano, Sept. 14, 1967, Presidential Task Force on the Quality of the Environment, box 196; office files of Horace Busby, boxes 25, 29; James Everett Katz, "Presidential Politics and Policy for Science and Technology, 1953–1973" (Ph.D. diss., Rutgers University, 1974).

38. OST Administrative History, vol. 2: "Environmental Quality," p. 1, Johnson Library.

39. Transcript, Donald F. Hornig oral history interview, p. 28.

40. See note 39; see also memo, Bennett to Nimetz, Mar. 18, 1968; memo, Phillip S. Hughes to Nimetz, Jan. 4, 1968; memo, Hornig to Califano, Dec. 15, 1967, President's Task Force subject file, box 38—both in WHCF.

41. Wandesforde-Smith, "National Policy," pp. 211–13; see also memo, Hornig to Califano, Dec. 15, 1967, Presidential Task Force subject file, box 38.

42. See list 1 in the Appendix; see also Davies and Davies, *Politics of Pollution*, p. 68.

43. Executive Branch Comments on "Report of the Task Force on the Preservation of Natural Beauty—November 18, 1964," Dec. 1, 1964, prepared by Department of the Interior, Task Force subject file; see also memo, Interior to the President, Dec. 2, 1964, FG 600.

44. Memo, E. Fenton Shepard to Director, Bureau of the Budget, Dec. 6, 1967, files of James C. Gaither, box 55.

45. Roderick Nash, *Wilderness and the American Mind* (New Haven, Conn.: Yale University Press, 1967), p. 221.

46. See Craig W. Allin, *The Politics of Wilderness Preservation* (Westport, Conn.: Greenwood Press, 1982), pp. 102ff.; Michael Frome, *Battle for the Wilderness* (New York: Praeger, 1974); Michael McCloskey, "Wilderness Movement at the Crossroads, 1945–1970," *Pacific Historical Review* 41 (1972): 346–61; Frank Graham, Jr., *Man's Dominion: The Story of Conservation in America* (New York: M. Evans & Co., 1971), pp. 301–9; Frank E. Smith, *Politics of Conservation* (New York: Harper & Row, 1966), pp. 295–96; Delbert V. Mercure, Jr., and William M. Ross, "The Wilderness Act: A Product of Congressional Compromise," in *Congress and the Environment,* pp. 47–64; Sundquist, *Politics and Policy,* pp. 336–40, 355–61; Petulla, *American Environmentalism,* pp. 45–47.

47. Frank Gregg, "Federal Government and Public Land Policy" (paper delivered at the Conference on the Evolution of American Environmental Politics, June, 1984, the Wilson Center, Washington, D.C.), pp. 13–17. In addition to the Natural Resources file, the following subject files in the WHCF at the Johnson Library are most useful in understanding the Johnson administration's wilderness and national park policy: FG 710: Outdoor Recreation Resources Review Commission; FG 738: President's Council on Recreation and Natural Beauty; FG 747: Public Land Law Review Commission; LE/NR 3: Legislation/Forests; LE/NR 4: Legislation/Land; LE/PA: Legislation/Parks-Monuments; LE/PA 3: Legislation/Parks; PA: Parks/Monuments; PA3: Parks. The following Aides files also include valuable information on key legislation: Horace Busby, box 4(1296); Joseph Califano, box 28(1736); James Gaither, box 4; Richard Goodwin, box 10(641); Harry McPherson, box 11(1412); and Bill Moyers, box 133(1577); see also Marion Clawson, *The Federal Lands Revisited* (Washington, D.C.: Resources for the Future, 1983), and *The Bureau of Land Management* (New York: Praeger, 1971); Alfred Runte, *National Parks: The American Experience* (Lincoln: University of Nebraska Press, 1979).

48. The courts were playing an increasingly important role in environmental policy by the mid 1960s. The landmark case of *Scenic Hudson Preservation Conference* v. *Federal Power Commission* in 1965 led the way for environmental organizations as effective litigants in the courts. For more details on environmental law see Joseph Sax, *Defending the Environment: A Strategy for Citizen Action* (New York: Knopf, 1971).

49. Crevelli, "Final Act," pp. 189–91.

50. The relationship between LBJ and Udall had been strained because of the Vietnam War. In fact, Udall had considered resigning, in part because of his differences of opinion over the war policy (see ibid., pp. 188–89).

51. Cited by Dennis G. Asmussen and Thomas P. Bouchard in "Wild and Scenic Rivers," in *Congress and the Environment,* p. 165; see also memo, Interior to the President, Dec. 2, 1964, FG 600.

52. Ibid.; see also 1967 Task Force on the Quality of the Environment, files of James C. Gaither, box 55.

53. Sundquist, *Politics and Policy,* pp. 372–73; Asmussen and Bouchard, "Wild and Scenic Rivers," pp. 163–74.

54. Udall oral history interview, tape 1, p. 39.

55. Memo, Hornig to Califano, May 18, 1967; draft letter, Hornig to Carl Hayden, May 18, 1967, NR 7, box 17; letter, Elmer B. Staats to Udall, May 25, 1964, and attachments, NR 7, box 14; letter, William L. Guy to Clifton C. Carter, Apr. 24, 1964, NR 7, box 14—all in WHCF. Additional information on various water projects and desalination can be found in NR 7, boxes 18–29; Ex UT 4, box 13; Ex FG 145, box 204; Gen FG 145, box 207; LE/NR 7, boxes 143–45; see also WHCF subject file for various commissions on waterways and river basins.

56. Keith W. Muckleston, "Water Projects and Recreation Benefits," in Congress and the Environment, pp. 112–29.

57. Memo, Bureau of the Budget to Califano, Jan. 17, 1966, WHCF, Ex NR 7, box 15.

58. Hays, "Structure of Environmental Politics," p. 721; Cooley and Wandesforde-Smith, Congress and the Environment, p. 235; see also 1966 Task Force on Resources and Recreation.

59. Thomas R. Dunlap, "The Federal Government, Wildlife and Endangered Species" (paper delivered at the Conference on the Evolution of American Environmental Politics, June, 1986, the Wilson Center, Washington, D.C.), pp. 21–24; see also Michael J. Bean, The Evolution of National Wildlife Law (Washington, D.C.: Environmental Law Institute, 1978); Howard P. Brokaw, ed., Wildlife and America (Washington, D.C.: Government Printing Office, 1978); Lewis Regenstein, The Politics of Extinction (New York: Macmillan, 1975).

60. Crevelli, "Final Act," pp. 179–80.

61. Aside from files on fisheries commissions and a few other distantly related files, the Johnson Library does not contain extensive materials on wildlife issues.

62. See Stephen Fox, John Muir and His Legacy: The American Conservation Movement (Boston, Mass.: Little, Brown, 1981), pp. 291–306; Thomas R. Dunlap, DDT: Scientists, Citizens, and Public Policy (Princeton, N.J.: Princeton University Press, 1981), pp. 3–5; Hays, "Three Decades," pp. 15–17.

63. Press release, Johnson to Hornig, Nov. 4, 1965, FG 11-9, box 122.

64. Report of the 1964 Task Force on Environmental Pollution, pp. 2–3, files of James C. Gaither.

65. Richard H. K. Vietor, Environmental Politics and the Coal Coalition (College State: Texas A & M University Press, 1980), pp. 127–54; Martin V. Melosi, "Energy and Environment in the Era of Fossil Fuels" (paper delivered at the Conference on the Evolution of American Environmental Politics, June, 1984, the Wilson Center, Washington, D.C.), pp. 25–26.

66. James E. Krier and Edmund Ursin, Pollution and Policy: A Case Essay on California and Federal Experience with Motor Vehicle Air Pollution, 1940–1975 (Berkeley: University of California Press, 1977); U.S., Department of Commerce, The Automobile and Air Pollution (Washington, D.C.: Government Printing Office, 1967), pp. 1–28; Rex R. Campbell and Jerry L. Wade, eds., Society and Environment: The Coming Collision (Boston, Mass.: Allyn & Bacon, 1972), pp. 145–62; Davies and Davies, Politics of Pollution, pp. 49–58.

67. Vietor, Environmental Politics, pp. 143, 148; Davies and Davies, Politics of Pollution, pp. 49–52.

68. Sundquist, *Politics and Policy*, pp. 368–71.

69. Memo, Califano to the President, May 31, 1967, WHCF, HE 8-1, box 22; see also memo, James Gaither to Fred Panzer, Oct. 30, 1968, Task Forces, box 19; memo, President to Secretary of HEW, et al., Apr. 21, 1967; memo, Wilbur J. Cohen to the President, July 14, 1967; memo, Udall to the President, Jan. 23, 1968, HE 8-1, box 22—all in WHCF; see also Hays, "Three Decades," pp. 56–57.

70. Davies and Davies, *Politics of Pollution*, pp. 28–35; Sundquist, *Politics and Policy*, pp. 363–67; see also memo, Kermit Gordon to Wilson, Mar. 6, 1965, HE 8-4, box 24; letter, President to Philip H. Hoff, June 24, 1965, NR 1, box 11, memo, Udall to Califano and Wilson, Aug. 24, 1966; memo, W. W. Rostow to the President, May 11, 1967; memo, President to Dean Rusk, no date; memo, Hornig to the President, June 1, 1967, NR 7, box 17; memo, Schultze to Califano, Dec. 11, 1967, Presidential Task Forces subject file, box 39—all in WHCF.

71. Davies and Davies, *Politics of Pollution*, pp. 35–39; see also memo, President to Udall and Secretary of Treasury, May 26, 1967, Ex NR, box 5; memo, Wilfred H. Rommel to Califano, Sept. 8, 1967; memo, Nimetz to Califano, Sept. 23, 1967; Rommel to Califano, Oct. 19, 1967; Briefing Paper on Oil Pollution, Nov. 12, 1968, Presidential Task Force subject file, box 39; memo, President to Clark M. Clifford, et al., June 7, 1968, FG 11-9, box 122—all in WHCF. For information on the Johnson energy policy see James C. Cochrane, "Energy Policy in the Johnson Administration: Logical Order versus Economic Pluralism," in *Energy Policy in Perspective: Today's Problems, Yesterday's Solutions*, ed. Craufurd D. Goodwin (Washington, D.C.: Brookings Institution, 1981), p. 337; Richard H. K. Vietor, *Energy Policy in America since Nineteen Hundred Forty-five: A Study of Business-Government Relations* (Cambridge, Eng.: Cambridge University Press, 1984), p. 135; Melosi, "Energy and Environment." For information on an array of energy issues in the presidential papers see, e.g., IT 5-2, Coal and Steel Community, box 2; LE/NR 5 Legislation/Minerals-Metals, boxes 142, 144; LE/NR 6 Legislation/Oil-Natural Gas, boxes 142, 144; Natural Resources, see subdivisions, WHCF; office files of Joseph Califano, box 7(1416); office files of Bill Moyers, box 78 (1391); office files of W. De Vier Pierson, boxes 8–10; 1964 Task Force on Natural Resources; see also "Oil, Oil Reserves, and the Environment; Energy Sources," a listing prepared by the staff of the Johnson Library.

72. Letter, David S. Black to John J. Laux, Jan. 5, 1968, WHCF, NR 6, box 13.

73. Material on various forms of pollution is interspersed throughout the NR files and other files dealing with natural resources, as well as most of the task-force reports, especially the 1964 Task Force on Environmental Pollution and the 1965 Task Force on Pollution Abatement.

74. Ann L. Strong, "The Rise and Decline of an Urban Conscience: Urban Environments, Recreation, and Historic Preservation" (paper delivered at the Evolution of American Environmental Politics Conference, June, 1984, the Wilson Center, Washington, D.C.), pp. 22–28.

75. Ibid., pp. 22ff.; see also Ann L. Strong, *Open Space for Urban America* (Philadelphia: University of Pennsylvania Press, 1965).

76. Martin V. Melosi, *Garbage in the Cities: Refuse, Reform and the Environment, 1880–1980* (College Station: Texas A & M University Press, 1981), pp. 199–201.

77. A. L. Strong, "Rise and Decline," pp. 50–52. Almost all of the task-force reports deal with some aspect of the urban environment.
78. Caldwell, *Environment*, pp. 56, 199–200, 207–8.

Appendix

Task Forces on the Environment

1964 Task Force on Environmental Pollution
   Task Force on Natural Resources
   Task Force on the Preservation of Natural Beauty
1965 Task Force on Pollution Abatement
1966 Task Force on Natural Resource Studies
   Task Force on the Quality of the Environment
   Task Force on Resources and Recreation
1967 Task Force on the Quality of the Environment
1968 Task Force on the Quality of the Environment

SOURCE: White House Central Files, Task Force Reports, Johnson Library

Major Legislation on the Environment, 1963–68

1963 Clean Air Act
1964 Canyonlands National Park
   Fire Island National Seashore
   Water Resources Research Act
   Wilderness Act
1965 Federal Water Project Recreation Act
   Highway Beautification Act
   Land and Water Conservation Fund Act
   Solid Waste Disposal Act
   Water Quality Act
   Water Resources Planning Act
1966 Clean Water Restoration Act
   Endangered Species Act
   Federal Coal Mine Safety Act
   Fish and Wildlife Conservation Protection Act
   Historic Preservation Act
   Indiana Dunes National Lakeshore
1967 Air Quality Act
   National Emissions Standards Act
1968 National Trails Act
   Redwood National Park
   Wild and Scenic Rivers Act

6 | Lady Bird Johnson and Beautification

Lewis L. Gould

MRS. LYNDON B. JOHNSON'S CAMPAIGN on behalf of the beautification of the United States has not as yet become part of the historical record of her husband's presidential administration. Although students of the environmental movement now recognize the contributions of Lyndon Johnson and his presidency to the emergence of a new ecological spirit in the 1970s,[1] Mrs. Johnson's similar efforts to improve the appearance and quality of Washington, D.C., and other places in the country, her advocacy of highway beautification, and her concern for the environment in general are still regarded as either a side show from the real work of the Johnson years or as a politically motivated task with which the First Lady could occupy herself.

These conclusions first appeared in the early comments about the beautification campaign after the Johnsons had left the White House. Best-selling memoirs of White House employees assigned credit to Mrs. Johnson's aides, Mrs. Elizabeth ("Liz") S. Carpenter and Mrs. Bess Abell, for having devised a program that enabled the First Lady to emulate, but not to imitate, the restoration work that Mrs. Jacqueline Kennedy had performed for the White House. Nancy Dickerson, writing in the mid 1970s, conceded the serious purpose of Mrs. Johnson's work but argued that "beautification was probably the only subject that LBJ would have let her handle without jealousy." The caustic Barbara Howar, in *Laughing All The Way* (1973), speculated on what Mrs. Johnson's impact on her husband and his presidency would have been "had she used her influence in matters more crucial than beautifying a troubled nation."[2]

More positive evaluations were less widely read. June Sochen, in a 1973 book on women activists and thinkers in this century, advanced the view that "Lady Bird's concern for the natural environment foreshadowed the much publicized ecology movement of the late sixties." More recent appraisals have extended Sochen's conclusions. In a comparison of First Lady activism with the model of Eleanor Roosevelt, Abigail McCarthy has observed that beautification, "despite the somewhat gimmicky tone of its title," bore real results by directing attention to the environment and by improving the quality of life in towns and cities, especially Washington, D.C. Vaughn Bornet, too, assigns credit to the Johnsons for having laid the groundwork for environmentalism in the 1970s; he calls the First Lady "well suited to being the organizer, propagandist, spokeswoman, and recruiter of talent for her cause of beautification."[3]

As the ample materials in the Johnson Library reveal, especially the recently opened beautification files, her role in the administration was even more extensive than the impression offered in previous accounts of her work. In pursuing beautification, the First Lady functioned as a legislative aide, adviser on appointments, shaper of policy, and public advocate for the administration. Tangible results of her efforts included the Highway Beautification Act of 1965; a lasting enhancement of the physical appearance of Washington, D.C., and other urban and rural places; and the involvement of environmentally minded individuals and groups in the shaping of government programs. Less immediately visible, but in the long run of equal importance, was the stimulus that she gave to an increased ecological consciousness in the nation at large. Like her husband, Mrs. Johnson had a significant role in providing a foundation for the environmental movement that burgeoned during the 1970s.

A sensitivity to her physical surroundings and their natural beauty marked the early life of Claudia Alta Taylor in Karnack, Texas, where she was born on December 22, 1912. Her mother, Minnie Patillo Taylor, introduced her youngest child and only daughter to music, books, and the arts at an early age. After her mother died when Claudia was nearly six, her busy father, Thomas Jefferson Taylor, the owner of a general store and "Dealer in Everything," often left her in the charge of a maiden aunt, Effie Patillo. Claudia played in the fields and on the lake near her home. "When I was a little girl," she said in 1976, "I grew up listening to the wind in the pine trees of the east Texas woods." Years after her childhood, she wrote about Caddo Lake: "I loved to paddle in those dark bayous, where time itself seemed ringed round by silence and ancient cypress trees, rich in festoons of Spanish moss. Now and then an alligator would surface to float like a gnarled log. It was a place for dreams." Already called "Lady Bird" by a family cook, she disliked the name but made her peace with it in early adolescence.[4]

After attending school in Marshall, Texas, Claudia went on to St. Mary's School for Girls in Dallas, where she pursued her love of the theater. In 1930 she entered the University of Texas, and friends remembered her affection for the out of doors during the ensuing four years. "She loved bluebonnets," her friend Gene Boehringer said; "she loved everything about Austin and Texas, and she loved the hills and the dirt and everything in Austin."[5] Though she concentrated in college on history and journalism, she also took a course in geology, "which stretched my perspective of the life of man on this physical planet." She wrote for the *Daily Texan*; she was publicity manager for the University of Texas Sports Association, the women's athletic organization on campus; and she read Dorothy Parker, D. H. Lawrence, and Emily Dickinson. She believed that at the University, "all the doors of the world suddenly were swung open to me."[6]

In November, 1934, after a brief courtship, she married Lyndon B. Johnson, then a congressional aide in Washington. Over the ensuing three decades, the rhythms of his political life shaped her career. Her initial reticence as a speaker gave way to facility by the early 1960s. She ran his congressional office during his wartime military service in 1942, and she successfully managed the radio station that they purchased in Austin and, later, their expanding television holdings. Two daughters were born in the 1940s and were raised around the demands of her husband's emerging prominence in the Senate after 1949. Lyndon Johnson was a demanding and affectionate, though often a difficult, spouse. He criticized her appearance, sometimes embarrassed her, and was faithful when he chose to be. He also stretched her abilities, and she had grown in self-confidence and skill as a public figure before he came to the presidency.[7]

A strong bond in the marriage, she believed, was their mutual interest in the land. They shared, she told an interviewer in 1964, "a deep sense of oneness with the land, a reliance on the land and the love of it." When Lyndon was directing the National Youth Administration in Texas from 1935 to 1937, she participated in the discussions that led to the idea of roadside parks along the state's highways. "I loved the trips across the country to Washington and I never got too many of them," she recalled. On these journeys and on the later campaign trips in Texas, she observed the changing shape of the land and the impact that billboards, junkyards, and buildings were having on scenic views. Her interest in nature also manifested itself in "quite a remarkable garden" that she raised in wartime Washington. "There is something remarkably more beautiful about flowers that you yourself have planted and divided and cared for than any other flowers," she observed in 1965. "It reminds one that creation of beauty is a happy experience."[8]

When she entered the White House as First Lady in the wake of John F. Kennedy's assassination, Lady Bird Johnson wanted neither to imitate what Jacqueline Kennedy had done nor to depart from it in a manner that might arouse criticism. Most of her first full year as First Lady was spent in feeling her way into a proper role. Until President Johnson decided to run in 1964 and was safely elected, her initiatives could only be exploratory. She made speeches in which she exhorted women to be "dedicated doers" on behalf of a better society, and she gave public support, through personal visits, to the administration's war on poverty and hunger. But even in this transitional phase, she thought about issues of conservation and the environment. In June, 1964, she discussed with Secretary of the Interior Stewart Udall and Secretary of Commerce Luther Hodges the effect that highway construction was having on national parks and wilderness areas. In the diary that she kept regularly, she noted that Udall was "a loud voice for preserving the wilderness, the National Parks, the shrines, the jewels of America." Two days later, Jane Jacobs, a critic of urban planning, spoke to the First Lady's "women doer" luncheon about the problems of the cities. Mrs. Johnson identified one issue in particular: "How to make a city beautiful."[9]

The primary political concern of the Johnsons in 1964 was success against Barry Goldwater in the autumn. In October, Mrs. Johnson made a flamboyant whistle-stop tour of the South on the "Lady Bird Special," which helped to keep more than half of Dixie in the Democratic column.[10] A similar motive underlay an earlier trip to the West with Udall in August, 1964, to visit Indian reservations and to assist Democratic senatorial candidates in Montana and Wyoming. The tour also laid the basis for the First Lady's close working friendship with Udall and provided some initial stirrings of the actual beautification program. As they flew in a propeller plane across the Rocky Mountain area, they sat side by side and found, in Udall's words, an "instant rapport" about the land and its resources. Mrs. Johnson had "an instinctive feeling for the beauty of the country," and Udall sensed that her commitment to conservation subjects grew during the trip.[11] Speeches that James Reston, Jr., of the Interior Department wrote for her spoke about the beauty of the region and the need to preserve it.[12]

The woman in the seat next to Stewart Udall in August, 1964, was five feet, four inches tall, with dark hair, prominent features, and a ready smile. To help her husband after his heart attack, she kept her weight at 110 pounds. Photographs and television cameras usually failed to capture her attractiveness and her outgoing public personality. Highly organized, very intelligent, and a perpetual reader, Mrs. Johnson had, one close friend said, "one of the most compartmentalized minds I've ever known." Those who worked closely with the First Lady learned that she was always prepared, and she expected others to have done their homework. Walter Washington recalled that Mrs. Johnson's eyes missed nothing on their walks around the capital city. Cautious with money and hard-headed about business matters, she also had an idealistic impulse to serve humanity and to better society. Above all, she knew how to influence her husband, and she knew the limits of that authority.[13]

The First Lady understood that access to news and publicity was central to success in Washington. She brought in Liz Carpenter as the first officially designated press secretary to a First Lady. Carpenter was ebullient and vocal, "the White House's female P. T. Barnum," as Helen Thomas has called her. Carpenter had an excellent sense of how the working press functioned. To help her with television appearances, Mrs. Johnson relied on Simone Poulain. The social secretary, Bess Abell, daughter of Senator Earle Clements, was a model of discretion and efficiency. Morale was excellent among those around Mrs. Johnson, and her staff exhibited few of the tensions that are often characteristic of work in the White House.[14]

As soon as Barry Goldwater had been defeated in November, 1964, Mrs. Johnson "began to think of what I could do to help" the president and his policies. The Head Start program for preschool children attracted her involvement in 1965/66, but the "whole field of conservation and beautification" had "the greatest appeal."[15] In mid November she asked a number of friends and advisers for ideas about how she could best pursue her general goals.

Suggestions came in rapidly. Mrs. Katie Louchheim, who had long been active in the Democratic party and who was a State Department official, surveyed what the administration was already doing about natural beauty; in a memorandum of November 20 she proposed that awards should be given for "preserving, improving, or beautifying the American scene." On that same day, Mrs. Johnson met with Udall at the LBJ Ranch. "It was her idea," Udall remembered, "to start out in the National Capital to demonstrate what could be done" and then to use Washington as a model for the rest of the country.[16] Elizabeth Rowe, the wife of a former aide to Franklin Roosevelt and a long-time friend of the Johnsons, was chairman of the National Capital Planning Commission. In early December she offered the complementary idea "that you extend your interest in the White House's beauty and history to the whole city." Rowe added that a White House Committee on Washington's Appearance might be a suitable vehicle to "support present and future programs on the city's beauty."[17]

During the early 1960s the physical situation of the nation's capital and the social problems that it reflected stimulated efforts to revitalize and reclaim the federal city. "Washington is a shabby city compared with most European capitals," Udall told the First Lady,[18] and critics outside of government spoke even more harshly. Wolf von Eckardt, who wrote on architecture and urban design for the *Washington Post*, said in 1963 that among Washington's disgraces were its "many lawns, dilapidated sidewalks, ugly and confusing clutter of traffic signs, decrepit benches, forbidding trash baskets, hideous parking lots, poorly lit, deserted, and crime-ridden city parks, and a desperate dearth of amenities" for residents and tourists.[19]

On a larger scale, such issues as pollution, controversies over highway location and construction, public transportation, and a deteriorating inner city made Washington an example of the urban dilemmas that were convulsing the 1960s. To that mix was added the city's subordinate relation to Congress, which left the city's eight hundred thousand residents without self-government. Even more salient was the presence of a black majority that was impoverished and segregated and a white minority that was in control both economically and politically. Touching one aspect of the capital city's problems meant becoming involved in a whole range of issues. As Antonia Chayes, who was a lawyer on the Planning Staff of the National Institute of Mental Health and an aide on Mrs. Johnson's 1964 campaign, observed in a memorandum "On the Cities" in December, 1964, the aim of improving urban life in Washington had large implications for the central domestic theme of Johnson's presidency: "These goals reach for the 'Great Society.'"[20]

At the outset the public plans for Mrs. Johnson's beautification initiative addressed only the issue of the city's appearance. By early 1965 the First Lady had decided to form a committee of approximately twenty private citizens and public officials to promote a greater awareness of Washington's beauty. She told her friends that her role would be advisory; she would act as a general sponsor who would make some awards to worthy beautification projects. The name of the panel evolved into the First Lady's Committee for a More Beautiful National Capital, and letters were sent out to the proposed members, inviting them to a meeting at the White House on February 11, 1965. "It is in our own communities," the letter from the First Lady said, "that we can best participate in creating an environment which has beauty, joyousness, and loveliness, as well as dignity." In addition to selecting Udall and Elizabeth Rowe, Mrs. Johnson tapped Laurance

S. Rockefeller; Walter Tobriner, a commissioner of the District; Mrs. Katharine Graham, publisher of the *Washington Post*; and Mrs. Mary W. Lasker of New York City, a benefactor of health and beautification causes. Other members came from the federal government, from the private sector, and from a group of prominent Washingtonians who were active in the District's affairs.[21]

The First Lady's beautification campaign also consciously drew inspiration from the Johnson administration's ambitious effort to beautify the nation in general. In his "Great Society" speech of May, 1964, the president had spoken about the need "to prevent an ugly America" because "once our natural splendor is destroyed, it can never be recaptured."[22] As his wife listened to Lyndon Johnson in 1964, "as I began to see the things he was applying himself to, there emerged the interests that made my heart sing, the ones that I knew most about and cared most about. Those were the environment and beautification." The extent of the First Lady's reciprocal influence on her husband remains unclear. Stewart Udall believed that "she influenced the President to demand—and support—more farsighted conservation legislation." Neither of the Johnsons committed much to paper on this and other subjects, and conclusions about the flow of ideas are only speculative. The exchange of views between the spouses was probably mutual, rather than a definite movement from the president to the First Lady.[23]

The Task Force on the Preservation of Natural Beauty was named in July, 1964, and it worked through the rest of the year on such topics as "the cost of ugliness" and "natural beauty and the public interest." Mrs. Johnson read the task force's report when it was issued in November, 1964, and discussed it with Udall when he visited the ranch. The president mentioned natural beauty in his 1965 State of the Union speech, the first chief executive to have alluded to the subject in that way. Mrs. Johnson noted in her diary: "I hope we can do something about that in our four years here."[24]

President Johnson opened the natural-beauty campaign on February 8, 1965, when he sent Congress a special message on "Conservation and the Restoration of Natural Beauty." The president called for "a new conservation," which would provide "restoration and innovation," and urged that "our planning, our programs, our buildings, and our growth" all have "a conscious and active concern for the value of beauty." Specific programs included highway beautification, clean-air legislation, an array of other conservation measures, and the White House Conference on Natural Beauty in May, 1965.[25]

At the same time, the First Lady prepared to launch her own beautification drive. She met with Laurance Rockefeller, who had already been selected as chairman of the Natural Beauty Conference, to discuss the subject. It was, she noted, "like picking up a tangled skein of wool—all the threads are interwoven—recreation and pollution and mental health, and the crime rate, and rapid transit, and highway beautification, and the war on poverty, and parks—national, state, and local." She was "desperately interested in something positive coming out of this program, something besides a lot of words and proliferation of committees."[26]

The public learned of the First Lady's plans when a lengthy interview appeared on "Ways to Beautify America" in the February 22, 1965, issue of *U.S. News and World Report.* "I am proud that this Administration has accepted the commitment to make our cities and country more beautiful for all the people." She observed that "the time is ripe—the time is now—to take advantage of this yeasty, bubbling desire to beautify our cities and our countryside."[27]

The First Lady's Committee for a More Beautiful National Capital assembled in the Blue Room of the White House on February 11, 1965. After hearing her read from Lord Bryce's description of Washington in 1913 to underscore the possibilities of the city's beauty, the committee members explored her charge "to implement what is already underway, supplement what should be underway, and to be the catalyst for action." They agreed to plant flowers in the traffic triangles and squares of Washington, to give awards for neighborhood beautification, and to endorse existing projects, such as the revitalization of Pennsylvania Avenue and the preservation of Lafayette Park.[28]

Mrs. Johnson's interview and news reports about the initial meeting of the committee evoked an enthusiastic popular reaction. To handle the accumulation of mail on beautification, the First Lady's staff was expanded. Sharon Francis, an aide to Secretary Udall, came to the White House, first as a part-time helper and then, by the summer of 1965, as a regular assistant to the First Lady for beautification. Cynthia Wilson had begun to work for Mrs. Johnson in early 1965, and by the middle of the year, Wilson had assumed beautification duties as well. The women gradually acquired their own office space in the East Wing. Francis handled the more public side of Mrs. Johnson's campaign, writing speeches and dealing with agencies and private citizens; Wilson oversaw the extensive correspondence that the First Lady received about beautification issues, wrote press releases, did advance work on trips, and helped with official events.

Both Francis and Wilson had ample personal energy and a good grasp of how Mrs. Johnson's mind operated. They served the First Lady well.[29]

The beautification work that Mrs. Johnson did between 1965 and 1969 spread out in many directions in response to burgeoning public concern and the mounting national awareness of environmental problems. Washington, D.C., may have been the center of her activity, but inevitably she was drawn into supporting and encouraging efforts that were occurring in the rest of the country. Both in regard to the District of Columbia and for national programs, Mrs. Johnson and her associates sought a more precise and inclusive word than *beautification* to describe their activities and purposes. "It sounds cosmetic and trivial and it's prissy," she told an interviewer in 1980. Critics mocked the term or pretended to agree on the aims while opposing their practical implementation, but nothing better ever came along, so the name endured.[30]

In the nation's capital, Mrs. Johnson began with a rush of activity in 1965. Her committee took inspection trips on the Potomac; they planted trees and visited schools. Katie Louchheim strongly pursued the program of competitive beautification awards for worthy projects in the District. In November, 1965, Mrs. Johnson escorted a national-network television audience on a tour of the city and asked her viewers: "What will we leave to those who come after us?" A year and a half later, in March, 1967, she accompanied the wives of the governors as they planted dogwood trees near National Airport. As the *Washington Star* noted in October, 1966, "With a green-thumbed glove and a gilt shovel, the First Lady has traveled all over town planting pansies, azaleas, chrysanthemums, dogwood and cherry blossom trees."[31]

Mrs. Johnson also worked extensively with the noted architect Nathaniel Owings on the revival of Pennsylvania Avenue, displaying what Owings called her "gentle urgency." They discussed the merits of underground parking, and she prodded him about the appearance of cherry trees at the Washington Monument and the time that it would take to have fountains constructed on the Mall. She also lobbied with legislators about Owings's bill to establish a permanent commission on Pennsylvania Avenue. Owings remembered one occasion when he, Secretary Udall, and the First Lady had unrolled some plans for the avenue on the carpet and had knelt down to inspect them. At that point, President Johnson walked in and said: "What in hell, Udall, are you doing there on the floor with my wife?"[32]

As the beautification campaign progressed in Washington, two alternative tendencies emerged within the committee and among those around the First Lady. Katie Louchhcim labeled one group "the daffodil and dogwood set," while the other became identified with Walter E. Washington, later to become the city's first mayor, and Polly Shackleton. The main exponent of those who wished to stress the planting of flowers, trees, and shrubs in the District was the New York City philanthropist and long-time advocate of expanded governmental medical research programs Mary W. Lasker, widow of the advertising executive Albert D. Lasker. She had used her ample fortune to spread trees and flowers throughout Manhattan with the same dedication that she had used to lobby senators and presidents to spend more to defeat heart disease and cancer. Her beautification slogan was "Plant masses of flowers where the masses pass," and she looked to the general improvement of what Sharon Francis called "the monumental and tourist parts of the city."[33]

Wise in the exercise of influence in Washington, Lasker operated through the National Park Service, which oversaw most of the District's government land. She enlisted the support of Sutton Jett—the regional director—and Nash Castro, Jett's assistant regional director. A member of the Park Service since 1939, Castro became a central figure in Mrs. Johnson's campaign in Washington. He met regularly with the First Lady at the White House, and he displayed a striking ability to see that plantings were made, materials were secured, and work was carried out on time. She came to regard him as "indispensable," and he reciprocated, by expressing ample respect for "the great work she has begun."[34]

Mary Lasker's desire to spread seeds, bulbs, and plants at the highway entrances to Washington and in the parks harmonized so easily with the mission of the Park Service that she was able to draw readily on the service's budget for planting, location, and maintenance. Her emphasis on "beautification through planting activities" struck a warm response in the First Lady, who herself admired flowers and trees; the New York benefactor also made herself useful to the Johnsons with her mailing lists, publicity machinery, and friendships on Capitol Hill.[35]

Knowing that private funds would be required to supplement what the government could allocate, Mrs. Johnson approved of Lasker's plan for the Society for a More Beautiful National Capital in 1965 as a nonprofit, tax-exempt body to receive donations from the public and to sponsor beautification endeavors. Initial hopes to raise more than $5 million did not work out, but the society did take in about $2 million from such donors as Laurance Rockefeller, Brooke Astor, Marjorie Merriweather Post, and other individuals and foundations. The society did not raise money professionally during these years, but Lasker, with the help of Carolyn Agger Fortas, was able to attract, through membership on the group's Advisory Council, in her words, "those who are rich and possibly sympathetic."[36]

The tangible outcome of Lasker's efforts was impressive. By April, 1966, Sutton Jett had reported to Mrs. Johnson that thirty-five park sites had been beautified. Four hundred thousand bulbs bloomed that spring along Rock Creek Park and the Potomac Parkway and in squares and triangles across the city. Cherry trees, some donated by the Japanese government, were planted on Hains Point; azaleas, cherries, and magnolias were added along Pennsylvania Avenue. In early 1967, Lasker reported to Douglass Cater of the White House staff that eighty park sites had been landscaped, along with nine schools and eight playgrounds. Half a million bulbs, one hundred thousand of which she had contributed, had been planted, as had, Lasker continued, "83,000 spring flowering plants, 50,000 shrubs, 25,000 trees, and 137,000 annuals." The First Lady recorded one White House discussion in early 1966 as evidence of her friend's irrepressible commitment to things floral. Mary Lasker "said with an absolutely straight face, 'How are we going to get the nurserymen to have enough stock to plant the whole United States?'"[37]

Lasker displayed less enthusiasm for having the committee deal with the social problems of the District; her interest remained fixed on flowers and plantings. When the question arose in 1967 of having landscape architect Lawrence Halprin speak about beautification in the neighborhoods, Lasker responded "Oh, no, that's not what we want to be doing." She believed that it would be easier to persuade wealthy donors to provide funds for parks and gardens than for projects in the city's black district. When she advocated the creation of community parks out of school facilities or sought recreational facilities for publicly financed housing projects as a way in which the government might discourage idleness and help to alleviate juvenile delinquency, Lasker sounded paternalistic and to a degree condescending. With its emphasis on wealthy contributors and the impact of beautification on the tourist population, Lasker's approach to Washington's appearance seemed to Sharon Francis, Walter Washington, and Lawrence Halprin to have elitist overtones that made what she did merely cosmetic in light of the capital city's complex urban difficulties.[38]

Walter Washington, at this time the executive director of the National Capital Housing Authority, advocated a beautification strategy that was directed at the needs of the black community as well. The fifty-year-old Washington, who chaired the Neighborhood and Special Projects Committee of the First Lady's Committee, emphasized the involvement of inner-city neighborhoods and schools in the campaign. Even as she backed Mary Lasker, Mrs. Johnson also supported Washington's approach. She offered her visible endorsement at a planting ceremony in the Greenleaf Gardens public-housing project in March, 1965, and at other similar occasions during the next four years. Two decades later, Walter Washington was still impressed with her courage, charm, and personal rapport with residents when she toured even the most impoverished sections of the city's ghetto.[39]

The First Lady's commitment went beyond these public events. In the summer of 1965, Washington's committee identified three public schools for demonstration cleanup projects and initiated a "clean-up," "fix-up," "paint-up," and "plant-up" program in the Forty-Ninth Census Tract in the city's Second Precinct. "The main focus," Washington wrote to Mrs. Johnson, "was an attempt to motivate the children, youth, adults, and family units in a long-range program of self-involvement for enhancing the physical appearance of the community."[40]

Project Pride, in the summer of 1966, represented a similar kind of central-city beautification effort. Polly Shackleton, a Democratic activist in Washington who was a member of the committee, selected the Shaw Urban Renewal Area, "one of the most deprived areas in the city," for a cleanup campaign. Residents caught rats and hauled off debris, garbage, and abandoned cars. The project employed more than one hundred local school dropouts and high-school students. Funding of $7,000 came from the Society for a More Beautiful National Capital, and the energetic Shackleton enlisted cooperation from diverse sectors of the District's government.[41]

In the following year, Shackleton organized Project Trail Blazers, which enrolled 110 youths in transforming a shuttered movie theater into the Anacostia Neighborhood Museum, in creating "play space" in housing projects, and in cutting nature trails in area parks. Shackleton noted that the participants came "out of a background of extreme deprivation which often makes its mark physically and emotionally." Again, the society underwrote the project, and Laurance Rockefeller added $50,000 to carry it through the summer and into the fall. The First Lady visited the Anacostia Museum in August and, according to Shackleton, "seemed pleased with what she saw."[42]

Another project that Mrs. Johnson pursued in the inner city was the beautification of the recreational facilities at the Buchanan School at Thirteenth and D streets, in southeast Washington. Walter Washington had taken her to see the school, which was "surrounded by a sad area of broken concrete and weeds." Later, Washington also showed the school to Mrs. Vincent Astor of New York City, whose good works there included the upgrading of school playgrounds and parks. In 1966 Brooke Astor's foundation donated $300,000 for an outdoor community center near Buchanan School, and a year and a half later Mrs. Johnson spoke at the dedication ceremonies. Sharon Francis reported that in the ensuing days, "Buchanan Plaza was overwhelmed with users."[43]

In April, 1967, the *National Geographic* did an article about Mrs. Johnson's campaign. Walter Washington summed up the benefits of her commitment to the projects that he and Shackleton had sponsored: "When this program started, there were some, I suppose, who regarded it as Marie Antoinette's piece of cake, I mean, out in east Washington, how many rats can you kill with a tulip? But it hasn't been that way at all. We started with mass plantings, then we moved on to Project Pride, and we are here."[44]

By mid 1966 the beautification campaign in the nation's capital was moving in an even more expansive way than the initiatives of Walter Washington and Polly Shackleton had envisioned. Stephen Currier, president of Urban America, first came to Mrs. Johnson's attention when his organization sponsored a conference on cities in September, 1966. The Johnsons hosted a reception at the White House, at which the First Lady said that "the challenge to America's cities is how to govern their growth boom with beauty and with compassion for every life and its fulfillment." Currier, who was married to a member of the Mellon family, pursued good works through his Taconic Foundation. He also gave money to civil-rights work in the South and, as Sharon Francis said, "had an orientation in the direction of helping the needy and black part of the city." Currier initiated conversations with Mrs. Johnson's associates about paying for another staff member who could "work with Washington's business community on a daily basis as a representative of Mrs. Johnson's committee" or could raise money for the committee itself. By the time of the cities conference, Currier and Francis had gone well beyond this initial proposal and had agreed to employ a landscape architect to make plans for Washington. Their choice was Lawrence Halprin of San Francisco.[45]

Mrs. Johnson herself learned about Halprin during a conservation and beautification trip in the West in September, 1966. Sharon Francis accompanied her and, in San Francisco, took the First Lady and Liz Carpenter to Ghirardelli Square, an old chocolate factory that Halprin had transformed into a shopping center and plaza. Mrs. Johnson was impressed, Francis told her about Halprin, and they decided to secure his services. The landscape architect came to Washington in October and toured the city with Walter Washington. As they drove and talked, ideas emerged for improving the black districts. As he rode with Mrs. Johnson, Halprin proposed to create vest-pocket parks and to transform school grounds into recreational spaces. Asked to comment, Mrs. Johnson said: "Well, I'm no expert in these fields. You experts who know how to do the things must make the judgments. All I would say is that any area this committee undertakes should be usable by lots and lots of people. It should be fun, and its maintenance should be easy because any project we sponsor will be a stepchild of the city."[46]

After consultation and planning in November and December, 1966, Halprin set out his proposals at a meeting of the First Lady's Committee on January 12, 1967. He described ambitious designs for a large park near the Anacostia River, conversion of a transit-car barn on East Capitol Street into a recreational center, and the development of inner blocks near the Capitol into vest-pocket parks and recreational places. To accomplish Halprin's vision, some adjustment of construction plans for a projected freeway would be necessary. Mrs. Johnson called it "an imaginative, exciting program with great potential. It will take a lot of hard work to implement it." A subcommittee, composed of Udall, Clifton Shackleton, Secretary Robert C. Weaver of Housing and Urban Development, Commissioner Tobriner, and others, was established to explore ways to bring Halprin's ideas into being.[47]

Within days of its unveiling, Halprin's initiative received a devastating setback. Stephen Currier and his wife were lost on a plane flight in the Caribbean. With their deaths went the assured funding for Halprin's work as a consultant, as well as the money that Currier had hoped to raise. It was, Sharon Francis recalled, "a very, very major blow that, of course, no one could have foreseen."[48]

Nonetheless, Mrs. Johnson, Francis, and Halprin went forward. They opened discussions with the local community, sought alternative funding from the Rockefeller Foundation, and started negotiations with the Department of Housing and Urban Development

(HUD) about federal beautification grants for the Capital East–Inner Blocks project. But changes in congressional funding for HUD grants slowed the process, as did the general turning away from Great Society programs that marked 1967/68. Consequently, the Halprin proposals remained largely unrealized possibilities during the Johnson years, though they underscored the ambitious range of Mrs. Johnson's definition of beautification.[49]

The First Lady's work with Walter Washington and Polly Shackleton, as well as her endorsement of Halprin's plans, did not, of course, prevent the city from undergoing serious violence and rioting in April, 1968, after the death of Martin Luther King, Jr. The conditions that fueled the riots were more deep-seated than even the programs of the Johnson years recognized. Nonetheless, Walter Washington believed then, as he did twenty years later, that Mrs. Johnson, between 1965 and 1968, did important work in improving the self-image and pride of the black community in Washington and that her efforts had reduced tensions and alleviated problems. "Her heritage as First Lady," he said at the White House in April, 1968, "is not in beautification per se; it is in communication. It is in the hope and desire to identify a human being with his environment."[50]

The legacy of Lady Bird Johnson in Washington, D.C., endured after her departure in 1969. The Society for a More Beautiful National Capital continued into the mid 1970s; but without the support of a First Lady, it experienced fund-raising and organizational problems that eventually caused it to disappear. Her floral contribution, however, pervaded the city. The Park Service and the District government did better maintenance in the monumental and tourist areas than in the black sections of the city, but all Washington residents felt the impact of Mrs. Johnson's work as the seasons turned. Each spring, say Washingtonians and visitors alike, when the cherry blossoms, the azaleas, and the other flowers bloom, the collective thought is "Thank God for Lady Bird Johnson."[51]

The First Lady's beautification campaign in Washington engaged her energies and filled her schedule. Yet she also carried on an equally ambitious program nationally. She used the drawing power of the institution to stimulate citizen action to improve the appearance of the nation's landscape. She encouraged participants in environmental affairs, the young, and the business community to meet and discuss common issues. She spoke widely on beautification topics. Most important, Mrs. Johnson involved herself deeply in the administration's effort to enact and implement legislation to regulate billboards and junkyards and to preserve the natural scenery of the nation's highways.

After the president's message on natural beauty and after the *U.S. News* interview, popular interest in Mrs. Johnson and beautification burgeoned. To meet the public's concern, she traveled widely for her cause and enlisted surrogates to assist her. Unable to meet all the invitations to speak that she received, in early 1966 she recruited cabinet and Senate wives, under Mrs. Henry Fowler, wife of the secretary of the Treasury, to serve on the Speakers Bureau. Beginning in the spring of 1965, Mrs. Johnson herself took numerous well-publicized well-organized tours for beautification. On May 11/12, 1965, she led a "Landscapes and Landmarks" excursion through Virginia to Monticello and on to the Blue Ridge Mountains. Later that year she went to Jackson Hole, Wyoming, to Milwaukee, Wisconsin, and to Buffalo, New York, on separate trips.[52]

Perhaps the most memorable of the conservation tours was the trip to the Big Bend region of Texas in April, 1966. Seventy-five reporters accompanied Mrs. Johnson, Secretary Udall, Liz Carpenter, and other officials through the rugged mountains and on rafts down the Rio Grande. "But mostly there were just the awesome spires of the canyon walls pierced by centuries of wind, eroded by centuries of water, with all sorts of tales to tell to a geologist," the First Lady recorded in her diary. When the party of one hundred and thirty camped at last after running the river, Liz Carpenter observed: "Frankly, I like the parks where all the concessions are run by the Rockefellers." This event impressed the media, but it also made the important point that what Udall called "a wilderness experience" had the direct support of the president's family.[53]

Mrs. Johnson also delivered dozens of speeches on beautification topics to groups across the country. In Jackson Hole in September, 1965, she told the National Council of State Garden Clubs and the American Forestry Association that beauty "cannot be reserved 'For nice neighborhoods *only.*'" She informed the American Roadbuilders Association in Denver in February, 1966, that "great roads not only get you from 'here' to 'there,' but they afford a revelation of America's great beauty along the way." Toward the end of the presidency, in May, 1968, she declared, in dedicating a park in Stamford, Connecticut: "We *can* make and re-make this land of ours into a land where people can not only prosper but where they can see and feel the beauty of our time and place."[54]

As the Johnson administration became mired in the Vietnam War, Mrs. Johnson encountered protests and hecklers on her travels. In October, 1967, at Williams College, where she received an honorary degree and gave a speech on the environment, picketers appeared, and some students walked out when she was introduced. On the next day, at Yale, there were eight hundred demonstrators outside and a "very quiet very attentive audience" of the same size inside for another speech on the environment, "one thing that all of us share." The experience, Sharon Francis concluded, left her "very, very disheartened and upset." Worried that she might not be able to visit campuses in the future, the First Lady wrote: "I want to know what's going on—even if to know is to suffer."[55]

Mrs. Johnson's political style was inherently inclusive. Accordingly, she saw the business community as an important and necessary ally of beautification. She wanted to move, as she wrote to a financial columnist in December, 1965, "from the garden club to the hardware stage of the problem." Responding to her campaign, corporations such as the Reliance Insurance Company, Giant Food, and major oil companies embarked on diverse beautification projects. Through Adam Rumoshosky of the American Petroleum Institute, the First Lady sought industry approval of the renovation and landscaping of automobile service stations in Washington and elsewhere. Some of these initiatives did not last beyond Mrs. Johnson's time in the White House, some projects were largely symbolic, and there was a certain inescapable distance between beautification goals and corporate profits that was never bridged. Yet the First Lady identified no villains herself, and she did not drive away any potential supporters from the business sector.[56]

In the field of her personal interest, Mrs. Johnson played a direct role in appointments to boards and commissions that dealt with beautification-related subjects. She watched the functioning of the Citizens Advisory Committee on Recreation and Natural Beauty with particular care. In March, 1968, John W. Macy, Jr., who handled federal appointments, sent her the names of potential nominees to the panel. "If you desire to retain any of the present membership," Macy told her, "I will be happy to recommend them to the President." She consulted with her husband, and two months later they "mutually agreed" on a list of appropriate selections. Mrs. Johnson's endorsements helped to obtain the appointment of several individuals who had backed her efforts for highway beautification and other conservation causes.[57]

Two beautification conferences in 1965 and 1966 also offered the First Lady a platform from which to promote beautification. Opening the White House Conference on Natural Beauty, she told the delegates that "ugliness is bitterness" and asked them, "Can a great democratic society generate the concerted drive to plan, and having planned, to execute great projects of beauty?" Eight hundred delegates spent two days listening to 116 panelists on such subjects as "The Townscape," "The New Suburbia," and "Citizen Action." Thirteen months later, in June, 1966, she welcomed to the White House the five hundred delegates to the first National Youth Conference on Natural Beauty and Conservation, a gathering arranged by her niece, Diana MacArthur. Again, Mrs. Johnson spoke, urging the young people "to consider making America's beauty a full-time vocation." Copies of the proceedings of the 1965 conference were sent out by the president to mayors, county officials, and Congress in a further attempt to create a constituency for natural beauty. Such conferences reflected the essence of Mrs. Johnson's approach to her responsibilities as First Lady. "She always liked to be in a position," Udall said, "of commending those and participating in ceremonies where you were, in effect, highlighting and dramatizing the good things that were happening in the country." Beautification meant consensus to Mrs. Johnson, and she pursued consensus long after her husband's administration had lost it to an unpopular war and to domestic unrest.[58]

The policy issue in the beautification area with which Mrs. Johnson became most closely associated and that best illustrates her role as First Lady was the campaign to regulate junkyards, improve the look of highways, and, most important, to control highway billboards and outdoor advertising. Neither of the Johnsons had been identified with the billboard regulation that emerged in the mid 1950s and culminated in the Billboard Bonus Act of 1958. In fact, as a senator, Lyndon Johnson was regarded as being friendly to the outdoor-advertising industry. By the early 1960s the 1958 law had few friends on either side of the issue. Only about half of the states had adopted laws to oversee billboards and thereby to obtain the extra federal highway funds that went to states that controlled such advertising. The law, which was scheduled to expire in mid 1965, did not please the billboard industry, the Bureau of Public Roads in the Department of Commerce, or the advocates of a more stringent approach to highway beauty. For some time the bureau and the lobbyists for billboards had been talking about the shape of a new law.[59]

In November, 1964, a few days after his election, President Johnson called Secretary of Commerce Luther Hodges and said: "Lady Bird wants to know what you're going to do about all those junkyards along the highways." The First Lady appears to have been a decisive element in her husband's conversion to a proregulation position on billboards. Under the pressure of the president's repeated expressions of personal interest in early 1965, the staff of the Bureau of Public

Roads entered into extended negotiations with key segments of the junkyard and billboard communities. These talks stretched out over four or five months. The First Lady and her staff were not kept informed of the discussions that Bill Moyers, in the White House; the new secretary of commerce, John T. Connor; and the undersecretary for transportation, Lowell K. Bridwell, were having with industry representatives. The administration's strategy was to gain the support of the Outdoor Advertising Association of America (OAAA), a pivotal section of the billboard forces, by allowing billboards in commercial and industrial areas in return for the OAAA's agreement to accept the exclusion of such advertising from scenic areas along interstate highways and the federally supported primary road system. These negotiations had been successfully concluded when the White House Conference on Natural Beauty assembled in late May, 1965.[60]

Because they were not aware of the extent of the administration's bargaining with the billboard industry's lobbyists, particularly with Phillip Tocker, president of the OAAA, the members of the roadside-control panel at the conference recommended a law that would have banned billboards even in commercial areas. To the surprise of the panelists and the advocates of billboard regulation, the president, in addressing the delegates, called for the banning of billboards and junkyards from highways "except in those areas of commercial and industrial use." Feeling betrayed, the members of garden clubs, roadside councils, and other beautification groups withdrew their support from the legislation that the administration sent to Congress on May 27, 1965. Highway beautification went to Capitol Hill without extensive grass-roots backing from the conservation forces. It also faced the resolute opposition of those who owned billboards in rural areas, of economic interests that were dependent on tourist travel and the signs that sought the trade of motorists, and of Congressmen who were indebted to the local billboard operators for campaign help or were sensitive to the impact of regulation on their constituents. "Lady Bird's bill," as it soon became known, needed all of the president's power and the sizable Democratic majorities that it could command.[61]

Mrs. Johnson became extensively involved with the billboard-control struggle during the late summer as the bill bogged down in committee in both houses. She had kept up with the legislative situation in midsummer through memoranda from Lawrence O'Brien, the administration's link with Congress, and she participated in a decision to drop some parts of the program that lacked support on Capitol Hill in mid August. Later in the month she met with Walter P. Reuther, of the United Auto Workers, who promised to assemble organized labor and civil-rights groups to push for highway beauty. "We'll keep our fingers crossed about the beautification legislation," she told Reuther, "I've lived through enough last days of congressional sessions to know that anything can happen. We'll hope for the best." Around Washington at the end of August, 1965, the verdict was that Mrs. Johnson was doing more than relying on hope. The word went out from the White House that "the highway beauty bill was one of the ones the President wanted this year, that he had to have this one, it was reported, 'for Lady Bird.'"[62]

The most significant aspect of Mrs. Johnson's activity on behalf of the highway-beautification bill began on September 11, 1965. By this time the administration had broken with the Outdoor Advertising Association and was seeking, in the House version of the bill, to secure stronger language that would give the secretary of commerce a greater voice in the regulation of billboards. To move minds and votes, a working group met with the president that Saturday afternoon. Mrs. Johnson received specific lobbying assignments at this gathering. She was to call four important congressmen, including the chairman of the pivotal Subcommittee on Roads, John C. Kluczynski (Dem., Ill.). She spoke to him that afternoon, and she talked with the others over the next few days. In regard to the Kluczynski call, one White House aide wrote: "Obviously Mrs. Johnson's call has had its effect and the Congressman is all for anything we want."[63]

As final action on the highway bill neared in early October, the involvement of the First Lady and her staff intensified. Liz Carpenter, having "put on my best Joy perfume and tightest girdle," went to see Texas congressmen on behalf of Mrs. Johnson. "No one in the Texas delegation likes the bill," George Mahon told Carpenter, "but no one wants to vote against Lady Bird." Carpenter also talked extensively with conservation lobbyists and friendly newspaper editors. Mrs. Johnson herself wrote letters, made more phone calls, and oversaw the lobbying effort on behalf of the bill.[64]

Passage of the bill in the House on October 7, 1965, further highlighted Mrs. Johnson's role. Debate took place on a Thursday afternoon, as congressmen were preparing to attend social events that night, including a "Salute to Congress" at the White House. The president insisted that House action must occur that day. One disgruntled Republican, Robert J. Dole of Kansas, moved unsuccessfully to insert Mrs. Johnson's name, instead of the secretary of commerce's, in the language of the bill. Late in the evening the solid Democratic majority put the bill through. After the Senate took action on the House bill, President Johnson signed the Highway Beautification Act on October 22, 1965.[65]

Mrs. Johnson's participation attracted criticism during the legislative process. "This legislation is a WHIM of Mrs. Johnson," a Texas billboard owner wrote to the president, and in Montana a billboard sought the "Impeachment of Lady Bird Johnson." Bill Mauldin turned the latter thought to the First Lady's advantage in a cartoon that depicted a motorist in a landscape filled with billboards, one of which read "Impeach Lady Bird." Garden clubs and roadside councils thought that the bill was weaker than it should have been, and they displayed continuing reservations about it. Yet, as a Pennsylvania activist conceded: "Lady Bird scored a notable victory." She agreed: "Isn't it wonderful that Congress has made highway beautification the law of the land," she said to a supporter. Still, she also decided to be a little less visible, if no less active, in pushing her programs.[66]

That decision governed how the First Lady performed in the next phase of the highway-beautification battle over the enforcement of the 1965 act. The billboard industry sought to use its congressional allies to weaken the regulatory standards that the administration was proposing in 1966 to implement the law. At the same time, efforts were proceeding in Congress to reduce or eliminate funding for billboard control. The First Lady and her staff kept a lower profile during 1965, but their participation behind the scenes showed little change in her actual role. In January, 1967, she helped to persuade a California state senator, Fred Farr, to serve as highway-beauty coordinator in the new Department of Transportation. When funding bills came up in Congress in 1967 and 1968, Liz Carpenter, Sharon Francis, and some presidential staffers wrote probeautification speeches and statements for legislators to insert in the *Congressional Record*. Mrs. Johnson also sought to limit the extent to which agencies of the federal government could rent billboards in order to advertise their programs.[67]

Mrs. Johnson and her allies had to fight rear-guard actions during her last two years in the White House to retain the substance of the Highway Act. Strengthening amendments that would have bolstered key provisions languished in committee. More important, appropriations for billboard control were slashed, and the administration had to retreat on key aspects of its enforcement standards. Congress limited, for example, the power of the secretary of transportation to set rules about the size, lighting, and spacing of billboards. Some conservation groups would have preferred to see the 1965 act die, convinced as they were that it had irremediable flaws. For her part, Mrs. Johnson did her best to preserve the law and to keep it funded, and she participated in the formal details of the legislative process to a degree that was unparalleled for the wife of the president. She believed that an important initial step had been taken, and she applauded the law's less controversial provisions to clean up junkyards and to acquire and maintain scenic areas along the highways. On balance, the Highway Beautification Act of 1965 represented the limit of what could have been achieved at the time, and it would not have been passed and enforced without Mrs. Johnson's support and active lobbying.[68]

Once President Johnson had announced his decision not to be a candidate in 1968, the thoughts of the First Lady and her colleagues turned to the related questions of the significance of her beautification work and the extent to which it might continue under the incoming president and first lady. In the summer of 1968 there was talk within the White House of an executive order raising the First Lady's Committee from informal to formal status. Arguments against the proposal included a recognition that "the First Lady has never been given official duties by law or executive order, and this would be a break with tradition." When the subject of approaching Russell Train, a prospective appointee to the Interior Department in the Nixon administration, about continuing the First Lady's Committee came up after the election, Mrs. Johnson said, "I never want there to be anything on paper that would indicate that we were instigating any self-perpetuation." She did agree to be the honorary chairman of the Society for a More Beautiful National Capital after January 20, 1969, and she accepted Udall's appointment of her to an advisory committee on national parks, historic sites, buildings, and monuments.[69]

Praise and honors accompanied her all through the concluding months of her husband's term. Eric Sevareid of CBS News told a luncheon of conservationists at the White House in November, 1968, that the First Lady had stimulated "a new popular consciousness about the precious American land." The editors of *Christian Century* concurred: "In a difficult time Mrs. Johnson has comported herself with dignity and charm and has exercised a great spirit of leadership." Her beautification associates, working through Secretary Udall, renamed Columbia Island, in Washington, Lady Bird Johnson Park, and they gave her benches and a planted area for the Johnson Library in Austin. Sharon Francis spoke for the staff: "Well, you've made us all better people, Mrs. Johnson."[70]

Even before leaving Washington, Mrs. Johnson planned to carry on her beautification work at the grass roots. She joined the garden clubs of Stonewall and Johnson City and made annual beautification awards to members of the Texas Highway Department. She rallied the city of Austin to construct parks and jogging paths along Town Lake. The lake trails represented, she said, "a big piece of my heart." In 1982, when she was seventy, she donated sixty acres of land and $125,000 to found the National Wildflower Center outside of Austin. The center began to conduct research on the economic and aesthetic uses of wild flowers, such as planting along highways to reduce mowing and other maintenance costs. The project would be, Mrs. Johnson told her friends, "my last hurrah," but her active schedule continued unabated.[71]

The historical impact of Mrs. Johnson's beautification campaign transcended her specific achievements in Washington and around the nation, important as they were. Her influence and encouragement rippled across the country over the succeeding years. Former colleagues have stressed that she brought people together—Laurance Rockefeller, Mary Lasker, Walter Washington, Lawrence Halprin, Stewart Udall, and Nathaniel Owings—in constructive and productive interaction. In an even larger sense she awakened Americans, as did others during the 1960s, to the environmental crises that lay just ahead. Citizens who wrote to her about the California Redwoods, the Grand Canyon, or a proposed New Orleans freeway received back from the First Lady a sense of concern about their protests that legitimized ecological issues for the future.[72]

"I came very late and timorously to the uses of power," Mrs. Johnson wrote in her diary in December, 1968. Hardly anyone who knew her during the 1960s would agree with that characteristic bit of self-deprecation and reserve. One associate calls her "the most consummate politician" he has known in Washington, because of her ability to persuade diverse and discordant individuals to serve her goals and purposes. The Johnson Library contains a large body of materials about her beautification activity; these offer much support to that positive judgment; they also provide fresh opportunities for studying how Americans saw the environment during the 1960s, how they responded to an activist first lady, and the diversity of issues that the Johnson administration dealt with under the heading of beautification. Mrs. Lyndon B. Johnson was a first lady of unusual influence and range, and her important place in the history of her husband's presidency is rooted in her commitment "to keep the beauty of the landscape as we remember it in our youth . . . and to leave this splendor for our grandchildren."[73]

Notes

For assistance in preparing this essay, I would like to thank Bess Abell, Liz Carpenter, Sharon Francis, Michael Gillette, Sally Graham, Lawrence Halprin, Linda Hanson, Helen Keel, William Leuchtenberg, Harry Middleton and the LBJ Foundation, Joseph Monticone, Craig Roell, Nancy Smith, Stewart Udall, Walter Washington, and Cynthia Wilson.

1. John P. Crevelli, "The Final Act of the Greatest Conservation President," *Prologue* 12 (Winter, 1980): 173–91.

2. Nancy Dickerson, *Among Those Present: A Reporter's View of 25 Years in Washington* (New York: Random House, 1976), pp. 106, 136 (quotation); James B. West, with Mary Lynn Kotz, *Upstairs at the White House: My Life with the First Ladies* (New York: Coward, McCann & Geogehegan, 1973), pp. 331–32; Traphes Bryant, with Frances Spatz Leighton, *Dog Days at the White House: The Outrageous Memoirs of the Presidential Kennel Keeper* (New York: Macmillan, 1975), p. 106; Barbara Howar, *Laughing All The Way* (New York: Stein & Day, 1973), p. 126.

3. June Sochen, *Movers and Shakers: American Women Thinkers and Activists, 1900–1970* (New York: Quadrangle, 1973), pp. 243–47; Abigail McCarthy, "ER as First Lady," in *Without Precedent: The Life and Career of Eleanor Roosevelt*, ed. Joan Hoff-Wilson and Marjorie Lightman (Bloomington: Indiana University Press, 1984), pp. 220–21; Vaughn Davis Bornet, *The Presidency of Lyndon B. Johnson* (Lawrence: University Press of Kansas, 1983), p. 137.

4. The first quotation from Mrs. Johnson comes from remarks at the dedication in 1976 of the LBJ Grove at the Lady Bird Johnson Park in Washington, D.C. (*Congressional Record*, 94 Cong., 2d sess., May 7, 1976, Extension of Remarks of Congressman J. J. Pickle, p. 13033); the second quotation is in Mrs. Lyndon B. Johnson, "Memories of the Wilderness," *Wild Places of North America: Engagement Calendar, 1984* (Washington, D.C.: National Geographic Society, 1984), p. 4. There is no good, thorough biography of Mrs. Johnson, but see Nan Robertson, "Our New First Lady," *Saturday Evening Post*, Feb. 8, 1974, pp. 20–24; and Ruth Montgomery, *Mrs. LBJ* (New York: Holt, Rinehart & Winston, 1964), for studies written when she became the first lady. Robert Caro, in *The Years of Lyndon Johnson: The Path to Power* (New York: Knopf, 1982), pp. 292–305, paints a picture of a shy, retiring young girl, which other sources contradict.

5. Eugenia Boehringer Lasseter oral history, Mar. 10, 1981, p. 19. All oral histories and manuscript documents are in the LBJ Library unless otherwise indicated.

6. The first quotation is from Mrs. Johnson's commencement address to the graduates of the centennial class of the University of Texas at Austin on May 21, 1983, author's copy; "The Doors of the World Swung Open," *Alcalde*, Nov., 1964, p. 21; "The University of Texas Sports Association," *The 1933 Cactus: Yearbook of the University of Texas* (Austin, 1933), p. 134.

7. There is no satisfactory treatment of the Johnsons' marriage. Caro, *Years of Lyndon Johnson*, pp. 302–5, 489–91, sacrifices complexity to the demands of his thesis about her husband's perfidy. Ronnie Dugger, *The Politi-*

cian: The Life and Times of Lyndon Johnson: The Drive for Power, from the Frontier to Master of the Senate (New York: Norton, 1982), pp. 193–94, 254–55, 267–68, is more balanced.

8. Robertson, "Our New First Lady," p. 23 (1st quotation); Katie Louchheim, ed., *The Making of the New Deal: The Insiders Speak* (Cambridge: Harvard University Press, 1983), p. 300 (2d quotation); the remaining quotations are from "Ways to Beautify America," *U.S. News and World Report,* Feb. 22, 1965, pp. 72, 74; Mrs. Johnson recalled her observations of the landscape in an interview with me on Sept. 16, 1984.

9. "Addresses by The First Lady: Mrs. Lyndon Baines Johnson, 1964," pamphlet in Johnson Library, address to the YWCA National Convention, Apr. 20, 1964, p. 19; Lady Bird Johnson, *A White House Diary* (New York: Holt, Rinehart & Winston, 1970), pp. 166, 170. Mrs. Johnson's published diary, representing about one-seventh of the original, is an indispensable source for her activities and thoughts during the White House years. While it gives due space to the public side of her beautification work, there is less in it about the formation of the Committee for a More Beautiful National Capital, her efforts on behalf of highway beautification in Congress, and such matters as Lawrence Halprin's initiative to reshape parts of Washington. The diary, in its original form, is not yet available for scholarly research.

10. Norma Ruth Holly Foreman, "The First Lady as a Leader of Public Opinion: A Study of the Role and Press Relations of Lady Bird Johnson" (Ph.D. diss., University of Texas at Austin, 1971), pp. 157–79; Liz Carpenter, *Ruffles and Flourishes* (Garden City, N.Y.: Doubleday, 1969, 1970), pp. 141–68; Beverly Smith Wakefield, "The Speechmaking of Mrs. Lyndon Baines Johnson, 1964–April 1968" (Master's thesis, University of Texas at Austin, 1968), pp. 20–23.

11. Stewart Udall to Lyndon B. Johnson, Aug. 19, 1964, Johnson to Udall, Aug. 24, 1964, July 15–October 1, 1964. EX/PP5/Lady Bird Johnson, White House central files (hereafter cited as WHCF), box 62; the quotations are from my interview with Stewart Udall, Apr. 11, 1984.

12. Drafts of Mrs. Johnson's speeches at Park City and at Flaming Gorge, written by James Reston, Jr., Aug., 1964, Liz Carpenter Subject File, Western Trip, White House social files (hereafter cited as WHSF), box 9.

13. Robertson, "Our New First Lady," p. 21 (quotation); my interview with Walter Washington, Aug. 9, 1984; Katie Louchheim, *By The Political Sea* (Garden City, N.Y.: Doubleday, 1970), pp. 220–26.

14. Helen Thomas, *Dateline: White House* (New York: Macmillan, 1975), p. 84; Carpenter's *Ruffles and Flourishes* is an engaging and informative memoir that well captures Carpenter's flamboyant style; my conversation with Bess Abell, Aug. 6, 1984.

15. Henry Brandon, "A Talk with the First Lady," *New York Times Magazine,* Sept. 10, 1967.

16. Katie Louchheim to Mrs. Lyndon B. Johnson, Nov. 20, 1964, two memoranda, box C33, Katharine Louchheim Papers, Manuscript Division, Library of Congress (hereafter cited as LC). I am indebted to Mrs. Louchheim for permission to consult her personal papers. The president's daily diary, Nov. 20, 1964, box 2, records Udall's presence at the LBJ Ranch; Udall interview, Apr. 11, 1984. The Stewart Udall Papers at the University of Arizona Library, Tucson, shed much light on his working relationship with Mrs. Johnson.

17. Elizabeth Rowe to Mrs. Lyndon B. Johnson, Dec. 8, 1964, Formation of Committee, Beautification files, WHSF, box 1. The Beautification files (hereafter cited as BF) consist of seventeen boxes of correspondence and documents, divided by subject, which form a central body of source material on Mrs. Johnson's activities in this field. Another six boxes contain pamphlets, photographs, and other miscellaneous materials.

18. Stewart Udall, memorandum for the First Lady, Dec. 9, 1964, box C29, Louchheim Papers.

19. Wolf Von Eckardt, "Washington's Chance for Splendor," *Harper's*, Sept., 1963, p. 55.

20. Antonia Chayes, memorandum on the cities, Dec. 9, 1964, box C29, Louchheim Papers; Andrew Kopkind and James Ridgeway, "Washington: The Lost Colony," *New Republic*, Apr. 23, 1964, pp. 13–17.

21. Mrs. Lyndon B. Johnson to Katie Louchheim, Jan. 30, 1965, box C33, Louchheim Papers; see also Udall to Liz Carpenter, Jan. 7, 1965; Mary Lasker, suggestions for a national landscape committee, Feb. 3, 1965; and Neill Phillips, suggestions for the First Lady's Committee for a More Beautiful Capital, Feb. 11, 1965, Formation of Committee, BF/WHSF, box 1; *Washington Star*, Feb. 2, 1965; *Washington Post*, Feb. 3 and 6, 1965.

22. *Public Papers of the Presidents of the United States: Lyndon B. Johnson, 1963-1964* (hereafter cited as *Public Papers*), 2 vols. (Washington, D.C.: Government Printing Office, 1965), 1: 705.

23. Lady Bird Johnson, *Texas: A Roadside View* (San Antonio, Texas: Trinity University Press, 1980), p. xvii; Stewart Udall to Lewis L. Gould, Oct. 1, 1984.

24. James Reston, Jr., to Richard Goodwin, May 4, 1964, Conservation—Natural Beauty, box 28; Paul Sears, "The Landscape: Its Health and Disease as Economic Factors: or The Cost of Ugliness," no date, Task Force on Beauty, box 14; and Natural Beauty and the Public Interest, Oct. 28, 1964, Natural Beauty—Background, box 14—all in office files of Richard Goodwin; on Mrs. Johnson's knowledge of the Task Force Report see Lewis L. Gould to Stewart Udall, Aug. 11, 1985, with Udall's marginal notations about her participation, copy in Lewis L. Gould Papers, LBJ Library; Lady Bird Johnson, *White House Diary*, p. 215; *Public Papers*, 1:8.

25. *Public Papers, 1965*, 1:156.

26. Lady Bird Johnson, *White House Diary*, p. 234.

27. "Ways to Beautify America," p. 78.

28. Lady Bird Johnson, *White House Diary*, pp. 240–42; *Washington Star*, Feb. 12, 1965.

29. Sharon Francis oral history, May 20, 1969, pp. 8–16; Gould telephone conversation with Sharon Francis, July 17, 1984; Gould conversation with Cynthia Wilson, Aug. 6, 1984; Christine Stugard to James Jones, Aug. 22, 1966, Sept. 11, 1965–Mar. 31, 1966, Ex/HI3, WHCF, box 5.

30. Barbara Klaw, interviewer, "Lady Bird Johnson Remembers," *American Heritage* 32 (Dec., 1980): 6; Sharon Francis oral history, May 20, 1969, p. 35; Carpenter, *Ruffles and Flourishes*, p. 237.

31. The most convenient guide to the work of Mrs. Johnson's committee is "Beautification Summary: The Committee for a More Beautiful Capital," 1965-1968, BF/WHSF, box 22, pp. 21, 22 (1st quotation), 47–48, 51; Washington, *Sunday Star*, Oct. 30, 1966 (2d quotation). There are stenographic

reports of each meeting of the First Lady's Committee in BF/WHSF, boxes 1–3. They will be cited hereafter by date and box number.

32. Nathaniel Alexander Owings, *The Spaces in Between: An Architect's Journey* (Boston: Houghton Mifflin, 1973), pp. 233–34; Nathaniel A. Owings to E. C. Bassett et al., May 28, 1965, box 34; Mrs. Lyndon B. Johnson to Owings, Sept. 16, 1965, and June 14, 1966, box 20, Nathaniel A. Owings Papers, L.C.; see also Pennsylvania Avenue Plan, BF/WHSF, box 7.

33. Louchheim, *By The Political Sea*, p. 232 (1st quotation); *Washington Post*, Feb. 6, 1965 (2d quotation); Sharon Francis oral history, May 20, 1969, p. 24 (3d quotation). For data on Mary Lasker see Elizabeth Brenner Drew, "The Health Syndicate: Washington's Noble Conspirators," *Atlantic Monthly*, Dec., 1967, pp. 75–82; Bornet, *Presidency of Lyndon B. Johnson*, pp. 142–43; and Clarence Lasby's essay, below. Lasker's correspondence with Mrs. Johnson can be traced in Mary Lasker file, alphabetical files, WHSF, box 1,340. The alphabetical file in WHSF has several thousand boxes of correspondence that are now being reviewed and opened in response to requests from researchers.

34. The Nash Castro Papers at the LBJ Library contain abundant materials on his work with Mrs. Johnson. The quotation is from Nash Castro to Sutton Jett, Jan. 12, 1966, Mrs. Johnson's file no. 2, Nash Castro Papers, box 3; Lady Bird Johnson, *White House Diary*, p. 318; see also Nash Castro oral history, Feb. 25, 1969.

35. Mary Lasker to Liz Carpenter, Sept. 24, 1965, Formation of Committee, BF/WHSF, box 1 (quotation); see also Lasker to Louchheim, July 26, 1965, box C29, Louchheim Papers; Lasker to Mrs. Johnson, June 25, 1965, Fund Raising for Washington, BF/WHSF, box 6.

36. Lasker to Louchheim, Oct. 12, 1965, box C29, Louchheim Papers (quotation); Carolyn Agger Fortas to Mary Lasker, Apr. 3, 1967, Society for a More Beautiful National Capital, BF/WHSF, box 7; Mrs. Johnson to Mrs. Vincent Astor, May 24, 1965, Liz Carpenter alphabetical file (hereafter cited as LCAF), beautification, special, WHSF, box 15. Liz Carpenter's alphabetical file contains in its beautification series much correspondence from the First Lady's program; it is second in importance only to the Beautification files themselves. It is, however, a separate file from the larger alphabetical files within the WHSF.

37. T. Sutton Jett to Mrs. Johnson, Apr. 13, 1966, Beautification Meeting, Apr. 13, 1966, BF/WHSF, box 2; Mary Lasker to Douglass Cater, Jr., Jan. 30, 1967, Highway Beautification folder 1, box 96, office files of Douglass Cater; Lady Bird Johnson, *White House Diary*, p. 352.

38. Sharon Francis oral history, May 20, 1969, p. 90; Mary Lasker to Mrs. Johnson, July 22, 1965, Suggestions of D.C. Projects, BF/WHSF, box 8; Gould telephone conversation with Sharon Francis, July 17, 1984; Gould interview with Lawrence Halprin, Apr. 5, 1984; *Washington Star*, Jan. 12, 1967; *Washington Post*, Jan. 13, 1967.

39. Walter Washington to Mrs. Johnson, Sept. 24, 1965, Suggestions of D.C. Projects, BF/WHSF, box 8; Walter Washington to Liz Carpenter, Oct. 20, 1965, "Give Till It's Beautiful," BF/WHSF, box 6; Gould interview with Walter Washington, Aug. 9, 1984.

40. Washington to Mrs. Johnson, Sept. 24, 1965, Suggestions of D.C. Projects, BF/WHSF, box 8.

41. Shackleton discussed Project Pride at the meeting of the First Lady's Committee, Oct. 5, 1966, box 2, pp. 22–40, quotation on p. 23. Press release on Project Pride, July 19, 1966, box C30, Louchheim Papers; Liz Carpenter to Mrs. Johnson, Aug. 23, 1966, Sharon Francis to Liz Carpenter, Aug. 25, 1966, Beautification Meeting, Oct. 5, 1966, BF/WHSF, box 2.

42. Polly Shackleton to Laurance Rockefeller, July 18, 1967 (1st and 2d quotations), Shackleton to Rockefeller, Sept. 1, 1967 (3d quotation), Trail Blazers, BF/WHSF, box 8.

43. The first quotation is from Mrs. Johnson's remarks at the dedication of the Buchanan School Plaza (U.S., House, *Congressional Record*, 90th Cong., 2d sess. [May 15, 1968], p. 13554); Sharon Francis to Mrs. Johnson, June 11, 1968, Buchanan School, BF/WHSF, box 5 (2d quotation); Mrs. Johnson to Brooke Astor, Apr. 3, 1967, Mrs. Vincent Astor file, alphabetical file, WHSF, box 45; Brooke Astor, *Footprints* (Garden City, N.Y.: Doubleday, 1980), pp. 338–40.

44. Joseph Judge, "New Grandeur for Flowering Washington," *National Geographic*, Apr., 1967, p. 520.

45. Beautification Summary, p. 35, quotes Mrs. Johnson's comments at the Urban American Conference; Sharon Francis oral history, May 20, 1969, p. 25, describes Stephen Currier's philanthropic work. Sharon Francis to Liz Carpenter, July 6, 1966 (final quotation), and Sept. 27, 1966, with cover note from Mrs. Johnson to Liz Carpenter, Currier offer, BF/WHSF, box 6. For biographical data on the Curriers see *New York Times*, Feb. 16, 1967.

46. Sharon Francis oral history, May 20, 1969, pp. 25–32, describes Mrs. Johnson's San Francisco trip, and quotes her on p. 32. Lady Bird Johnson, *White House Diary*, p. 423; Gould interview with Lawrence Halprin, Apr. 5, 1984.

47. Mrs. Johnson is quoted by Roberta Hornig in "Beauty Planned For Capital East," *Washington Star*, Jan. 13, 1967; A report from Lawrence Halprin Associates to Mrs. Johnson's Committee for a More Beautiful Capital, Jan., 1967, BF/WHSF, box 18, gives Halprin's proposals in detail. Taconic Foundation, Dec. 7, 1966, Lawrence Halprin Papers, San Francisco, outlines his preparations for the January, 1967, meeting. I am indebted to Mr. Halprin, for his kindness in making his papers available to me, and to Ms. Dee Mullen for her assistance as well.

48. Mrs. Johnson to Mrs. David Bruce, Jan. 17, 1967, Halprin Report, BF/WHSF, box 6; Sharon Francis oral history, May 20, 1969, p. 34.

49. For a sample of the rich Halprin material see Progress Report—Halprin Proposals—Apr. 1, 1967. Sharon Francis to Mrs. Johnson, May 12, 1967, Halprin Report, BF/WHSF, box 6; Francis to Liz Carpenter, May 23, 1967; Francis to John Simon, June 23, 1967; Francis to Mrs. Johnson, June 30, 1967, Capital East—Inner Blocks, BF/WHSF, box 5; Alan Boyd to Francis, Nov. 28, 1967, Lawrence Halprin to George B. Hartzog, Jr., Dec. 1, 1967, Francis to Halprin, May 13, 1969, Halprin Papers.

50. Remarks of Walter Washington at the First Lady's Beautification Luncheon in the East Room, Apr. 17, 1968, Mayor's Remarks, BF/WHSF, box 6; Sharon Francis oral history, June 27, 1969, p. 10; Lady Bird Johnson, *White House Diary*, pp. 665–67; Gould interview with Walter Washington, Aug. 9, 1984.

51. Colman McCarthy, in "Tiptoeing through NW Tulips," *Washington Post*, May 12, 1970, describes how beautification had faltered in the black

areas of Washington. Carolyn Agger Fortas to the trustees, Mar. 8, 1973, box C31; Wayne H. Dickston, memorandum to all trustees, Feb. 21, 1974, box C33, Louchheim Papers; statement of Elizabeth H. Rowe, Mar. 19, 1984, in "Gold Medals to the Daughter of Harry S. Truman: Lady Bird Johnson; and the Widow of Roy Wilkins," *Hearings before the Subcommittee on Consumer Affairs and Coinage of the Committee on Banking, Finance and Urban Affairs, House of Representatives, Ninety-eighth Congress Second Session, on H.R. 3614, H.J. Res. 394, H.R. 3240*, ser. no. 98-74 (Washington, D.C.: Government Printing Office, 1984), p. 58.

52. For the work of the Speakers Bureau see Speakers Bureau, 1965–67; BF/WHSF, box 13; Mrs. Johnson's travels are recorded in Beautification Summary, passim, and in Liz Carpenter's subject file, WHSF, under the date and location of each trip.

53. Lady Bird Johnson, *White House Diary*, pp. 376–83, 381 (3d quotation), 382 (1st quotation); Carpenter, *Ruffles and Flourishes*, p. 88 (2d quotation); Shana Alexander, "Lady Bird's Boat Ride," *Life*, Apr. 15, 1966, p. 34.

54. Beautification Summary, pp. 17 (on Jackson Hole), 75 (on Stamford, Conn.); "Conservation's One-Two," *American Forests* 72 (Apr., 1966): 61, road-builders speech.

55. Lady Bird Johnson, *White House Diary*, pp. 575–78, 579, 580, 581 (1st and 2d quotations), 582 (last quotation); Sharon Francis oral history, June 4, 1969, p. 24.

56. Mrs. Lyndon Johnson to Sylvia Porter, Dec. 28, 1965, "P" Folder, LCAF/WHSF, box 14; Paul S. Forbes to Sharon Francis, Oct. 15, 1968, Report to the President, BF/WHSF, box 12, for Giant Food; Francis to Liz Carpenter, Feb. 23, 1967, Reliance Insurance Event, BF/WHSF, box 12; Rumoshosky report, June 6, 1967, service stations, BF/WHSF, box 12; Reader's Digest Event, BF/WHSF, box 12, outlines that magazine's support for Mrs. Johnson in 1965 and later. Lady Bird Johnson, "America Can Be More Beautiful with Your Help," *Reader's Digest*, Sept., 1968, pp. 142–49.

57. John W. Macy to Mrs. Johnson, Mar. 22, 1968 (1st quotation), Oct. 23, 1968; Matthew Coffey to Macy, May 4, 1968; Coffey to Mrs. Johnson, June 28 and July 2, 1968, Citizens Advisory Commission on Recreation and Natural Beauty, John W. Macy files, WHCF, box 815; Macy to Lyndon B. Johnson, May 11, 1968, President's Council on Recreation and Natural Beauty, Jan. 1–June 30, 1968, FG 738, WHCF, box 404 (2d quotation).

58. For Mrs. Johnson's remarks at the 1965 White House Conference see *Beauty for America: Proceedings of the White House Conference on Natural Beauty, Washington, D.C., May 24–25, 1965* (Washington, D.C.: Government Printing Office, 1965), p. 17; Beautification Summary, p. 35; Stewart Udall oral history, May 19, 1969, p. 13. For White House dissemination of the recommendations and proceedings of the 1965 conference see Lyndon Johnson to George C. Wallace, Jan. 17, 1966, Sept. 1, 1965–Jan. 16, 1966, Natural Resources, WHCF, box 5.

59. Jack Valenti to B. W. Bordages, Jan. 23, 1965, responding to Bordages to Valenti, Dec. 21, 1964, Nov. 22, 1963–Feb. 17, 1965, Highways 3, WHCF, box 6; Gould interview with Phillip Tocker, Feb. 7, 1984; James L. Sundquist, *Politics and Policy: The Eisenhower, Kennedy, and Johnson Years* (Washington, D.C.: Brookings Institution, 1968), pp. 340–45, 373–74; Thomas E. Redard, "The Politics of Beautification in the Johnson Administration" (Master's

thesis, University of Texas at Austin, 1976); Lewis L. Gould, "First Lady as Catalyst: Lady Bird Johnson and Highway Beautification in the 1960s," *Environmental Review* 10 (Summer, 1986): 77–92.

60. Mrs. Johnson is quoted in Maxine Cheshire, "Mrs. Johnson Digs New Landscape Role on Capitol Hill," *Washington Post*, Jan. 5, 1965; Luther Hodges to Lyndon Johnson, Nov. 19, 1964, Nov. 22, 1963–Sept. 10, 1965, HI3, WHCF, box 5. Evidence of Johnson's personal interest is apparent in his handwritten comments on the letter of Lyndon B. Johnson to the secretary of commerce, John T. Connor, Jan. 19, 1965, Bill Moyers office files, Highway Beautification, box 79; the letter, without the comments, is available in *Public Papers, 1965*, 1:81–82, where it is dated Jan. 21, 1965. For the negotiations with the Outdoor Advertising Association see Donald S. Thomas to Lyndon Johnson, Mar. 28, Apr. 30, and May 7, 1965, Phillip Tocker to Moyers, Apr. 22, 1965, Thomas to Moyers, Apr. 23, 1965, Moyers to Thomas, Apr. 26, 1965, Bill Moyers office files, Highway Beautification, box 79.

61. For the president's recommendations see *Beauty for America*, p. 681; and for the events at the White House Conference see Elizabeth Brenner Drew, "Lady Bird's Beauty Bill," *Atlantic Monthly*, Dec., 1965, pp. 68–72. The reaction of proponents of billboard regulation is evident in Fred Farr to Lyndon B. Johnson, May 27, 1965, with cover memorandum of Lawrence McQuade to Richard Goodwin, July 16, 1965, chronological correspondence, box 15, Papers of Alan Boyd; and Maurine Neuberger to Mrs. Cyril G. Fox, July 12, 1965, box 7, Maurine Neuberger Papers, University of Oregon. I am indebted to John Simpson of the University of Oregon for locating and copying materials in the Neuberger Papers relating to highway beautification.

62. Charles Schultze, Memorandum for the President, Aug. 17, 1965, Bill Moyers office files, Highway Beautification, box 79; Mrs. Johnson to Walter Reuther, Aug. 26, 1965, Beautification Special, BF/WHSF, box 15; Drew, "Lady Bird's Beauty Bill," p. 71.

63. Joseph Califano to Lyndon Johnson, Mrs. Johnson, et al., Sept. 11, 1965, Nov. 22, 1963–Oct. 20, 1964, Legislation/Natural Resources, WHCF, box 142, summarizes the results of the conference and lists the First Lady's telephone assignments. Jake Jacobsen to Lyndon Johnson, Sept. 11, 1965, Sept. 11, 1965–Mar. 30, 1966, HI3, WHCF, box 5, reports on Kluczynski's reaction.

64. Liz Carpenter to Mrs. Johnson, Oct. 4, 1965, Highway Beautification, BF/WHSF, box 14, for both quotations; see also Activities on Behalf of Highway Improvement Bill, Oct. 5, 1965, Esther Peterson to Hayes Redmon, Oct. 15, 1965, Highway Beautification, BF/WHSF, box 14.

65. For the Dole amendment see U.S., House, *Congressional Record*, 89th Cong., 1st sess. (Oct. 7, 1965), p. 26306; Jack Anderson, "Sharp Battle on Beautification Bill," *Washington Post*, Oct. 15, 1965.

66. Lee Ray Page to Lyndon Johnson, Sept. 10, 1965, Oct. 1, 1965–Dec. 8, 1965, NR, WHCF, box 7; "Apology to Lady Bird Johnson," U.S., Senate, *Congressional Record*, 89th Cong., 1st sess. (Oct. 13, 1965), p. 26860, remarks of Senator Mike Mansfield (Dem., Mont.); for the Mauldin cartoon, "Signs along the Road," *New Republic*, Oct. 2, 1965, p. 7; Mrs. Cyril G. Fox to Maurine Neuberger, Nov. 3, 1965, box 7, Neuberger Papers; Mrs. Lyndon Johnson to W. Robert Amick, Nov. 19, 1965, Four H. Clubs, Beautification, alphabetical file, WHSF, box 113.

67. John H. Steadman to Bess Abell, Oct. 14, 1966, "Implementation of Highway Beauty," BF/WHSF, box 16, deals with the Department of Defense and its use of billboards; Leon Janos to Jim Keefe, Mar. 26, 1968, Beautification, Robert Hardesty office files, box 18, conveying a statement for Senator Thomas McIntyre (Dem., Vt.) to put in the *Congressional Record*; Sharon Francis to Mrs. Johnson, Jan. 9, 1967, Highway Beautification Act, BF/WHSF, box 14, and Alan Boyd to Mrs. Johnson, Jan. 4, 1967, Status Report on Highway Beautification Program, in Highway Beautification, BF/WHSF, box 15, discusses Farr's candidacy. Gould interview with Phillip Tocker, Feb. 7, 1984, provided the position of the billboard industry; Gould interview with Ruth R. Johnson, Aug. 9, 1984, supplied the perspective of a billboard regulator in the Department of Transportation.

68. The legislative struggles of 1966–68 are too complex to be dealt with here. Evidence of Mrs. Johnson's involvement in the details of the process includes Sharon Francis to Mrs. Johnson, June 30 and July 3, 1968, Barefoot Sanders to Mrs. Johnson, June 29 and July 16, 1968, Liz Carpenter and Francis to Mrs. Johnson, July 10, 1968, Highway Beautification—1968, BF/WHSF, box 15. Charles F. Floyd and Peter J. Shedd, in *Highway Beautification: The Environmental Movement's Greatest Failure* (Boulder, Colo.: Westview Press, 1979), pp. 91–106, offer a critical look at the early years of the act. A recent evaluation of the whole billboard control program is *The Outdoor Advertising Control Program Needs to Be Reassessed* (Washington, D.C.: General Accounting Office, Jan. 3, 1985), a report made to Senator Robert Stafford (Rep., Vt.).

69. Matthew Nimetz to Joseph Califano, July 31, 1968, with attached statement on First Lady's Committee for a More Beautiful Capital, Beautification, James Gaither office files, box 257; Sharon Francis oral history, June 27, 1969, p. 67, quotes Mrs. Johnson; Lady Bird Johnson, *White House Diary*, pp. 736–37.

70. Eric Sevareid's remarks, Conservation Luncheon, Nov., 1968, in Conservation Luncheon, Nov. 13, 1968, BF/WHSF, box 5; "Lady Beautiful," *Christian Century*, Nov. 27, 1968, p. 1523; Lady Bird Johnson, *White House Diary*, pp. 736–37; Sharon Francis oral history, June 27, 1969, p. 80.

71. Gould interviews with Liz Carpenter, Aug. 13, 1984, and with Mrs. Lyndon Johnson, Sept. 16, 1984; Klaw, "Lady Bird Johnson Remembers," p. 6 (1st quotation); Mary Barrineau, "Last Hurrah for Lady Bird," *Westward: Dallas Times Herald*, pp. 5, 7–10, 18–20; Liz Carpenter, "The Incomparable Lady Bird," *Ultra*, Nov., 1983, pp. 86–87; I attended the Highway Beautification award ceremony at the LBJ Park on Oct. 3, 1984.

72. Gould interviews with Lawrence Halprin, Apr. 5, 1984, with Stewart Udall, Apr. 11, 1984, and with Walter Washington, Aug. 9, 1984. Cynthia Wilson kindly put at my disposal a set of sample letters that Mrs. Johnson's staff sent out about particular issues, which is now part of the Beautification files.

73. Lady Bird Johnson, *White House Diary*, p. 752; Gould interview with Spencer Smith, Aug. 6, 1984; Lady Bird Johnson, "Foreword," *Texas in Bloom: Photographs from Texas Highways Magazine* (College Station: Texas A & M University Press, 1984), p. 10.

Part 3 | Science and Public Policy

7 | The War on Disease

Clarence G. Lasby

ON APRIL 7, 1966, LYNDON JOHNSON entered the Cabinet Room to receive the Special Albert Lasker Award for leadership in health—a gold statuette of the Winged Victory of Samothrace. The Greeks had set up the statuette to honor Nike, goddess of victory; now a jury of scientists was giving it to honor a president who, to an "unparalleled degree," had sought victory over death and disease. The citation saluted the recipient for his specific legislative achievements—bills for Medicare, research laboratories and libraries, community health centers, medical manpower, and the Regional Medical Program to combat heart disease, cancer, and stroke. "We glory in your impatience with things as they are," the medical experts told their president, and they went on to predict new victories and greater glory: "We know that children not yet born will one day venerate the name of Lyndon Baines Johnson for leading this God-inspired crusade against needless disability and death."[1]

Years later, Lyndon Johnson was more restrained when he surveyed the health accomplishments of his presidency. In *The Vantage Point* he spent seven pages describing the legislative history of Medicare, a program of "overriding importance" because it "foreshadowed a revolutionary change in our thinking about health care." He was obviously proud to have given Medicare top priority, and he was pleased that the nation "had begun, at long last, to recognize that good medical care is a right, not just a privilege." But he gave most of the credit to others, in his sense that "the times had caught up with the idea" and that "the voters of America passed the law." He did engage in one boastful flourish; he listed some other achievements: raising health expenditures from $4 to $14 billion; extending the fruits of medical research to more people; fighting heart disease, cancer, strokes, and mental retardation; eliminating measles as a cause of serious concern; building new hospitals and nursing homes; and training more doctors and nurses. "During my administration," he recorded, "forty national health measures were presented to the Congress and passed by the Congress—more than in all the preceding 175 years of the Republic's history."[2]

Like the president, commentators have focused on Medicare as the great health accomplishment of his administration. As early as 1966, journalist Richard Harris set the tone when he portrayed the long and bitter struggle for hospital insurance as a victory of reform over reaction, culminating in the grand summer of 1965. Aides of the president furthered that image. Larry O'Brien considered Medicare "one of the glories" of the Great Society, and Jack Valenti deemed it "worthy of hall-bursting applause." Scholars agreed. Eric Goldman saw the program as "monumental" and "far-reaching," and William O'Neill placed it among the best of the legislation that "established Johnson's place in history." This initial interpretation of Medicare as one of the "big three" legislative victories of the Eighty-ninth Congress persists in contemporary histories. Vaughn Bornet, for example, though sensitive to its soaring costs, pays homage to the "memorable" law. This interpretation, however, is under attack. Sociologist Paul Starr, in his prize-winning study of American medicine, stresses the limitations of Medicare-Medicaid and decries the "politics of accommodation" that give such unfortunate advantages to the hospitals and doctors. Historian Allan Matusow, in his New American Nation Series volume on the 1960s, is even harsher; he uses the program as a case history of failure in the Great Society. For these influential revisionists, yesterday's triumph seems tarnished.[3]

Much as historians continue to reflect on Medicare, they continue to ignore Lyndon Johnson's other hopes and accomplishments in the field of health. From Goldman to Bornet, the president's multifarious activities earn only passing mention, if any at all, and then are consigned to a listing of a few bills passed. Only political scientist Theodore Marmor, in a 1976 article, has touched meaningfully upon the president's "widespread effort to reach problems across all the areas of health industry." But he is quick to point out, in his two-and-one-half page summary of the administration's diverse initiatives, that all of them were starkly overshadowed, in budget terms, by Medicare and Medicaid and that none of them "dramatically altered the distribution of access to medical care services." On the rare occasion when a scholar has sought to add to the historical record, as in Paul Starr's one-page assault on the President's Commission on Heart Disease, Cancer and Stroke, the poverty of sources has led to confusion. Citing a misleading contemporary article and the preface to only the first volume of the commission's report, Starr sets forth a series of charges that are simply wrong.[4]

The abundant collection of health papers in the Johnson Library—which far surpasses similar collections in the Truman, Eisenhower, and Kennedy Libraries—proves conclusively that Lyndon Johnson was more deeply committed to and achieved greater benefits for his nation's health than did any other president. The papers also should lead scholars away from a single-minded emphasis on Medicare to a broader conception of the president's interests, although with varying results. For example, the papers do not significantly enlarge our understanding of a number of activities—such as the construction of health facilities, the education of health manpower, the establishment of community health centers—which were essentially initiatives from previous administrations but which expanded dramatically in size and scope between 1963 and 1968. These were not small accomplishments, but still they must depend for assessment on such statistical testimonials as the training of 100,000 doctors, nurses, and dentists; the treatment of 460,000 crippled children; the addition of 123,000 new and improved hospital beds; and a 13 percent decline in infant mortality.[5]

What is new in the library and what serves as the basis for this essay is a wealth of material in which Lyndon Johnson appears as a "can-do dreamer," to use a phrase of Harry C. McPherson, who was personally and politically involved in a crusade against disease. Johnson was not content merely to deliver the blessings of American medicine to every citizen; he would deliver the world from every such scourge as heart disease, cancer, stroke, malaria, and measles. Early in his administration he entered a war that he sincerely believed he could win, and for several years thereafter he summoned his people to action. Assuming the role of commander in chief, he appointed a special presidential commission to provide the strategy; he sponsored legislation of many kinds to further the cause; and he teamed with health advocate Mary Lasker in an extraordinary, almost unique, relationship to chastise the bureaucrats for their tactical errors and their lack of faith. In this war against disease the president was a visionary, a politician who spoke constantly of the miracles of modern medicine. Obviously he won no final victory, and he came to know the meanng of unfulfilled expectations. But more than any president before or since, he sought to have his people suffer less and live longer.[6]

On the Battleground against Disease

In August, 1965, President Johnson journeyed to the National Institutes of Health (NIH) in Bethesda, Maryland, to sign the Health Research Facilities Act. Dr. James Shannon was pleased; he had invited Presidents Eisenhower and Kennedy to visit, but they had shown little interest and had declined. This president, in contrast, Wilbur Cohen had told Shannon, "is very anxious to identify himself on the whole development of health." The visitor made that evident. "Here on this quiet battleground our Nation leads a worldwide war on disease," he said to the assembled scientists. "The experience of the past 10 years assures us that war can be won." Johnson promised leadership and vision at the onset of a "staggering era for medicine," mentioned "the miracles of which today we only dream," and set forth some of his goals—the elimination of rheumatic heart disease among children, the reduction of the tragic toll of heart disease among adults, and the eradication of malaria and cholera from the entire world. He was determined "that research and discovery yield results which not only increase man's knowledge but the strength of his body and the length of his life." In the days ahead, he vowed, the government and Americans were "going to successfully conclude that war you have declared on those ancient enemies."[7]

The president's visit to Bethesda was largely symbolic; eighteen months before he had already assumed leadership in the nation's war against disease. That war had come to life out of another conflict—World War II—with its victories over infectious diseases, its triumphs of technology, and above all, the development of the atomic bomb. On the day that U.S. planes bombed Nagasaki, a United States senator asked President Truman to marshal the same stupendous scientific and engineering effort to "discover causes and cures for the deadly diseases of mankind . . . which have up to now baffled scientific effort." Harry Truman did not take the initiative, but he did respond to a group of citizens who believed American science could accomplish everything. Foremost among them was Mary Woodward Lasker, a successful businesswoman who founded Hollywood Patterns during the depression and was the wife of Albert D. Lasker, who sold his advertising firm in 1942 for a fortune that allowed them to pursue an interest in health. Mrs. Lasker was inspired by a perception of disease as an enemy—she had experienced illness as a child, had lost her parents to heart disease, and would lose her husband to cancer in 1952—and by a belief that "the human being on fire can do so much." As early as 1948, working with her close friends Anna Rosenberg, an assistant secretary for defense under Truman, and Florence Mahoney, whose husband owned the Cox newspaper chain, she convinced Congress to establish the National Heart Institute. The American people, she explained, "are assaulted by killers from within, whose victims from these diseases total twice as many persons each year as were lost by our armed services on all fronts during the last war."[8]

During the 1950s, Mary Lasker had mobilized a remarkable group of allies who were passionately committed to the war against disease and were eminently successful in winning ever-increasing budgets for medical research. She hired, as her lobbyist, a crusading journalist, Mike Gorman, one of the most proficient ever to serve in Washington; she worked closely with Congressman John Fogarty of Rhode Island, whose heart attack in 1953 had enhanced his concern about dread diseases; she became a very close friend of Senator Lister Hill, who controlled Senate health appropriations; and she benefited from the support of Dr. James Shannon, who served as director of the National Institutes of Health (NIH) after 1955 and who could always make a case for more money. She also organized a number of "citizen witnesses" to appear before Congress—Dr. Howard Rusk, who was famous for his work in rehabilitation; Dr. Sidney Farber, an authority on cancer; and Dr. Michael DeBakey, the nation's leading heart surgeon. Each year these or other experts testified before congressional committees as to progress in their fields and opportunities for the future.[9]

The health lobby had a grand design, adorned in the analogue of war. As the director of the National Heart Institute explained, "The campaign must be carried on patiently, must consist of actions, skirmishes, attritions, as scientific knowledge encompasses first new conceptions, later practical applications on a modest scale, and finally total victory." Mary Lasker coordinated that campaign with consummate skill. She used her financial resources to support responsive congressmen of both parties; she used the Albert Lasker Medical Research Awards to honor scientific excellence; she published annual "fact sheets" through her National Health Education Committee to inform politicians and the public about the realities of the conflict; and she served for eighteen years on citizen advisory committees for the National Heart and Cancer Institutes. The crusade was so effective as to raise expectations dramatically. As early as 1956 the science editor of the *New York Times*, Pulitzer Prize recipient William Laurence, predicted that heart disease, cancer, and polio would be conquered within a decade. "Ten years from now," he assured his readers, "we will be 10 or even 20 years younger."[10]

Lyndon Johnson enlisted in the war against disease even before he became president. "Perhaps there is no more important problem facing us," he wrote to a constituent in 1959, "than finding the solution to the dread diseases." He always supported increased funds for medical research, and he explained why to a friend in Fort Worth: "I have a personal interest in research on the problem of heart disease, of course, and the death by cancer of Senator Taft a few years ago and former Secretary of State Dulles this week, should certainly dramatize these needs." He had also become an ally of Mary Lasker. In 1948, Albert Lasker had contributed $500 to the Johnson campaign (along with a message that he would soon be sending recommendations in the field of health), but it was not until the mid 1950s that Mrs. Lasker met the senator. Within a few years they were on a first-name basis, and in June, 1959, in the midst of a struggle with President Eisenhower, who told his cabinet that "money alone isn't going to keep him or anyone else from having a heart attack," Mary Lasker approached Johnson: "I know you can get anything done that you want. . . . I am convinced that in the area of medical research we are pre-eminent in the world, and we must stay pre-eminent. We seem to be lagging in other areas of science as compared with the Russians. More breakthroughs in medical research will give us the energy, as a Nation, to go forward and stay ahead in the other scientific fields!"[11]

Soon thereafter the majority leader responded with a powerful speech, written in large part by Mike Gorman, denouncing Eisenhower's position. The nation should not try to balance the budget at the expense of medical research, which had saved 1.8 million lives since World War II, thereby providing the federal government with $623 million in taxes every year. Disease was still cutting into our economic system at an annual cost of $30 billion and was striking "at the very core and strength of our posture in the free world." The United States was facing a "medical Sputnik," the senator claimed, for Russia had already launched a fifteen-year program to conquer heart disease and cancer. Shortly after making his presentation, Lyndon Johnson informed his friend of their victory for health research. "The Senate certainly succumbed to the irresistible pleas of Mary Lasker" and to the "words which were so very good because they reflected the thinking and outlook of a great and fine lady." These expressions of mutual interest and friendship were to become important several years later, the more so because of the health advocates' disappointment with John Kennedy.[12]

During the early 1960s the coalition of Lasker, Fogarty, Hill, and Shannon continued to seek increased funds for the NIH, almost always with success. But Mary Lasker and, to a lesser degree, her congressional allies became disenchanted because the scientists had failed to produce victories. After more than a decade of accelerated research, heart disease and cancer were claiming more lives. Now she wanted to speed up the action by means of a massive national assault against the two most dreaded diseases. To that end she induced the Democratic National Committee to pledge, in its 1960 platform, that a Democratic president would "summon to a White House conference the Nation's most distinguished scientists in these fields to map a coordinated long-range program for the prevention and control of these diseases."[13]

John Kennedy did call the Conference on Heart Disease and Cancer, but it was a disaster: the scientists failed to come forth with any new ideas, and the president refused to make their recommendations public. Submitted on April 21, 1961, the results of the conference survived in inner circles as a bad memory and came to be known as the "Bay of Pigs Report." For the next two and one-half years, Mary Lasker struggled to convince the administration—over the objections of the surgeon general and of James Shannon—to appoint a presidential commission that would be empowered to seek the ultimate conquest of heart disease, cancer, and strokes (the latter having been added to take cognizance of Joseph Kennedy's illness). President Kennedy, whose interest in health was limited essentially to Medicare and mental retardation, remained lukewarm to Lasker's solicitations until shortly before his death, when he promised to establish a commission sometime in the future.[14]

Lyndon Johnson became the true pioneer on this New Frontier of medicine, in large part because of the influence of Mary Lasker. Building upon her earlier association, she remained friends with the Johnsons during the vice-presidential years and gained the most precious asset of would-be policy makers—access. During the first two months of Johnson's presidency, she met with him three times, spoke with him on the telephone several times, had Mrs. Johnson for lunch and the couple for dinner at her New York town house, and spent a night at the White House. There is no record of their conversations, but there is no question about the result. On February 10, 1964, in his message on health, the president announced the establishment of the Commission on Heart Disease, Cancer and Stroke (HCS). He acted, he explained later, "with the grim facts in mind"—over a million productive citizens would die each year unless action were taken—and "at the insistence of that lovely lady, Mrs. Mary Lasker."[15]

Lyndon Johnson was also unusually amenable to such an initiative. On philosophic grounds he completely accepted the responsibility of government to fight mankind's ancient enemies, which he defined in many speeches as disease, ignorance, poverty, and discrimination. And from his own experience he believed it was possible for science to conquer disease; he had seen it happen on a grand scale during his lifetime, with infectious diseases during the 1940s and with polio a decade later. He was sympathetic, as well, to such observations about the nation's priorities as in Mary Lasker's trenchant comparison: "$51.2 billion to defend ourselves against possible enemy attack from without as compared to . . . $918.4 million to defend ourselves against *disease enemies within our bodies*"; or in David O. Selznick's letter of complaint: "I am not alone in thinking that it is absurd that a nation that can spend countless billions to reach the moon cannot devote some small fraction of this amount to an all-out drive on the two great killers."[16]

Above all, Johnson's family history of heart disease and stroke, as well as his own heart attack, made him attentive to the future of medicine. He spoke often about his gratitude to the doctors who had "saved" his life, and he was ever mindful that such a day could come again. As Lady Bird wrote on the ninth anniversary of his misfortune (1964): "For the first few years we passed those milestones stepping softly with great trepidation. Now we act almost as though the heart attack had not been, though Lyndon and I will not forget." Nor could they, for there were sobering reminders, such as the stomach pains during a night in September, 1965, followed by the initial fright, as the president was "stretched out on the bed with the wires of an electrocardiogram machine attached to his body," and finally the relief in learning that it was only gallstones. It was little wonder that he welcomed Mary Lasker's impatient search for a solution to cholesterol or the message that he received on January 31, 1966: "Dr. DeBakey predicts a fully functioning dacron heart in five years."[17]

The president blessed the war against disease in the spirit of a true believer on the morning of April 17, 1964, when he formally greeted the members of his commission in the Rose Garden. "Health is something that we treasure in this house," he assured the gathering, but his health meant little in the light of their opportunities. "What can be more satisfying than to feel that you have preserved, not a life, but millions of them, for decades?" So he called them to the challenge, the "hardest fight" they would ever have. Departing from his prepared speech, he asked them "to give their talents and their energies and their imaginations, and stay awake at night and roll over and go get a glass of water and come back and think some more on how to get the results that we know are within our reach." In an electrifying passage that stunned even the most sanguine of his guests, he explained why they must find the answers and what it would mean:

> The point is, we must conquer heart disease, we must conquer cancer, we must conquer strokes. This Nation and the whole world cries out for this victory. I am firmly convinced that the

accumulated brains and determination of this commission and of the scientific community of the world will, before the end of this decade, come forward with some answers and cures that we need so very much. When this occurs—not "if," but "when," and I emphasize "when"—we will face a new challenge and that will be what to do within our economy to adjust ourselves to a life span and a work span for the average man or woman of 100 years.[18]

The president was not alone in having grandiose expectations for the commission. Mary Lasker was enthusiastic because in a fundamental sense the commission was hers. Her friends made up the majority of the membership, and her ally Dr. Michael DeBakey, who served as chairman, remembered that "whenever Mrs. Lasker would call me to ask me to do certain things, I would drop what I was doing to do it." With good reason she expressed hope that the commission would be as historic in its province as the revolutionary Flexner Report had been for medical education after the turn of the century. Presidential aide Myer Feldman told a plenary session that the advances should constitute an achievement "so great that if nothing else was done this would represent a major event in a successful administration." The commission's executive secretary insisted that it could make a smashing impact by stating flatly: "Dear American People. We are going to Bring the Wonders of Medical Science to You," and then really doing so. "I think people are tired of reading about scientific marvels and then watching Mom die." And at the first meeting of the Executive Council, Dr. Sidney Farber interrupted a DeBakey pep talk about challenge and imagination: "May I just read you in reference to your imaginative approach the origin of the term 'Cloud 9,' which is where you are now?" the doctor asked. "This comes from the Medieval idea of the ninth heaven of Dante's Paradiso. This is the diaphanous spirit of love that rules the action of all other spirits and is, therefore, beyond time." There was silence, and then applause.[19]

The establishment of the HCS Commission (for which the Johnson Library has an incomparable collection, including verbatim transcripts of its deliberations) was the major health event of 1964. Its members went to work with a surge of excitement, moved by a need to go beyond the mere support of medical research to some new strategy that would really make a difference. For seven months they collected information, wrote comments, exchanged letters, gathered at fifty-six meetings, and made a penetrating inquest into the conduct of the war against disease. They saw theirs as the chance of a lifetime to influence policy at the highest level, and they were in a hurry to give the president something to use in his next State of the Union address, something practical, "something other than poetic expressions." But after all the discussions about prosaic topics—available resources and facilities, the nature of research, the application of knowledge, the education and training of manpower, research grants, organizational deficiencies, and the diseases themselves—they ended with a report that was filled with the promise of miracles.[20]

At a meeting to approve the final draft of the commission's report, Dr. Philip Handler of Duke University complained of its evangelical fervor: "The word miracle I think occurs three different times and on one page it says miracles are just around the corner . . . and that just isn't fair because I don't know it is true and I don't think Presidential Commissions should make such statements in good conscience. I am serious about this." Michael DeBakey took issue: "I am not sure I would agree with you. Miracles have been around the corner for a long time." Handler retorted that "when you say miracles, it is still around the same corner, sir." "Yes," DeBakey conceded, "and they have been going on for 20 years or more." After a few moments, Emerson Foote, a former advertising executive with Albert Lasker's firm, ended the discussion: "As far as promising people great things, what was the Salk vaccine, penicillin, what is operating on an aorta aneurysm, except a miraculous thing?" he asked. "I am sure people accept those as miracles and I am sure there are more around the corner. . . . And if you think this is evangelical, I refer you to President Johnson's remarks about living to a hundred, which shocked even me. I was told I should not have been shocked."[21]

The commission's report, which was submitted on December 9, opened with a detailed account of a national disaster: in 1962, heart disease, cancer, and strokes had claimed 1.2 million American lives, 71 percent of the deaths in the country, at a cost of $40 billion. But the prognosis was bright: the nation stood at the threshold of a historic breakthrough. The people no longer needed to tolerate the loss of several hundred thousand lives a year because "yesterday's hopeless cause has become today's miracle cure." The commission set forth a $2.94 billion prescription for the "ultimate conquest" of the three killers, in the form of a five-year battle plan with thirty-five specific recommendations. It asked for more research, more training, more continuing education, more hospitals, more doctors, more nurses, more state and community services, better communications, and a new National Library of Medicine.[22]

The commission's one "major innovative thrust" called for the establishment of a national network of 60 regional centers, 550 diagnostic and treatment stations, and 30 medical complexes to unite the world of scientific research and patient care. Its members held to an overriding assumption—namely, that a serious gap existed between discovery and application, between science and practice, between what experts knew in the great medical centers and what doctors delivered to patients across the land. And they argued that access was often a matter of money, for "medical miracles are in many instances available only to the fortunate few who can get to the unique medical institution or specialist who can perform that miracle." The network of medical complexes would address that paramount issue; it would make available the most advanced methods of diagnosis and treatment to every doctor in America, and thus to all the people when and where they needed them.[23]

The publicity surrounding the commission's report was extensive; in the words of a surprised cardiologist, "it rivalled one of the better scandals." It was also overwhelmingly favorable. The press described the report with such adjectives as bold, sweeping, vast, and massive; praised it as a sneak preview of the way to health in a Great Society; and seemed pleased, as the Boston Globe put in headlines, that "LBJ Declares War on 3 Killer Diseases." There were some misgivings about the cost ("huge gobs of taxpayer money," to the dismay of the Washington Daily News); about the approach ("an all-out federally financed fight," in the words of the Wall Street Journal); and about the prospects ("Without the cooperation of the powerful AMA . . . it will inevitably run into trouble," in the view of the New York Herald Tribune). But DeBakey and his colleagues had inspired wonder and hope, even among the skeptical. The prestigious New England Journal of Medicine, despite doubts, cynicism, and caution, wrote nonetheless that the commission had "painted with such a broad, sweeping brush and with such magnificent colors that the average practicing physician, despite his sophistication, cannot but gasp in awe at the picture the minds of men have wrought, and look upon it with some embarrassment. For here in words and phrases is a glimpse into an idealistic state of future well-being that he cannot quite comprehend because of its magnitude."[24]

The president joined the euphoric chorus when he accepted the commission's report, proclaiming a "day of electric possibilities." The three diseases "can be conquered," he asserted, "not in a millennium, not in a century, but in the next few onrushing decades." His optimism continued into the new year, and as part of his special health message to Congress on January 7, he pledged to sponsor the most important item of the commission's report—the five-year program for a system of regional medical complexes. Every American deserved access to the newest, the most specialized and expensive services, whether of open-heart surgery, high-voltage radiation, or advanced diagnostic techniques. The time had come to "turn otherwise hollow laboratory triumphs into health victories." He fulfilled his pledge only twelve days later, when he rushed to Congress, with high priority, the "Heart Diseases, Cancer and Stroke Amendments of 1965." It would provide $50 million the first year and whatever might be necessary for the next four years to establish and operate "medical complexes," which would be located at existing institutions or at newly constructed facilities; would pay for such patient care as was incidental to research, training, or demonstration; but could not interfere with the "existing patterns or financing of patient care, professional practice or hospital administration."[25]

The president had high expectations for the HCS's regional-medical-centers bill, which he believed would help the less fortunate people of America. Its purpose, as he explained to Lady Bird, was to set up "a bunch of little Mayos" around the country, "so Dale Malechek and Alvin Sultemeier can get to them." Next to Medicare, he considered it his most important health program, and during two days of hearings before Lister Hill's Subcommittee on Health, senators from both parties promised their support. Republican Jacob Javits described the bill as a "most patriotic and honorable effort to add yet another milestone thing to the great history which has been written in recent years in this tremendous war of the Federal Government on disease." But thereafter, during the next nine months, political combat and compromise marked the legislative history, until only a semblance of the bill remained. Even Lyndon Johnson, in his best year, could not translate this dream into reality.[26]

A Shortfall in Aspirations

The HCS bill, which came to be known as the Regional Medical Program (RMP), was in trouble from the outset. On the day before it went to Congress, the president's science adviser warned that its overall intent "gives the American Medical Association (AMA) further grounds for contending that the Federal Government intends to gradually take over medical care." Written primarily by two commission members, Dr. Michael DeBakey and Dr. Edward Dempsey, it had two threatening provisions—the construction of a network of federal hospitals and the government's payment of patients' fees. For several months the AMA ignored the RMP, in part because of a single-minded devotion to the defeat of Medicare. And too, there was some risk in an early attack on an extremely popular program. The *Washington Post* had warned the organization not to try to halt this venture, for it would constitute "a piece of folly which can end only in making itself regarded as an enemy rather than a benefactor of mankind." But late in April, when the course of Medicare was clear, the AMA issued a three-page staff report denouncing the DeBakey Commission for planning "to reorganize the American system of delivering medical care"—a system that was already more advanced and more sophisticated than any other in the world.[27]

Individual physicians expressed intense fears. Dr. Thomas Townsend of Pine Bluff, Arkansas, who was already "on the ropes" because of Medicare, conjured up a frightful future for the likes of him. Skillful young men from the huge federal medical complexes would appear in the rural areas to tell doctors what to do, would take their patients to distant centers with special facilities, and would then return to the "boondocks" periodically, like "circuit riders," to entice patients away from their own physicians. "This is what is driving us crazy," he explained to an unusually attentive congressional committee—the prospect of a team of salaried federal specialists infringing on the traditional fee for service practice, until there is "no place in medicine for such as myself." And most of the medical practitioners resented the central message of the legislation—that they were not keeping up to date on new developments, thus short-changing their patients. "What's wrong with the way we physicians and surgeons in Lake Charles, Louisiana, treat or diagnose a heart attack, a stroke or a cancer?" asked one of Senator Russell Long's constituents. And he offered some advice popular among his colleagues: "This country of ours can declare war on poverty, war in Viet Nam, but *not* war on cancer or strokes or heart attacks. It just doesn't work this way, and I think it is cruel to so mislead the American people."[28]

The legislation did pass the Senate in June, although it was stripped of a crucial provision for construction funds, but by August it was in trouble in the House. Congressman Oren Harris, the Democratic chairman of the Commerce Committee, blamed angry general practitioners, expressed a preference for an abbreviated three-year program, decided to ignore the Senate bill, and predicted that he was two votes short of getting the legislation out of his committee. A presidential aide blamed HEW itself, because its testimony "apparently has been miserably vague and contradictory. And you could read anything you want into the bill itself, which says nothing." Larry O'Brien portrayed the bill as "the big tough one." Harris is "all the way with us," O'Brien told the president, "but the A.M.A. is working hard and this bill obviously will require at least a couple of weeks work." He was overly optimistic. HEW spent several weeks working with the Harris committee to make the House bill more specific and to sway undecided members, but with little success. Nor was the president able to move the legislation. On August 18 he went out of his way at the swearing-in ceremonies for John W. Gardner, his new HEW secretary, to reaffirm his commitment: "This Administration intends to bring the healing miracle of modern medicine to everyone in this country," Johnson said, "no matter how remotely they live from the city." But when he asked Congress to act within the week so that he could launch an all-out assault to "track down, isolate and destroy" the three great killers, there was no response.[29]

The AMA would not retreat, and in late August it went on the offensive. Dr. James Appel asked the administration to defer action for a year, insisting that a bill of such far-reaching implications, which "many physicians presently consider a greater threat" than Medicare, needed more study and dialogue. If the president would desist, the AMA would convene a National Congress on Regional Medical Centers to seek a consensus. On the other hand, if the pending legislation should pass, Appel warned, it would compromise his efforts to ensure the full cooperation of his colleagues in implementing Medicare. The attempt at blackmail did not move Douglass Cater, the president's aide on health matters; he asked permission to phone the AMA and promise cooperation, but to refuse to surrender. The president checked the yes box on his memorandum, and in one of those rare occasions, added a handwritten comment: "Tell him for weeks we have been seeing these would be stalling tactics. We will work with them—for them but they stalled many health items for years and we must act now and coordinate later. I'll spend all fall trying to help—L."[30]

The help came much sooner. Within days, HEW officials met in an afternoon session with the AMA to work out a compromise. Wilbur Cohen, bargaining for the administration, rejected the AMA's three major requests: to delay action; to modify the program so that it would affect only research and training; and to provide only such patient care as was indispensable to research. Then, to pacify the doctors, he proposed ten amendments, the most important of which assured the participation of local physicians in planning and approving projects, and restricted treatment to only those patients who were referred by practicing physicians. The AMA remained fearful. They could tolerate Medicare, an official told Cohen, but the RMP was a "much more radical concept," and they insisted on talking with the president. Gardner, Cohen, and Harris agreed; at the least, a discussion would permit the doctors to tell their constituents that they had had their day in court. On that same evening the president met with AMA leaders, assured them that the RMP would be a cooperative effort, promised that he had no intention of interfering with traditional medical practices, and instructed Cohen to work out the objections to the bill. "We've got to pass this Heart, Cancer and Stroke bill," he told DeBakey. "You know, you've just got to do everything you can to get this passed. I know that we are only going to be able to have this good relationship with Congress for so long. Then it's going to be all over."[31]

With the president's personal intervention, the negotiations proceeded swiftly and ended in a victory for the AMA. The RMP, or, officially, the Heart Disease, Cancer and Stroke Amendments of 1965, which emerged from the Harris Committee on September 8 and subsequently became law, differed substantially from the administration's original bill. The revised legislation shortened the duration of the war against disease from five to three years; decreased its costs from $1.2 billion to $340 million; and lowered its status from "program" to "pilot projects." The war would proceed without any new construction, without any diagnostic stations, and cleansed of the word *coordination*, because it smacked too much of federal control. The enterprise even had a new name: the old "regional medical complexes," which had aroused fears of newly constructed federal facilities scattered across America, staffed with government employees, which had threatening implications for patient care, gave way to the new "regional cooperative arrangements," which were designed to ensure local control and to protect traditional methods of financing medical care.[32]

When the president signed the RMP bill on October 6, there was little of the Rose Garden excitement of eighteen months before. He recited again the grim facts; he thanked DeBakey, Hill, Fogarty, Harris, and Mary Lasker; and he improvised engagingly about the hopes for a longer life, "not just for ourselves, but for all the little ones that look up with their trusting faces and expect us to do right by them." Some of the old words were there—"to speed the miracles of medical research from the laboratory to the bedside"—but much of the magic was gone. The president had merely accepted the political reality; Congress would not create a network of federal hospitals that would be open to the general public. But there was no way to put a pleasant face on defeat. Nor could he deny the charges in the *Chicago Daily News*—namely, that medical lobbyists had operated quietly for nine months to cripple the HCS Commission's sweeping national attack on disease and that they had "succeeded dramatically." The administration, giving in to pressure, had helped to "gut" the bill until it was a "mere shadow."[33]

Two months later the president added to the disappointment with his request for reductions in the 1967 budget. In order to support increases for defense and for the cost of Vietnam, there would be less for the NIH, health-manpower training, and the regional medical complexes. When the news leaked to the press, letters and telegrams from more than three hundred health advocates (among whom were his friend Senator Lister Hill; his cardiologist, Dr. Willis Hurst; and his family physician, Dr. James Cain) pleaded with him to reconsider the budget cuts. A damning complaint appeared publicly on January 2 in the *New York Times* and, surprisingly, from Dr. Howard Rusk, who only months before had served as LBJ's special envoy to study health problems in Vietnam. The doctor could sympathize and understand the president's dilemma, with his dual commitments to the defense of freedom and the Great Society, but he could not accept LBJ's attack on health, a common denominator of both: "It is inconceivable that President Johnson, who is primarily responsible for the great gains in the attack on death and disease, would give the indiscriminate axe treatment to the budget that is necessary for this continuing crusade."[34]

On December 21, Mary Lasker and Michael DeBakey went to the White House to complain to Douglass Cater about the RMP. They told him that the reductions (from $90 to $45 million) and the elimination of $90 million for the construction of health-research facilities would be disastrous. Two days later, DeBakey sent a powerful and impassioned 15-page telegram to the LBJ Ranch. After voicing initial praise for Johnson's bold and imaginative program to launch the nation into "a new era of action," DeBakey denounced the proposed cuts. They could shake the confidence of the people and the scientists in the administration's commitment to health, they could harm the national defense, and they would virtually destroy the RMP, which had already been gravely compromised by the sacrifice of construction funds. "Should these prospective limitations indeed come to be," he bemoaned, "it would be difficult to discern the sense of attempting to initiate this critical venture."[35]

The president's friends, who were now his critics, felt abandoned. They perceived him as having moved away from his earlier all-out support, and they sensed that his war abroad was eclipsing theirs at home. They tried to call him back to his earlier commitments: "I applaud the incredible progress in health legislation that your leadership has achieved in the past year," wrote Mary Lasker's sister, Alice Fordyce. "Won't you please make it possible to implement the high hopes you have stirred?" But the president did not waver; he was listening, instead, to his budget chiefs. In their view, the RMP had the potential for a far-reaching impact on American life; but it was also an excellent illustration of the kind of newly authorized program they should "phase in slowly." As of early 1966, the Bureau of the Budget (BOB) argued, medical groups were still in conflict and "maneuvering for power"; the NIH had not set forth the appropriate regulations; the Advisory Council had met only once; the chief of the program would not be at work until February; and the NIH likely could not make a grant until May. It was a time for deliberate caution in spending, and the $40 million was "a pretty good allowance."[36]

The president did not reply to most of his critics, but politics required a response to a five-page letter from John Fogarty. The old warrior for health waited until his subcommittee had finished its hearings on the budget, and then he told the president that the administration's budget would "fall far short." It could not meet the challenges "outlined so eloquently in your three Health Messages and in the truly historic health legislation which provides the blueprint for an unprecedented war upon disease." Fogarty was more specific: he wanted additional funds for the regional medical centers, without which there could be no all-out attack on heart disease, cancer, and strokes; and he wanted additional funds for a task force on breast cancer, for a heart drug study, and for the artificial heart. He reminded the president of the latter's promise "to speed the miracles of medical research from the laboratory to the bedside"; and he observed that the proposed budget "does not provide for many miracles." The president sent a letter prepared by BOB (with copies to Lasker, DeBakey, Cain, and Hurst), which defended the "slower rate of advance" as being necessary in order to meet "our international commitments" and to press forward confidently with the Great Society.[37]

The Regional Medical Program limped along after the spring of 1966. Congress did not add to its appropriations, and, more important, the "Mike DeBakey pressure" failed to convince the medical profession or the BOB of the need for construction funds. As the months passed, no one could challenge what one observer called "a short fall in terms of the aspirations" regarding it. "Because the law and the idea behind it are new, and the problem is so vast," the president explained to Congress in November, 1967, "the program is just emerging from the planning stage." A few months later, in his special message "Health in America," he was more specific: fifty-four regions, spanning the nation, had begun planning, but only eight had action programs. The gap between the high expectations and the lack of accomplishment was stunning. Four years before, Mary Lasker had hoped for a massive assault on heart disease, cancer, and strokes; by 1968 the bureaucracy had been able to spend only $90 million of the $340 million that Congress had authorized. Three years before, Michael DeBakey had submitted a blueprint for a system of federal complexes; in 1968 there were only eight cooperative arrangements. The president was alert to the developments. When Congress approved a two-year extension of the RMP in the fall of 1968, he ignored it. There would be no special signing ceremony and no words of hope. Three years before, in announcing the program, he had aspired for miracles; now he accepted the mundane—notwithstanding the RMP, the great killers remained abroad in the land, stubborn and unyielding.[38]

In recognizing the realities, the president did not abandon the war against disease; he merely extended the timetable for victory. In October, 1968, while celebrating the twentieth anniversary of the National Heart Institute, he conceded that the murderous disease was not ready for "a knockout blow." He asked his audience to pledge themselves to be "missionaries of progress in health legislation" for the next twenty years. "If you do these things I have no doubt that when we meet again in the East Room, God willing, twenty years from now, we will have an even happier birthday celebration," he predicted. "On that day, I believe we can boast not only to have slowed down the killers . . . but we can brag that we have banished them and all the fear and the waste and the tragedy that went along with it is no longer with us." Always the optimist, he would not give up on the miracles of modern medicine. He was hopeful, too, because of another of his initiatives.[39]

"Results Are Better"

Shortly after leaving office as secretary of HEW, Wilbur Cohen was reminiscing about how things "got done" in the Johnson administration. He mentioned four individuals who, in order of importance, were more influential with the president than almost any others—Lady Bird Johnson, Mary Lasker, Mathilde Krim, and Florence Mahoney. "I was more successful in working through these four women," Cohen recalled, "than I was with the White House staff." The president sought their advice, but sometimes he got "sick and tired" of their pressure: "Oh, you're getting all these women to talk to me, and they're talking and talking and talking. And look, Wilbur, they don't know what they're talking about." Lyndon Johnson's ambivalent moods—from inviting advice to fuming about it—were especially evident with Mary Lasker. "Several times the President indignantly said to me," Cohen remembered, " 'I wish Mrs. Lasker wouldn't try to interfere and pressure me to do this and do that,' but I'm quite sure that if Mrs. Lasker didn't do it for about a week he'd probably call her up and say, 'Where have you been? Why haven't you been telling me what you think?' "[40]

Rarely did Mary Lasker wait for a telephone call to offer advice. She had extraordinary access to the White House by virtue of the respect that Lyndon Johnson accorded to her as an expert on health, the appreciation that the first lady felt for her help on beautification, and the friendship of both. Mary Lasker consulted many times with the president alone or in small groups; she was present at dozens of parties and ceremonies; she was on occasions an overnight guest at the White House and at the ranch; and she opened her home in New York to the Johnson family. The relationship was mutually beneficial. She gave the president the Lasker Award, and he gave her the Medal of Freedom. He supported her proposals, and she praised his accomplishments. Their friendship survived the strains of the policy process. "The greatest joy of passing years is that friendships, too, grow older," the president wrote to her in 1968. "Happiness in life is measured by many things—but friends like you are foremost on the list."[41]

Johnson relied on several experts on health—notably, Wilbur Cohen; oftentimes, Douglass Cater; on particular issues, Michael DeBakey; and sometimes, specialists in BOB and HEW. Mary Lasker had a singular role; she became the "spark plug" for health with the president, and as a mutual friend saw it, she "prodded him a lot." On no occasion was she more persistent and the final results more unsettling than when she induced the president to involve himself, deeply and personally, in her struggle to obtain more practical benefits from the biomedical scientists. Through that partnership he aligned himself against his NIH-HEW bureaucracy, and he challenged the bias of the larger scientific community. One research cardiologist, Julius H. Comroe, Jr., was so shocked that he spent the rest of his life in a quest to discover "whether President Johnson was correct when he implied in 1966 that we then knew all we needed to know and that all we had to do was apply it." Shortly before his death in 1984 the scientist concluded that there was "no real basis for the President's view" and that the government cannot "order up specific medical discoveries on a specific schedule as one would order up a McDonald's hamburger or even as one would plan for the takeoff of a space shuttle." Thus did the elite get its historical revenge against a practical-minded president; they created the image of a man who was beyond his depth in matters of the mind.[42]

For years, as she sought ever-increasing budgets for medical research, Mary Lasker tried, through congressional allies, to force the NIH to place more emphasis on "breakthroughs" to bring immediate health benefits. In particular, she wanted task forces to study specific forms of cancer, and she wanted clinical trials to find a drug to control cholesterol. "I am depending upon you," she wrote to Congressman Fogarty about drug trials in 1962, "I am really desperate about it, and people's lives are being lost because of the lack of information on what these drugs will do." Even though she convinced Fogarty and Hill to appropriate the funds, she could not move James Shannon, who disliked any peripheral and expensive enterprise that might detract from his primary devotion to basic research. Her failure to move the NIH was the primary motive in her desire for a presidential commission. Indeed, in her one appearance before the President's Commission on Heart Disease, Cancer and Strokes (HCS Commission)—a dramatic Sunday-evening session in the Governor's Room at the New York Hospital—she expressed concern about what "you do for people who are already very arteriosclerotic, to prevent the ravages of it." She presented her case through the testimony of two supporters, Dr. Jessie Marmorston of the University of Southern California, who had spent a decade experimenting with female hormones to control cholesterol, and Dr. Jeremiah Stamler of Northwestern University, who was renowned for his work in preventive medicine and who wanted the NIH to "proceed with speed" on a national cooperative test of antiatherosclerotic drugs.[43]

Shannon, a devotee of pure science, was a powerful opponent. He intended for the NIH to focus its efforts on a broad program in the investigation of life processes, rather than on a search for the direct cure or prevention of a specific disease. In his appearance before the commission, he deplored the work of "conventional scientists therapeutically oriented," who wanted quick answers for small parts of the problem, rather than the pursuit of the fundamental problem of the "vessel wall." When a colleague pointed out that a diet study that would take care of 20 percent of the coronary disease problem could save about one hundred thousand lives a year, he replied: "I might say that I don't take figures very seriously because everybody has to die of something. . . . And before you go further, I do not say it is unimportant to save 20% of the coronaries, but I use this as an example of group emphasis in the field at the amelioration of the condition rather than causation." Even if a drug could modify a disease, it would not answer the ultimate questions.[44]

The HCS Commission surprisingly gave little satisfaction to Mary Lasker. Its report ignored the need for task forces, made only passing reference to the importance of clinical field trials of drugs, and had an astonishing omission—it never mentioned the word *cholesterol.* She tried to influence the RMP legislation by asking Senator Hill to include task forces when the bill went to conference. "Without such specific aims," she wrote to Hill, "the Centers may not get organized with sufficient focus and on a large enough scale to bring us the information to save people's lives in the next few years." When the House ignored the Senate bill, she sent Cater a statement for the president to incorporate in his speech upon signing the bill, or even for use in an executive order. It would have had him get tough: "It is, therefore, the policy of this Administration to urge the spending of at least 15% of these Institutes' budgets for clinical trials. It is my policy to make these diseases targets for intensive task force clinical and basic research efforts in order to prolong the prime of life of our people." Again Mary Lasker lost. The experts in HEW deemed it unwise to make a flat 15 percent commitment, and the president made no mention of task forces or clinical trials.[45]

It was not until early 1966 that Mary Lasker went to work on the president again. In reply to his Christmas greeting, she sent a powerful New Year's message from her farm in upstate New York, in which she set forth her dream of a decade:

> New eras in saving of lives through medical research can be started if you go ahead with present plans of 1965. The average age can be brought to 75 in your administration, before 1972, if you will call the directors of the National Institutes of Health to give you *specific plans* to put ideas now at hand to the test, in clinical trials with patients, on a large scale. Some funds now being used in other ways could be diverted to this if you will ask for plans to *reduce the death rate;* and *prolong* the prime of life. Doctors must be told this is *urgent* by *you.*

For the next six months, during which time the president held to his budget cuts and accepted the Lasker Award, nothing happened. But Mary Lasker was persistent. At the President's Club Ball at the Waldorf

Astoria Hotel on June 11, she sat at LBJ's table and, during the evening, urged him again to meet with the NIH directors and to ask them to review their plans for reducing death and disability during his administration. She followed up with her usual detailed memorandum, and she won a convert.[46]

On June 15, at an East Room gathering with several hundred medical and hospital leaders, called solely and specifically to arrange for the launching of Medicare, the president dropped a bombshell. He would soon call a meeting of the secretary of HEW, the surgeon general, the director of NIH, and the directors of nine institutes ("I want to serve notice on Secretary Gardner publicly because I don't want to give him a chance to object privately"), so that "in the days ahead we can put as much effort into prolonging the prime of man's life as we are in extending our knowledge of outer space." The president wanted to hear "what plans if any, they have for reducing deaths and for reducing disabilities and for extending research in that direction." He was not primarily interested in basic research; he had been supporting those appropriations for years. "But I think the time has now come to zero in on the targets by trying to get this knowledge fully applied." Until we spend more money on clinical research to test new drugs and treatments, "we won't have any major new ways of reducing deaths and disabilities."[47]

This was no timid commander in chief, content to leave the strategy of his war to the experts in the field. Presidents, he declared, need to show more interest in the specific results of medical research during their lifetimes, during their administrations. He would do so: "Whether we get any or not I am going to show an interest in them." He would watch the NIH scientists and bureaucrats, and he would return in several months with his "checksheet" to see just what they had accomplished, "like when you take a car in to get it filled with— the tires filled and the radiator checked and all those things—we will go down their checklist and we will see what specific efforts they are going to make to reduce deaths among the leading killers, especially arteriosclerosis of the heart and brain, and various forms of cancer, and to reduce disabilities such as arthritis and severe mental and neurological diseases or illness." Then, for whatever time was allotted to him in the White House, he would come back about every six months to ensure that the scientists were investing their funds as wisely as possible to "prolong the prime of life for all of our people." With a president showing such sympathy, interest, and leadership, "we will be able to get more results for the survival of our people than anyone else has ever done in the history of mankind. Think about what a laudable objective that is."[48]

In less than two weeks, armed with an agenda that had been prepared by Cater, Lasker, and Gorman, the president held his first meeting with the NIH. He called the twenty medical doctors and five administrators to the Cabinet Room, named them his "health strategy council" in the war against disease, asked for their help, and outlined his concerns: the life expectancy of the average American was not increasing, the child mortality rate was higher than in many other countries, and the killing and crippling diseases continued to take their heavy toll. The solution, he told them, was not simply more money; it was also a better selection of priorities. They were already spending more than $800 million a year, and he was "keenly interested to learn not only what knowledge this buys but what are the payoffs in terms of healthy lives for our citizens." Then, with words that were sure to provoke and that soon sent shock waves throughout the scientific community, he continued: "Some of my friends tell me that too little effort is going into clinical research to test new drugs and new treatments. They say there is too much love of research simply for the sake of research. In my judgment, *research* is *good*, but *results* are better."[49]

The president pressed his point with a series of tendentious questions that had been written by Mary Lasker and were aimed at each of the directors. He forced Dr. Kenneth Endicott to admit that technical problems had delayed the creation of task forces for research on solid tumors, and he forced Dr. Robert Grant to concede that his National Heart Institute was spending only 4.5 percent of its budget for drug studies, a proportion that the president observed was rather small. Only Dr. Shannon fought back. He insisted that drug studies to lower blood fats, no matter how successful they might be, would "contribute nothing to the prevention of heart disease." But the president had the last word through the official statement issued at the end of the meeting. "We began a review of the targets and the timetable they have set for winning victories in the war," he told the American people. "We must make sure that no life-giving discovery is locked up in the laboratory."[50]

The president's meeting evoked intense reactions. Dr. Shannon admitted that it "was surely an historical event," but he was angry, so he went to work on a report to show that there was already a balance between basic and targeted research within the NIH. Scientists in all fields were stunned; they considered that basic research was synonymous with prestige and freedom, in contrast to the less rarefied and highly directed area of applied research. They could respond only with shock to the politician with his practicality, the mechanic with his checksheet. And only a fool could believe that numerous discoveries of importance to health were hidden away in some laboratory. Scientists reacted so negatively that the administration, sensitive to the outcry, wondered at first if the NIH was organizing the protest and then, as if in retreat, sent forth Secretary Gardner to soothe the ruffled feathers. Only Mary Lasker was content, and excited. The president had sanctioned her strategic design; now she would provide the tactics. In October she and other members of the National Advisory Cancer Council sent their chief an "ideal" budget, with an increase of $41 million, to support a series of new task forces to attack the most common forms of cancer and thus speed up the progress years sooner than would be possible through individual efforts.[51]

Two months passed, and Lasker, seeing no action, sought an audience with her friend. "I want to avoid this if I can," the president told his staff. "I'll have to see her if she just has to, but I much prefer that she give me a memo. See if Bird can't handle it. I'll be busy with other things." Mary Lasker was not content to talk with Gardner or Cater; she insisted on conveying her ideas directly to the president, if only for ten minutes. It was a measure of her influence that the president relented, and on December 14 she assured him that an intensified attack was feasible and that it would come about much more quickly if he directed it be done. She even provided a draft letter to the surgeon general for Johnson's signature. "I direct the National Cancer Institute to establish Task Forces in lung cancer, cancer of the intestines and colon, cancer of the uterus and ovary, cancer of the stomach and cancer of the prostate, which annually cause over 142,000 deaths, and in other major types of cancer." She followed the meeting with a letter two days after Christmas: the task forces would be a benefaction to "change the average length of life of mankind" from a president who was "deeply sympathetic" to "people's suffering." Her persistence finally paid off. Johnson, in his health message to Congress in February, directed John Gardner to appoint immediately a Lung Cancer Task Force.[52]

In May, 1967, Mary Lasker was at the White House again, accompanied by Lister Hill, to suggest a replacement for James Shannon, who would reach compulsory retirement age in the summer of 1968. She wanted a successor who would be publicly committed to translating the results of research into health benefits. To accentuate her concern, she proposed that the president meet a second time with the NIH to review their progress. She stayed afterwards to tell him privately about a new drug—Atromid-S—for which Shannon had delayed trials for six years but which might lower cholesterol and might be a breakthrough in dealing with heart disease. She wanted LBJ's physician to consider it.[53]

Unbeknownst to Mary Lasker, her timing was ill-fated. There were different forces at work in the White House. John Gardner and his highly respected assistant secretary, Dr. Philip Lee, had already approached Cater about another meeting, one in which they wanted the president to express strong support for basic research, praise the contributions of the universities and their medical schools, and pay tribute to the leadership of Dr. Shannon. Their conviction echoed that of Donald F. Hornig, the president's science adviser, who wanted to combat the "unhappy feeling" and "deep suspicion" among scientists, which was based upon the 1966 meeting and budget restrictions, that the administration was suppressing basic research in favor of practical applications. Hornig spoke with the passion of a convert. In 1964 he had advised the president to improve the nation's health through the application of existing data and techniques; by 1967 he had come to believe the "treatment of disease is limited by a lack of basic knowledge."[54]

Douglass Cater, who had been one of Mary Lasker's foremost allies, decided to quell the political fallout through another presidential meeting with the NIH. But this time, in setting the agenda, Cater ignored Lasker and Gorman; instead, he consulted with Gardner, Shannon, and Lee. The contrast with 1966 was dramatic. The president flew to Bethesda, accompanied by a host of press and photographers, and made a grand tour of the open-heart-surgery amphitheater, the new computerized laboratory, and a new nuclear medical facility. From there he went to the board room to listen to the directors' progress reports on infant mortality (the most significant drop in ten years occurred in 1966); on heart disease (the nation was about to see the first leveling off in mortality in its history); on cancer (prevention is no idle dream); and on blindness (further advances were under way with the establishment of eleven clinical centers for eye research).[55]

In the auditorium, flanked by cameras, the president made his peace with the scientific community. He had come this time to renew his commitment to the "world's greatest research enterprise" and to applaud the efforts of its directors; indeed, he elevated them to "Chiefs of Staff" in the war against the ancient enemies. Progress was "going up instead of down," he declared; and departing from his prepared speech, he took issue with the "hotshots" who "think we have reached what you might call a stalemate, because we have not found all the answers to all the questions in all the 365 days since we last ran our check—our final exam." To ensure that no cloud should darken his day of reconciliation, he omitted from his prepared speech any potentially provocative comments about the need for the "swift application of knowledge" and the formation of the long-delayed Task Force on Lung Cancer. In final obeisance he gave basic research a "first and foremost" position in a healthy society. "Because we are human, we explore; we seek to understand the deepest mysteries of our world," he told the practitioners of pure science. "The government supports this creative exploration because we believe that all knowledge is precious; because we know that all progress would halt without it." And twice he told them, in words that would thunder across the nation, that the NIH was "a billion dollar success story."[56]

The meeting at Bethesda had several effects. It mollified the NIH. Before the president left, a friendly Dr. Shannon presented LBJ with some sun-tan lotion and with the report that had been requested a year before, a 200-page volume entitled *The Advancement of Knowledge for the Nation's Health*, which could only elicit praise for the research programs. But the rapprochement did not extend to the scientific community. A September poll in *Science* reported diminished support for the president, because of the war in Vietnam, among the "Scientists and Engineers for Johnson" of 1964. "The fact that the President has passed more legislation and given more realistic support for science and education than any other President," Michael DeBakey complained, "is apparently completely disregarded by some of these scientists and engineers." He considered their lack of appreciation "unforgiveable," but there was no changing it.[57]

The president's foray into the field of biomedical policy did not earn him plaudits, then or later. In a seminal article in the *Atlantic Monthly* at the end of 1967, journalist Elizabeth Drew portrayed him as the victim of a "do-gooder" who was "too covetous of power, too insistent on her own pursuits, too confident of her own expertise in the minutiae of medicine," and who led him into "distortions" of health policy. Reflecting the bias of James Shannon and the NIH, the journalist found fault with the HCS Commission, the cancer chemotherapy program, the field trials of drugs, and above all, the idea to push for "payoffs" from research. The latter was too complex a problem to be "decided on the basis of who has the President's ear," and it damaged the chief executive by causing scientists to see him as "an anti-intellectual, unsophisticated president who could never understand such things."[58]

Experts in the politics of science have cited Drew as their primary source in evaluating the Johnson administration, although with differing degrees of emphasis. Paul Starr, for example, repeats Drew's strictures against Mary Lasker—and, by implication, the president—almost verbatim. Sociologist James Katz, in the best of the policy studies, accords Johnson a more aggressive role as the chief policy maker and describes his pro-Lasker bias toward practical results and his "dressing down" of the NIH as parts of LBJ's broader desire to bring biomedical science under executive control. Katz's portrait is nonetheless negative: a populist president who possessed little understanding of the world of science and who, lacking the sympathy and understanding of Eisenhower and Kennedy, "completely ruptured" the intimate relationship that had existed between scientists and government since World War II. Julius Comroe, Jr., writing from the perspective of the scientists and after having made a seventeen-year study of innovation in research, could not forgive the president for having made "unreasonable" billion-dollar decisions on the basis of "personal opinions or prejudices, gut reactions, pressure from special interest groups, and a few fascinating, convincingly spun anecdotes."[59]

On this issue, President Johnson has had consistently unfair evaluations. He was not an unschooled pragmatist who was opposed to pure science and who had been misled by a dilettante into meddling with the experts. He continued to support fundamental scientific research even when he was pushing for practical results. And although there can be no certainty as to the proper balance between targeted and basic research, he and Mary Lasker were almost surely correct in pressuring the NIH to conduct trials of heart drugs and to establish task forces for cancer. The Coronary Drug Project, which got under way in 1967, tested four lipid-influencing drugs; eight years later it concluded that none of them was effective. But in 1972 the National Heart Institute began a randomized double-blind study of a potent cholesterol-lowering drug, cholestyramine, and in 1984 it issued a landmark report, which demonstrated conclusively that lowering cholesterol could reduce coronary heart disease and thereby promised a reduced risk for tens of millions of Americans.[60]

There has been no equally startling result for cancer, but the current optimism of the National Cancer Institute gives new meaning to the words of Dr. Kenneth Endicott, its director in 1967. Endicott, who was slow in getting started on the president's order to establish the Lung Cancer Task Force, promised to have a substantial program ready by 1969. "I think we should probably emulate the Manhattan Project and simultaneously explore the various perceived alternatives," he wrote, "in the hope of emerging with a definitive answer in a period of twenty years instead of having the thing drag on for fifty." His acknowledgment that a greater effort might bring earlier results was a tribute, albeit private, to the president and to Mary Lasker. A breakthrough in less than fifty years would be their testimonial.[61]

"Pretty Visionary"

In 1966, when presenting John Fogarty with the Heart-of-the-Year Award, President Johnson remarked that some people considered him to be "pretty visionary," and he admitted, "We cannot conquer all disease" and "We cannot educate all humanity." But his philosophy of progress demanded that "we can hope for them and we can work for them and we can give what we have to them, and we can urge them and provide leadership and try to move along." For five years the president served as an indefatigable booster to conquer disease and "move along" the nation's health. He made his case not only through his presidential commission but also with the White House Conference, numerous task forces, five special health messages, and more than fifty relevant statements and signing ceremonies. Over and over again he stressed the basic themes. His generation of Americans had arrived at a historic moment of challenge and opportunity. If they had the will and would make a commitment, they could revolutionize their way of living. The war on disease would call a halt to the wholesale murder of the past and would extend human life to one hundred years. The effort made sense from a strictly business standpoint, for it would save the nation $32 billion a year; but it was more a matter of necessity, for "the health of our people is, inescapably, the foundation for fulfillment of all our aspirations."[62]

The president's leadership elevated the war against disease to a far-more-permanent position in American life, both for the people and for the government. He admittedly used extravagant rhetoric and promised far more than he could deliver; but this was not necessarily unfortunate. Unrealized expectations have a different effect in areas such as civil rights and health. In the former they can lead to anger and frustration and can even erupt in public violence; in the latter they can lead to disappointment and sadness but can endure as private sorrow. For Johnson, the promise of the miracles of modern medicine was essentially a challenge. If he could raise the expectations of the American people and the scientific community, they would persist in his war. And they did. His years of rhetoric helped set the stage for a renewed effort. Indeed, President Richard Nixon, under the tutelage of the Lasker forces, would have the nation declare a "war on cancer."[63]

One of Johnson's favorite health stories was about his heart attack. "I know what it is to have your blood pressure go to zero and go into shock," he told an audience shortly before leaving office. "I know it well enough that I would like to see the day come when that did not happen to anybody, and if it did . . . that you would have the implements to get the same result that the Good Lord and Lady Bird and Dr. Hurst all working together back in 1955 had." He could not provide such a benign setting, even for himself. In retirement, when his angina returned, there was no drug to control cholesterol and no fully functioning dacron heart. The experts at the Mayo Clinic told him that there was nothing they could do, and Michael DeBakey in Houston explained that his heart was too damaged to risk the newest "miracle," coronary by-pass surgery. In early 1973, racked by sharp pains and with an oxygen tank next to his bed, he moved toward death. But he had left a health legacy that the American people would embrace. In the most humane and compassionate sense, he wanted everyone to have what he could afford, and more.[64]

Notes

1. Jack Valenti to the President, with attached citation "1965 Albert Lasker Award for Leadership in Health," Mar. 10, 1966, diary backup, box 32. All manuscript documents and oral tapes are in the Johnson Library unless otherwise indicated.

2. Lyndon Baines Johnson, *The Vantage Point: Perspectives of the Presidency, 1963–1969* (New York: Holt, Rinehart & Winston, 1971), pp. 213–20.

3. Richard Harris, *A Sacred Trust* (New York: New American Library, 1966), Lawrence F. O'Brien, *No Final Victories* (Garden City, N.Y.: Doubleday, 1974), p. 188; Jack Valenti, *A Very Human President* (New York: Norton, 1976), p. 383; Eric F. Goldman, *The Tragedy of Lyndon Johnson* (New York: Knopf, 1969), pp. 284, 332; William O'Neill, *Coming Apart: An Informal History of America in the 1960's* (New York: Quadrangle Books, 1971), p. 129; Vaughn Davis Bornet, *The Presidency of Lyndon B. Johnson* (Lawrence: University Press of Kansas, 1983), p. 134; Paul Starr, *The Social Transformation of American Medicine* (New York: Basic Books, 1982), p. 376; Allen J. Matusow, *The Unraveling of America: A History of Liberalism in the 1960s* (New York: Harper & Row, 1984), pp. 220–21. The records at the Johnson Library do not contain any major surprises regarding Medicare, and they provide nothing new on the progenesis of Medicaid. They do record the president's remarkable effort to integrate the nation's hospitals

through Medicare, and they document his attentiveness to every aspect of the program.

4. Theodore R. Marmor and James A. Morone, "The Health Programs of the Kennedy-Johnson Years: An Overview," in *Toward New Human Rights: The Social Policies of the Kennedy and Johnson Administrations*, ed. David C. Warner (Austin, Texas: LBJ School of Public Affairs, 1977), pp. 157–82; Starr, *Social Transformation*, p. 370.

5. Two documents are valuable for a general appraisal of the achievements of the Johnson administration: Wilbur J. Cohen, "Health, Education and Welfare Accomplishments 1963–1968, Problems and Challenges, and a Look to the Future," White House central files (hereafter cited as WHCF), FG 165, box 242; and National Health Education Committee, *What Are the Pay-offs from Our Federal Health Programs: A Progress Report on the Johnson Administration—1963 to 1968* (New York: National Health Education Committee, 1968), WHCF, Douglass Cater files, box 68.

6. Harry McPherson, *A Political Education* (Boston, Mass.: Little, Brown, 1972), p. 250.

7. Wilbur Cohen to James Shannon, Aug. 2, 1965, NIH microfilm records, roll 1; *Public Papers of the Presidents: Lyndon B. Johnson, 1965*, 2 vols. (Washington, D.C.: Government Printing Office, 1966), 2:844–47.

8. Brian McMahon to President Truman, Aug. 9, 1945, official file, box 466, Truman Library, Independence, Mo.; *Time*, Aug. 30, 1948, p. 41; U.S., House of Representatives, Committee on Interstate and Foreign Commerce, *Hearings* on H.R. 3059, 80th Cong., 2d sess., May 5–6, 1948, p. 98. The early activities of Albert and Mary Lasker are discussed by John Gunther in *Taken at the Flood: The Story of Albert D. Lasker* (New York: Harper, 1960); Elmer Bobst, *Bobst: The Autobiography of a Pharmaceutical Pioneer* (New York: McKay, 1973); and "Fanning the Fire," *Time*, Aug. 30, 1948, pp. 40–41.

9. Stephen P. Strickland, in *Politics, Science, and Dread Disease: A Short History of the United States Medical Research Policy* (Cambridge, Mass.: Harvard University Press, 1972), gives a solid account of the politics of the crusade against disease, especially for the 1940s and 1950s. His analysis of the role of Congress is excellent, but his coverage of the presidents, especially Kennedy and Johnson, is weak, reflecting his lack of access to the presidential libraries.

10. U.S., House of Representatives, Subcommittee of the Committee on Appropriations, *Hearings* on Departments of Labor and H.E.W., 83d Cong., 2d sess., Apr. 8, 1954, p. 323; "Moving Force in Medical Research," *Medical World News*, Nov. 20, 1964, pp. 83–89; William L. Laurence, "Four Great Medical Triumphs Just Ahead," *Collier's*, June 8, 1956, pp. 25–27.

11. London Johnson to Mrs. Lamar E. Miles, Aug. 28, 1959, Senate subject files, box 676, 1959; Lyndon Johnson to Mrs. Gordon Smith, May 28, 1959, ibid.; Anna M. Rosenberg to Lyndon Johnson, Aug. 26, 1948, LBJ-A file, box 8; notes on legislative leadership meeting, July 7, 1959, Ann Whitman files, box 3, Eisenhower Library, Abilene, Kans.; Mary Lasker to Lyndon Johnson, June 16, 1959, LBJ-A file, box 6.

12. Lyndon Johnson, "Medical Research Pays Big Dividends to Our People and to Our Economy," Senate speech, June 24, 1959, President's Commission on Heart Disease, Cancer and Strokes (hereafter cited as HCS), box 21; Lyndon Johnson to Mary Lasker, June 24, 1959, LBJ-A file, box 6.

13. Abraham Ribicoff to Frederick Dutton, "Proposed President's Conference on Heart Disease and Cancer, " Mar. 3, 1961, WHCF, box 338, Kennedy Library, Boston.

14. For the formation of the Conference see Boisfeuillet Jones to Frederick Dutton, Mar. 10, 1961, WHCF, box 338, Kennedy Library. "Report of the President's Conference on Heart Disease and Cancer," Apr. 21, 1961, HCS, box 18. For the presidential commission see Luther L. Terry to Wilbur Cohen, "Proposed President's Commission on Cancer, Heart Disease and Strokes," Aug. 1, 1963, HCS, box 1.

15. The index to the Daily Diary, at the Johnson Library, reveals the close association between Mary Lasker and the Johnsons. *Public Papers, 1965*, 2:1044.

16. National Health Education Committee, "Does Medical Research Pay Off?" WHCF, Douglass Cater files, box 68, 1964, p. 54; David O. Selznick to Eric Goldman, Feb. 4, 1964, WHCF, Health files, box 7.

17. Lady Bird Johnson, *A White House Diary* (New York: Holt, Rinehart & Winston, 1970), pp. 173, 316-17; Douglass Cater to the President, Jan. 31, 1966, WHCF, Cater files, box 14.

18. A draft of the president's speech is in box 44 (1310) of the Horace Busby files in WHCF; *Public Papers, 1963-1964*, 1:478-79.

19. Michael DeBakey oral history, tape 1, p. 34; minutes of the first planning meeting for the President's Commission, Mar. 20, 1964, and Myer Feldman, Opening Statement, Proceedings of Commission, Apr. 17, 1964, HCS, box 20; Stephen Ackerman to Michael DeBakey, no date, HCS, box 1; minutes of the meeting of the Executive Committee, President's Commission, Apr. 16, 1964, p. 51, HCS, box 24.

20. The library has fifty-three boxes of records of the President's Commission. For a review of activities see "Progress Material" on President's Commission, Sept. 10, 1964, attached to Lea Martin to Abraham Lilienfeld, Sept. 10, 1964, HCS, box 3. The citation is in Emerson Foote to Dr. Abraham M. Lilienfeld, May 29, 1964, HCS, box 1.

21. Minutes of the meeting of the Executive Committee, President's Commission, Nov. 4, 1964, HCS, box 23, pp. 200, 214-15.

22. President's Commission on Heart Disease, Cancer and Stroke, Report to the President: A National Program to Conquer Heart Disease, Cancer and Stroke (Washington, D.C.: Government Printing Office, 1964), vol. 1, esp. pp. xii, 1-69.

23. Ibid.; *New York Times*, Dec. 10, 1984.

24. Dr. Irvine Page, cited in the U.S., House of Representatives, Committee on Interstate and Foreign Commerce, *Hearings* on H.R. 3140, 89th Cong., 1st sess., July 20-30, 1965, p. 221. The newspapers and journal cited— *Boston Globe*, Dec. 10, 1964, *Washington Daily News*, Dec. 9, 1964, *Wall Street Journal*, Dec. 10, 1964, *New York Herald Tribune*, Dec. 10, 1964, and the *New England Journal of Medicine*, Feb. 18, 1965—are in a collection attached to Stephen J. Ackerman to Douglass Cater, Apr. 2, 1965, WHCF, FG 645, box 378.

25. *Public Papers, 1963-1964*, 2:1650-51; *Public Papers, 1965*, 1:12-21; U.S., Senate, Subcommittee on Health of the Committee on Labor and Public Welfare, *Hearings* on S. 596, 89th Cong., 1st sess., Feb. 9, 1965, pp. 1-12.

26. Lady Bird Johnson, *White House Diary*, p. 326; U.S., Senate, Subcommittee on Health, *Hearings* on S. 596, Feb. 9, 1965, pp. 35–36.

27. Donald Hornig to Bill Moyers, Jan. 18, 1965, Hornig Papers; Edward W. Dempsey to Douglass Cater and attached "Answers to Bureau of the Budget Jan. 19, 1965 Questions for H.E.W. Regarding Proposed Bill, Authorizing Regional Medical Complexes," Feb. 4, 1965, WHCF, EX F14/FG 165, box 28; *Washington Post*, Dec. 13, 1964; *New York Herald Tribune*, Apr. 28, 1965; *Houston Chronicle*, Apr. 23, 1965.

28. U.S., House of Representatives, *Hearings* on H.R. 3140, pp. 216–19; Dr. Robert O. Emmett to Senator Russell B. Long, Aug. 18, 1965, HCS, box 44.

29. Robert N. Hills to Wilbur Cohen, Aug. 2, 1965, and Henry Wilson to Jean Lewis, Aug. 23, 1965, WHCF, Henry Wilson Papers, box 8; Larry O'Brien to the President, Aug. 9, 1965, WHCF, LE/Health Papers, box 58; *Public Papers, 1965*, 2:892–93.

30. James Appel to Douglass Cater, Aug. 25, 1965, WHCF, Cater files, box 65; Cater to the President (with handwritten note on bottom), Aug. 26, 1965, WHCF, LE/Health Papers, box 58.

31. Douglass Cater to the President and attached notes of Wilbur Cohen concerning meeting with the AMA, Aug. 30, 1965, WHCF, Cater files, box 14; Wilbur Cohen oral history, tape 4, pp. 22–24; Dr. Philip R. Lee oral history, tape 1, pp. 12–13, 21–22.

32. The text of the bill and an analysis of the adjustments to the original legislation are in U.S., House of Representatives, Committee on Interstate and Foreign Commerce, *Report No. 933* on H.R. 3140, 89th Cong., 1st sess., Sept. 8, 1965, pp. 1–5, 7–12, 23–25.

33. *Public Papers, 1965*, 2:1044–46; Douglass Cater to the President, Sept. 21, 1965, and attached article, *Chicago Daily News*, Sept. 17, 1965, WHCF, Cater files, box 14.

34. The letters and telegrams in response to the president's decision are in WHCF, GEN F1 4/FG 165, box 34; *New York Times*, Jan. 2, 1966.

35. Douglass Cater to the President, Dec. 21, 1965, WHCF, Mary Lasker name file, box 69; Michael DeBakey to President Johnson, Dec. 23, 1965, box 57a, Lister Hill Papers, University of Alabama, Birmingham.

36. Alice Fordyce to President Johnson, Dec. 10, 1965, WHCF, F1 4/FG 165, box 34; Sam Hughes to Joseph Califano, Dec. 28, 1965, WHCF, EX F1 4/FG 165, box 28.

37. John Fogarty to President Johnson, Mar. 15, 1966, WHCF, EX F1 4/FG 165, WHCF, box 28; Lyndon Johnson to John Fogarty, Apr. 25, 1966, attachment to Harry H. Wilson, Jr., to Mary Lasker, Apr. 26, 1966, WHCF, Mary Lasker name file, box 69.

38. Irving Lewis to Douglass Cater, Feb. 9, 1967, WHCF, Health papers; Irving Lewis to James Gaither, Sept. 11, 1967, WHCF, Gaither files, box 191; Lyndon Johnson to John McCormack, Nov. 8, 1967, WHCF, Health 1, box 7; *Public Papers, 1968*, 1:328.

39. *Public Papers, 1968*, 2:1124–25.

40. Wilbur Cohen oral history, tape 3, p. 31, and tape 4, pp. 3–4.

41. Lyndon Johnson to Mary Lasker, Aug. 28, 1968, WHCF, Health files, box 3.

42. Anna Rosenberg Hoffman oral history, tape 2, pp. 6–7; Julius H. Comroe, Jr., *Exploring the Heart: Discoveries in Heart Disease and High Blood Pressure* (New York: Norton, 1984), pp. 20, 319, 324.**

43. Mary Lasker to John Fogarty, July 20, 1964, F4, box B2, John Fogarty Papers, Providence College, Providence, R.I. Minutes, Subcommittee on Heart Disease, July 26, 1964, HCS, box 26, pp. 65–67.

44. Minutes, Subcommittee on Heart Disease, May 15, 1964, pp. 9, 31, HCS, box 11.

45. Mary Lasker to Lister Hill, July 26, 1965, box 63, Lister Hill Papers; Mary Lasker to Douglass Cater and attached suggested statement for the President, Sept. 10, 1965, and Wilbur Cohen to Douglass Cater, Sept. 24, 1965, WHCF, Health papers, box 61.

46. Mary Lasker to President Johnson, Jan. 4 and 14, 1966, WHCF, Mary Lasker name file, box 69.

47. *Public Papers, 1966*, 1:605, 609–10.

48. Ibid., 1:609–10.

49. Douglass Cater to the President, Jun. 20, 1966, and Douglass Cater to the President, with attached "Talking Points for Meeting with NIH Directors" and "Questions for President at Meeting of NIH Directors on Rapid Application of Research Knowledge," Jun. 25, 1966, WHCF, Cater files, box 15.

50. Ibid.; Irving Lewis to Douglass Cater, July 14, 1966, and attached "Resume of the Meeting with the President and Federal Health and Medical Officials," WHCF, FG 165-6, box 249; *Public Papers, 1966*, 1:652–53.

51. James Shannon to John Gardner, July 13, 1966, and Irving Lewis to Douglass Cater, July 28 and Aug. 10, 1966, WHCF, FG 165-6, box 249; Mary Lasker to President Johnson, Oct. 11, 1966, attached to Mary Lasker to Douglass Cater, Dec. 27, 1966, WHCF, Cater files, box 18.

52. Marvin Watson to the President, with LBJ note attached, Dec. 3, 1966, and Marvin Watson to the President, Dec. 11, 1966, WHCF, Mary Lasker name file, box 67; Mary Lasker to Douglass Cater, Dec. 27, 1966, and attachment "Need for More Task Forces in the Major Types of Cancer," WHCF, Cater files, box 18; Mary Lasker to the President, Dec. 27, 1966, WHCF, Health papers, box 7; *Public Papers, 1967*, 1:253.

53. Juanita Roberts to Marvin Watson, May 8, 1967, Diary Backup, box 65; Douglass Cater to the President, May 17 and 18, 1967, WHCF, Cater files, box 16; Dr. Philip Lee to Douglass Cater, and attached "Memorandum Recommending Atromid Drug Trial," May 24, 1967, WHCF, Cater files, box 65.

54. Dr. Philip Lee to Douglass Cater, May 10, 1967, WHCF, Cater files, box 16; Donald Hornig to the Vice President, Apr. 21, 1967, Hornig papers, box 5; Donald Hornig to Douglass Cater, June 20, 1967, WHCF, FG 165-6, box 248.

55. Douglass Cater to the President, July 11 and 19, 1967, WHCF, Cater files, box 16; Sherwin Markham to Marvin Watson, July 20, 1967, Diary Backup, box 71.

56. *Public Papers, 1967*, 2:711–14; Sherwin Markham to Marvin Watson and attached prepared speech, July 20, 1967, and "Summary of Presentations to the President at the National Institutes of Health," July 21, 1967, Diary Backup, box 71.

57. Lyndon Johnson to James Shannon, July 24, 1967, WHCF, FG 165-6, box 249; Elinor Langer, "Scientists and Engineers for LBJ: A War and Three Years Later," *Science*, Sept. 29, 1967, pp. 1533-36; Michael DeBakey to Douglass Cater, Oct. 17, 1967, WHCF, Cater files, box 65.

58. Elizabeth Brenner Drew, "The Health Syndicate: Washington's Noble Conspirators," *Atlantic Monthly*, Dec., 1967, pp. 75-82.

59. Starr, *Social Transformation*, p. 370; James Everett Katz, *Presidential Politics and Science Policy* (New York: Praeger, 1978), pp. 151-52, 160-63, 235; Comroe, *Exploring the Heart*, p. 319.

60. Coronary Drug Project Research Group, "Clofibrate and Niacin in Coronary Heart Disease," *Journal of the American Medical Association*, Jan. 27, 1975, pp. 360-80; *New York Times*, Jan. 13, 1984.

61. Kenneth M. Endicott to James Shannon, Apr. 12, 1967, NIH microfilm records, roll 1.

62. *Public Papers, 1966*, 1:140; *Public Papers, 1965*, 1:12.

63. President Nixon's "War on Cancer" is analyzed by Richard A. Rettig in *Cancer Crusade: The Story of the National Cancer Act of 1971* (Princeton, N.J.: Princeton University Press, 1977).

64. *Public Papers, 1968*, 2:1125; Leo Janos, "The Last Days of the President: LBJ in Retirement," *Atlantic Monthly*, July, 1973, pp. 35-41.

8 | Lyndon B. Johnson and the Politics of Space

Robert A. Divine

ON OCTOBER 4, 1957, THE SOVIET UNION began the space age with the launching of Sputnik, the first man-made satellite to orbit the earth. Lyndon Johnson, who was then serving as Democratic majority leader in the Senate, exploited the sluggish response of the Eisenhower administration to this dramatic breakthrough and thus established his own credentials as the nation's leading political spokesman on the challenge of outer space. From that time on, LBJ's political career would be closely associated with every major policy decision relating to space, from the creation of the National Aeronautic and Space Administration (NASA) to the development of the Apollo program to put men on the moon.

Although nearly all observers agree that Johnson became identified in the public mind with the effort to conquer space, there is considerable controversy over the exact nature of his role. In his memoir *The Vantage Point*, LBJ asserted that from the first moment he learned about Sputnik until Americans landed on the moon in July, 1969, he was personally involved in every aspect of the American space program. Other commentators, notably George Reedy, disagree, claiming that Johnson initially seized on space for political advantage and that he never developed the deep commitment to this issue that he did to civil rights, education, and the war on poverty.[1] In fact, LBJ did develop a strong interest in America's space program, but it came about haltingly and only reached its full potential after he had become president. And even then, the competing demands of the Vietnam War prevented him from doing all that he could to advance the American effort in space.

I

Johnson's initial involvement in space issues reflects the ambiguity that marked his entire approach in this area. He was slow to respond to the opportunity presented by Sputnik, but once he had grasped its potential, he exploited it skillfully to gain maximum political advantage.

LBJ was at his Texas hill-country ranch when the Russians sent up Sputnik on Friday October 4, 1957. In *The Vantage Point*, Johnson claimed that on that very evening he conferred by telephone with aides in Washington, telling them to begin gathering data on the American missile and satellite programs. In a 1969 interview with Walter Cronkite, Johnson recalled having stared up at the sky that once seemed so friendly and now "seemed to have question marks all over it because of this new development" and realizing "that this country of mine might, maybe, perhaps not be ahead in everything."[2] Yet the record indicates that it was his mentor, Senator Richard R. Russell of Georgia, who urged him to take the lead in investigating the American failure to be first in space and that it was George Reedy, his chief Senate political aide, who pointed out the historical and political significance of Sputnik.

At his home in Winder, Georgia, Senator Russell, chairman of the Armed Services Committee, was bombarded with telegrams from other senators who demanded that his committee investigate the American missile program. Senator Stuart Symington of Missouri, who was already a possible Democratic presidential candidate in 1960, wired Russell on October 5, 1957, that he considered Sputnik "proof of growing communist superiority in the all-important missile field" and urged Russell to hold "complete hearings" before the full Armed Services Committee so that "the American people can learn the truth."[3] Symington, a former secretary of the air force in the Truman administration, had long been a critic of the Eisenhower defense program, and Russell apparently feared that Symington would turn Sputnik into a partisan crusade. The Georgia senator had long considered Lyndon Johnson as his protégé, a relationship that LBJ had nurtured, so Russell now decided to let the majority leader frame the Democratic response. As he explained later, "I had more or less turned this whole matter over to Senator Johnson."[4]

At Russell's suggestion, Johnson reactivated the moribund Defense Preparedness Subcommittee of the Senate Armed Services Committee in order to conduct a preliminary inquiry into the American satellite program. On Monday, October 7, Johnson telephoned members of his Senate staff, instructing them to notify the Pentagon of his intent; and on the same day, Russell told Symington and others who were calling for hearings before the full committee that he had authorized Lyndon to have the staff of his subcommittee "look into this matter and assemble all available facts for evaluation."[5]

Over the next ten days, Johnson took full command. At his direction, Preparedness Subcommittee staff members Solis Horwitz and

Gerald Seigel received a preliminary Pentagon briefing on missile and satellite programs and made arrangements for a fuller presentation to Senator Johnson and other key members of the subcommittee in early November. Meanwhile, Johnson flew back to Washington and met with the ranking Republican member of the subcommittee, Senator Styles Bridges of New Hampshire, and assured him that he would not turn the inquiry into a partisan attack on the Eisenhower administration. Johnson made the same point to Secretary of Defense Neil McElroy, telling him that Russell wanted to cooperate with the administration in an orderly inquiry that would have "a rather stabilizing effect" on Symington and other senators who were still demanding a full-scale committee investigation under Russell's leadership.[6]

II

Johnson shifted from behind-the-scenes maneuvering to public advocacy on Sputnik in mid October, largely under the prodding of George Reedy. Reedy himself was slow to grasp the impact of Sputnik until Charley Brewton, a former aide to Senator Lister Hill, flew to Texas to persuade Reedy that Sputnik offered both the Democrats, who were on the defensive because of the desegregation issue in the public schools after the Little Rock crisis, and Lyndon Johnson, personally, a chance to seize the initiative. On October 17, 1957, Reedy sent LBJ a long memo, urging him "to plunge heavily into this one."

Reedy stressed two points. First, Sputnik marked the opening of a new age in history: "The Russians have left the earth and the race for control of the universe has started." Just as the Romans had used roads to establish their dominion, the British had used control of the sea, and Americans had used their mastery of the air, the nation that could conquer outer space would dominate the world of the future, Reedy argued. In view of the importance of the issue and the failure of President Eisenhower to reassure the American people after Sputnik, it fell to Lyndon Johnson to take the initiative in educating the public on space by leading a congressional inquiry into the American missile and satellite program. By identifying himself with the new age of space, Johnson could advance his own political career and at the same time perform a vital national service. Above all, Reedy counseled, LBJ must rise above partisanship to conduct a fair and impartial inquiry, one that would be directed at uncovering the facts, not at assigning blame. "This may be one of those moments in history," Reedy concluded, "when good politics and statesmanship are as close to each other as a hand in a glove."[7]

Johnson quickly followed Reedy's shrewd advice. In two speeches in Texas, one at Tyler on October 18 and another at Austin on the next day, LBJ staked his claim to leadership on the space issue. In both addresses he spoke about the magnitude of the Russian achievement, declaring that the "Soviets have beaten us at our own game—daring, scientific advances in the atomic age"—and that "the Communists have established a foothold in space." He repeated, almost word for word, Reedy's comparison to the Roman and British empires to stress the importance of catching up with the Russians in space. And then he made space "a direct responsibility of mine," stating that he planned to use his Preparedness Subcommittee to "take a long careful look" at the American missile and satellite program. Finally, Johnson promised an impartial investigation, one that would be devoid of "charges and counter-charges. . . . Our need is to put aside our angers and to work together as we step into a new age of history."[8]

Two weeks later, after a long Pentagon briefing on the American satellite effort that Johnson, Russell, and Bridges attended, Russell authorized LBJ to "launch an all out investigation into all aspects of our missile and satellite programs" in hearings before his Preparedness Subcommittee. In private, Russell explained to Johnson that he had chosen LBJ over Symington, who "has a lot of information and would raise a lot of Hell, but it would not be in the national interest."[9] In his public statement on November 4 that announced these hearings, Johnson said they were not intended "to fix blame or put anybody on trial." Instead, the hearings would focus on "the question of what is to be done" and the search for "bold, new thinking in defense and foreign policy."[10]

In a telephone conversation with Bridges on the next day, November 5, Johnson lamented the administration's refusal to take Sputnik seriously, claiming that Secretary of State John Foster Dulles had told him that there had been no adverse reaction abroad. LBJ said that while he was not going to search for scapegoats, he was not going to cover up any wrongdoing either. And he added, "There is no question but to admit the Russians are ahead of us on this." When Bridges asked what he should say to the press about the hearings, LBJ replied, "Say you are in complete agreement with Senator Johnson and that this should be a national investigation instead of a partisan one."[11]

Thus, in the first month after Sputnik, Johnson, after a slow start, had taken control of the space issue. He used his close relationship with Richard Russell to outmaneuver his potential rival in 1960, Stuart Symington, who actually had better credentials in the missile field, and LBJ capitalized on Reedy's advice to take a nonpartisan approach to win over Republican Styles Bridges. Most important, Johnson was establishing himself as the nation's leading political spokesman on space.

III

Lyndon Johnson moved quickly to organize the Preparedness Subcommittee's hearings. He asked Donald C. Cook, a utility executive who had worked with him on an investigation during the Korean War, to head the staff. When Cook declined, Johnson followed Cook's suggestion of Edwin L. Weisl, Sr., a partner in a prestigious New York City law firm, who accepted when Johnson stressed the importance of the inquiry to national security. LBJ allowed Weisl, who brought his son, Edwin L. Weisl, Jr., and a younger partner in his firm, Cyrus R. Vance, as his assistants, to plan the hearings and to select the witnesses. Johnson maintained close supervision over the preparations, with two trusted staff members, Solis Horwitz and George Reedy, working closely with Weisl. At the same time, LBJ kept Richard Russell informed about the subcommittee's plans.[12]

Once again it was Reedy who supplied Johnson with the best advice on procedure. Reedy reiterated the need to keep the proceedings strictly bipartisan in spirit, and he laid out the basic strategy that Johnson would follow at the hearings. To avoid excessive defeatism over Sputnik yet not to engage in the apparent complacency of the Eisenhower administration's reaction, Reedy suggested that Johnson present Sputnik to the American people as a challenge—one that would require "a call to action instead of a summons to a siesta." Comparing the Soviet achievement to Pearl Harbor, Reedy wanted Johnson to point out that the initial defeat had led ultimately to victory over Japan; "We lost the battle but we won the war." And so, Reedy argued, there was still time for the United States to rally from the shock of Sputnik and to beat the Russians in space.[13]

Johnson also received more practical advice on how to proceed. Reedy urged him to open the hearings with testimony by well-known scientists, who could suggest ways in which the United States could move ahead in its space program. In particular, Reedy warned against becoming bogged down in details of the missile program and advised him to avoid air-power advocates such as General Curtis E. LeMay. Instead of focusing on the issue of intercontinental ballistic missiles (ICBMs), the hearings should explore "what we can do to raise our level of technology and place ourselves in a position where we can meet any Soviet challenge." But another of Johnson's advisers, lawyer James H. Rowe, Jr., also reminded LBJ of the political necessity of creating "a sense of urgency to counteract the complacency of the administration. . . . Lyndon Johnson's greatest contribution can be—and should be—to carry on psychological warfare against Eisenhower."[14]

Johnson displayed his mastery of the situation at a meeting of the subcommittee on November 22, 1957, three days before the hearings were due to open. He gained quick approval for his staff appointments, deftly outmaneuvered Symington's attempt to include General LeMay in the list of witnesses, and succeeded in limiting each senator to only ten minutes of questioning for each witness by what he termed "a gentleman's agreement." Above all, despite Rowe's advice, Johnson stated his intention of keeping politics out of the hearing chamber. Praising Styles Bridges for his cooperation, Johnson declared that "the sole objective of the inquiry is to determine ways and means of securing the defense of the United States." Appealing to patriotism, he vowed that there would be "no 'guilty party' in this inquiry except Joe Stalin and Nikita Khrushchev." The material that the subcommittee's staff had assembled, he warned, was so "deeply disturbing" that even "the most hardened ward-heeler would forget politics if he knew the facts." Therefore, Johnson promised, he would do nothing to embarrass the "one man who can give the orders that will produce the missiles. That man is the President of the United States."[15]

In stressing a bipartisan approach, Johnson was heeding Reedy's initial observation that Sputnik was a case in which good politics and statesmanship were "as close to each other as a hand in a glove." Undoubtedly, Johnson knew that the facts that he would bring out in the hearings would reflect badly on the Eisenhower administration and would force it to admit that mistakes had been made. But he also believed that he would be performing a patriotic service in forging a new national consensus to meet the Soviet challenge in space. He expressed his hope to President Eisenhower that the hearings "will make a constructive contribution to the security of our country."[16]

IV

Whatever Johnson's motives may have been, he conducted the hearings in such a way that the entire country would be fully aware of his role in responding to Sputnik. From the opening session in late November until the hearings concluded in January, 1958, LBJ was at center stage. He introduced each witness, made sure he was the first senator to engage in cross-examination, and summarized the highlights of each day's testimony in his closing remarks. When witnesses discussed classified information in secret sessions, it was the chairman who briefed reporters afterwards about what had been said behind closed doors.

Senator Johnson set the tone for the hearings in his opening statement on November 25, 1957. Calling Sputnik a threat to the nation's security, "perhaps the greatest that our country has ever known," he cautioned against excessive pessimism. Asserting that the nation should accept the Soviet action in space as a challenge, LBJ asked Americans "to respond with the best that is within them." Again he stressed bipartisanship by declaring, "There were no Republicans or Democrats in this country the day after Pearl Harbor." Declaring that Sputnik was "an even greater challenge than Pearl Harbor," he expressed his belief that the facts that would be disclosed at the hearings would "inspire Americans to the greatest effort in American history."[17]

Johnson shrewdly allowed prominent scientists such as Edward Teller and Vannevar Bush to monopolize the early sessions, postponing testimony on the military implications of Sputnik and the tangled missile program until December. Teller was especially effective, advocating a trip to the moon, which he said would "have both amusing and amazing . . . consequences." Other witnesses, notably General James Gavin and Wernher von Braun, favored large rocket boosters that would be capable of sending a spacecraft to the moon. Such an ambitious effort, Gavin claimed, would require "the solution of many complex, difficult, challenging, scientific problems that all in themselves will contribute a great deal to understanding about the environment of man on the earth." Von Braun was even blunter, arguing that the conquest of space was of "tremendous military importance." In launching Sputnik, the Russians were in effect saying, "If we want to control this planet, we have to control the space around it," von Braun concluded.[18]

While the hearings continued, Johnson developed a carefully thought-out position on space, which he articulated in press conferences, public addresses, and letters to his constituents. The basic theme was familiar—the United States was facing "the most serious challenge to its security in our history" as a result of Sputnik, "a disaster . . . comparable to Pearl Harbor." Opportunity accompanied the danger, however. "The world is entering the Age of Space," he declared again and again, and there was still time for the United States to regain its rightful role of leadership. Comparing Sputnik to the Alamo, Johnson told a Texas audience that "history does not reward the people who win the battles but the people who win the war." By rising above partisanship and pulling together, Americans could turn the new space era into "our finest hour." Johnson always closed his letters and speeches on a positive note. "The unknown is beckoning to us," he proclaimed. "Flights to the moon are just over the threshold," as the Age of Space gave promise of stirring times that "made his blood tingle."[19]

LBJ's attempt to identify himself as the nation's foremost spokesman on space came to a climax in early January. In an effort to preempt President Eisenhower's annual State-of-the-Union message on January 8, 1958, Johnson called a special caucus of Democratic senators for January 7, explaining to Richard Russell, "I cannot overemphasize what I believe to be the importance of this meeting."[20]

At this Democratic conference, Johnson made his boldest statement yet on the space race with the Soviet Union. In contrast to Eisenhower's attempts to play Sputnik down, LBJ pointed out the high value that the Russians were placing on outer space. In a rare partisan thrust, he blamed the administration's concern over a balanced budget for limiting the American satellite program; but Johnson's focus was on the future, not the past. "Control of space means control of the world," he stated bluntly. "From space, the masters of infinity would have the power to control the earth's weather, to cause drouth and flood, to change the tides and raise the levels of the sea, to divert the gulf stream and change temperate climates to frigid." He went on to warn that Soviet control of space, "the ultimate position," would be more dangerous than "any ultimate weapon." There was only one possible American response to the Russian effort to seize "the ultimate position," he concluded; "our national goal and the goal of all free men must be to win and hold that position."[21]

After this deliberate effort to seize the initiative from the administration on the space issue, Johnson moved to block efforts both by the staff of the Preparedness Subcommittee and by Senator Symington to issue a minority report that would be critical of the Eisenhower administration. Instead LBJ prepared a seventeen-point program that stressed such future goals as building large rocket motors for space flights and creating a new federal agency to direct the nation's space program. In what Cyrus Vance later described as "one of the most skillful pieces of diplomatic statesmanship that I have run across," Johnson won approval for his report in the course of one morning's subcommittee meeting, making only a few slight changes to ensure unanimity. Then he overcame a final roadblock by calling Stuart Symington, who had missed the crucial meeting, and reading him the report over the telephone. Warned that if he dissented he would be alone, the Missouri senator, who was in the bathtub at the time, had no choice but to agree.[22]

By the time the subcommittee had completed its hearings in late January, 1958, Lyndon Johnson had succeeded in turning Sputnik into a personal political triumph. In their astute account of Johnson's techniques as Senate majority leader, Rowland Evans and Robert Novak cite this episode as a "minor masterpiece" in the larger Johnson tactic of advancing the interests of the Democratic party without directly confronting a popular Republican president. Yet the beauty of Johnson's approach was that he wrapped his political purposes so artfully in bipartisanship that someone as close to the scene as Edwin Weisl, Sr., could argue that LBJ had scrupulously avoided playing politics with the Preparedness Subcommittee hearings. "I admired your passion for unity," Weisl wrote to Johnson, "on matters concerning the survival of our beloved country."[23]

Johnson, quite rightly, gave much of the credit to Richard Russell, especially for serving as a "brake" on his "impetuosity." In a letter to the Georgia senator in late January, 1958, LBJ expressed his "heartfelt thanks for the way you stood by me during a very difficult and trying period."[24] Johnson's private correspondence also suggests that he was moved by more than purely political concerns. Apparently he did feel that Eisenhower's lack of concern over Sputnik was endangering the nation. As he wrote to a friend on the eve of the hearings, "It may be essential to infuse boldness into those who have not exhibited it in the past, but who are obviously the only people in a position to act." And after the hearings were over, he took pride in "arousing our people to the implications of the present danger. . . . There is certainly more a sense of urgency in Washington now than there was several months ago."[25]

In responding to Sputnik, Johnson appears to have been moved both by political expediency and by a genuine sense of national peril. As George Reedy had pointed out, this was one of those rare times when what was good for Lyndon Johnson politically was also good for the nation. From this time forward, Johnson would be identified in the public mind as an advocate of an expanded American effort in space. Unfortunately, LBJ's fondness for hyperbole had led him to overstate the military importance of exploring outer space and to play down its scientific value. As a result, Johnson was responsible for popularizing the concept of a space race with the Soviet Union that would distort the American space effort in the 1960s.

V

In 1958, Johnson adopted a more statesmanlike pose as the leading architect of the new American space agency. Shifting his attention from the contest with the Russians to the control and direction of the national effort in space, LBJ once again used his legislative skill to serve both the nation and his own growing political ambitions.

On February 6, 1958, the Senate voted to create the Special Committee on Space and Aeronautics, which was to frame legislation for a permanent space agency. Johnson packed the committee with senior senators, all busy with their own committee chairmanships and all heavily indebted to LBJ. It was not surprising, therefore, that at the first meeting of the special committee on February 20, LBJ was unanimously chosen as its chairman and was given free rein to select its staff and to decide on its agenda. The key question to be resolved, Johnson explained to his colleagues, was who in government "should have jurisdiction over scientific aspects of space and astronautics."[26]

In his dealings with the Eisenhower administration about the formation of the new space agency, LBJ displayed his usual deft touch. Careful not to overplay his hand, he let the administration take the lead in proposing new legislation; he would prefer to be a watchdog, looking out for loopholes and weaknesses to correct. As he explained to the president, the American effort in space could not be "wrapped into one neat little package. It reaches into practically every aspect of human endeavor and it is going to require an extraordinary effort." But Johnson did promise "wholehearted cooperation" in "what we anticipate will be a joint enterprise."[27]

President Eisenhower responded on April 2 with draft legislation that would expand the thirty-year-old National Advisory Committee for Aeronautics (NACA) into the new National Aeronautics and Space Administration (NASA). A director, who would be appointed by the president, would head the new agency, aided by a seventeen-member advisory board, which would have no administrative responsibility. The staff of Johnson's special committee immediately focused on the chief weakness of this clumsy arrangement—the failure to provide for a central policy-making body that would resolve potential conflicts between civilian and military space projects. Aware of the jurisdictional disputes that had plagued the American missile program, Johnson's aides warned that the administration's proposal did not give NASA the clear-cut "authority over the entire space program so that it can be handled with foresight rather than on a trouble-shooting basis." Therefore they recommended that the Senate insist on a small "Policy Board" of five to seven members, which would be charged with formulating "the aeronautic and astronautic policies, programs and projects of the United States."[28]

In the ensuing legislative process, which included brief public hearings and protracted redrafting sessions, Johnson let his staff do most of the work. He became absorbed in other issues, especially attempts to alleviate heavy unemployment, which had been caused by the 1958 recession. Gerald Seigel and Edwin Weisl, Sr., did the actual legislative drafting, aided by George Reedy, who was distressed by Johnson's lack of interest. "We'd shove the bills into Johnson's hands and get him to introduce them and that's the way the act emerged," Reedy recalled twenty-five years later.[29]

Johnson, however, did involve himself personally; he insisted on a central board to set policy and to decide between conflicting civilian and military proposals about space. At the special committee's hearings, he grilled administration witnesses on this point, asking the director of NACA, "Under this bill. . . , who is going to make the decision as to who controls what? Now who . . . is going to decide what is civilian and what is military?" At Johnson's insistence, the Senate bill included a provision for the nine-member Space Council, including the secretaries of State and Defense, the director of NASA, and the head of the Atomic Energy Commission (AEC), to set comprehensive space policy and to designate specific programs.[30]

President Eisenhower refused to accept the Space Council at first, fearing that it would be a powerful body, on the order of the National Security Council, that would consume too much of his time and attention. When the legislation became stalled in a conference committee, Ike finally asked for a personal meeting with LBJ in order to explain his desire for a purely advisory body, "not one which makes decisions." The two men met on Sunday July 7, 1958, and quickly reached agreement. When Eisenhower expressed his concern that the Space Council would make too many demands on him, Johnson suggested making the president chairman of that body. Ike accepted this compromise, telling James R. Killian, his science adviser, that he did so "in order to see the bill move ahead."[31]

President Eisenhower signed the act creating NASA on July 29, 1958. Lyndon Johnson could take pride that it contained the Space Council that he had fought so hard to create. Ike knew, however, that he had outmaneuvered Johnson. Over the next three years, the Space Council met on only rare occasions, and then with Killian, not Eisenhower, presiding. Johnson could not force the president to use the Space Council to give central guidance to the nation's space program, but he did have enough power to block an administration move in 1960 to eliminate this body entirely.[32]

In the long run, Johnson was once again the real winner. He had continued to enhance his reputation as the nation's leading spokesman on space by appearing to be the father of NASA. At the same time, he had softened his image by toning down his hard-line rhetoric on the space race with Russia. Instead, he had gone out of his way to speak about working for a space effort that "will bring peace in our time." At the opening of the spring hearings, he had spoken of striving "to convert outer space into a blessing for mankind, rather than a threat of the destruction of civilization," adding that he had "no intention of rattling sabers among the stars." His real goal, he told one correspondent in April, 1958, was to engage in "the greatest of mankind's adventures" by promoting programs aimed at "searching out new galaxies of human thought." He even accepted the president's invitation to give a speech before the United Nations in November, 1958, in which he stressed American support for the peaceful exploration of outer space. In contrast to his nationalistic response to Sputnik, Johnson used the creation of NASA to develop a constructive approach to the challenge of space.[33]

VI

Lyndon Johnson's next major contribution to the American space program came in 1961, when he was serving as vice-president under John F. Kennedy. During his last three years in office, Dwight Eisenhower had kept careful budgetary limits on NASA, approving the Mercury program for manned flights around the earth in the early 1960s but rejecting plans for a lunar landing, which was estimated to cost $30 billion. When NASA advocates compared it to Columbus's voyage, Ike replied that he was "not about to hock his jewels" to send men to the moon. Although neither Kennedy nor Johnson made space a major issue in the 1960 election, most observers expected the new administration to speed up the American effort to catch up with the Russians in space.[34]

Even before JFK had taken office, he had decided to put his running mate in charge of the space program, both to exploit Johnson's reputation as a leading authority on space policy and to give him something useful to do. On December 20, 1960, after a meeting in Palm Beach, Kennedy announced that he would ask Congress to make the vice-president the head of the Space Council. Congress approved this change in April, 1961, enabling LBJ to become the formal head of the agency that he had forced on Eisenhower and that now could begin to frame the comprehensive program that Johnson felt had been so conspicuously lacking in the previous administration.[35]

LBJ's first task was to help Kennedy find a new head for NASA. Jerome Wiesner, the president's science adviser who favored scientific experiments over manned space flight, had originally been given this assignment, but the scientists whom he asked to serve all declined, in part because they feared that Johnson would not give them a free hand in running NASA. In late January the vice-president conferred with Senator Robert Kerr of Oklahoma, who had succeeded LBJ as chairman of the Senate Space Committee. At Kerr's suggestion, Johnson met with James E. Webb, an experienced bureaucrat who had served in the Truman administration and who subsequently had managed one of Kerr's oil companies in Oklahoma. A shrewd "off-the-ballot politician," as Tom Wolfe has described him, Webb at first resisted LBJ's blandishments. But when Johnson persisted and Kennedy made a personal request, in which he assured Webb that he would be free to run NASA, subject only to the president's wishes, Webb agreed to serve. In time a close bond would develop between Webb and Johnson, but the new head of NASA made sure from the outset that the vice-president would not interfere with the way in which he ran the agency. Also, as Webb noted later, he sensed that while Kennedy wanted to use Johnson's expertise and reputation on space, the president was determined to make all the important policy decisions himself.[36]

Johnson quickly learned the limits of his power. In a memo to the president shortly after the inauguration, LBJ proposed that Kennedy delegate supervision over all national-defense and space agencies to the vice-president. On January 28, 1961, after a face-to-face meeting in the Oval Office, JFK sent Johnson a formal reply, turning him down gracefully. Instead of the general supervision that LBJ had requested, Kennedy asked Johnson to preside over National Security Council meetings when the president was out of Washington and to maintain close liaison with all governmental agencies that were concerned with national defense and space. To help Johnson carry out these duties, Kennedy told Johnson that he had asked these agencies, including NASA, "to cooperate fully with you in providing information."[37]

The first major decision on space policy during the Kennedy administration came in late March, 1961. James Webb, after spending six weeks in studying NASA's programs and budget, submitted a request for a 30 percent increase in NASA's Fiscal Year (FY) 1962 budget, so as to permit a possible moon landing, tentatively scheduled for the mid 1970s, to take place before the end of the decade. David E. Bell, the director of the Bureau of the Budget, immediately raised objections, pointing out that such a large increase, slightly more than $300 million, could only be justified if Kennedy wanted to reverse Eisenhower's decision and make a moon landing part of JFK's effort "to catch up to the Soviet Union in space performance."

This dispute forced the president to turn his attention to the space program for the first time since taking office. In White House meetings that Johnson attended on March 21 and 22, 1961, Webb and Bell debated the question of expanding the space effort to include a moon landing in the 1960s. Johnson spoke out strongly in behalf of Webb's plans for a bigger program, but Kennedy finally decided to delay any decision on a moon shot. Instead, he compromised by approving $125 million in additional funds for NASA, which would be enough to speed up the work on the big boosters that would be necessary for flights to the moon.[38]

Events soon forced the president to act more quickly than he had intended. On April 12, Soviet cosmonaut Yuri Gagarin became the first man to orbit the earth; once again, the United States, which had postponed its first suborbital flight until May, had been outstripped by the Russians in space. Two days later, Kennedy discussed the possibility of an American flight to the moon as a way to get ahead of the Soviets, but he delayed making any decision when Webb told him that such an effort would require a program on the order of the Manhattan Project and might cost as much as $40 billion.[39]

A week later, after the fiasco at the Bay of Pigs had added a new sense of urgency to the effort to restore American prestige, Kennedy called Johnson to the White House to ask him to convene the Space Council and to consider how the United States could catch up with the Russians in space. In a brief memo the next day, April 20, the president spelled out the issues that he wanted LBJ to address. As part of "an overall survey of where we stand in space," Kennedy specifically wanted to know if "we have a chance of beating the Soviets . . . by a rocket to go to the moon and back with a man. Is there any other space program which promises dramatic results in which we could win?"[40]

Although the president would wait for Johnson's report before announcing his decision, it is clear that Kennedy had already made up his mind. His criticism of the Eisenhower administration for having fallen behind the Russians in missiles and space, his campaign theme of getting the nation moving again, and his intense sense of competition with the Soviets in the Cold War—all pointed to a moon shot as the only possible way of recapturing the respect of the world. And the choice of Johnson, the foremost advocate of an expanded American space effort, to conduct the study and to make the recommendations suggests that Kennedy was only ensuring that the moon shot would bear the stamp of authority. Johnson's role was to confirm a decision that the president had already made.

Whether or not LBJ understood the part that he had been asked to play, he performed it with skill and enthusiasm. Over the next two weeks, he met regularly with the Space Council to ponder the questions that Kennedy had asked. For technical advice, Johnson relied heavily on NASA officials, especially Dr. Hugh Dryden, a strong advocate of the moon-landing program that Eisenhower had refused to promote but that was still being planned for the 1970s as Project Apollo. On April 22, Dryden informed Johnson that there was "a chance for the U.S. to be the first to land a man on the moon and return him to earth if a determined national effort is made." The earliest possible date would be 1967, Dryden wrote, and the cost would be about $33 billion, $10 billion more than the projected NASA budget for the next ten years.[41]

LBJ then set out to develop a consensus for an accelerated Project Apollo. He expanded the Space Council deliberations to include Senators Robert Kerr and Styles Bridges, the chairman and the ranking GOP member of the Senate Space Committee, and he personally chose three private citizens to represent the general public—Frank Stanton of CBS, Donald Cook of American Electric Power Service, and George Brown, head of Brown and Root, the major Houston construction firm. All three were businessmen, and two, Cook and Brown, had been closely associated with Johnson in the past. LBJ also went outside the Space Council to consult with the leaders of the House Space Committee and with three key governmental military and scientific spokesmen, General Bernard A. Schriever of the air force, Admiral John T. Hayward of the navy, and NASA's Wernher von Braun.

The advice that Johnson received from these different sources all pointed to the same conclusion. Speaking for the businessmen, Cook stressed the importance of gaining "leadership in space," commenting that to strive for anything less would mean "a second-rate program, worthy only of a second-class power." General Schriever thought that it was "overridingly important" for the United States to win the space race with the Russians. Johnson at first kept relatively silent, letting others air their views, but as the meetings of the Space Council progressed, he began to speak out for a vigorous approach, and he challenged those who expressed doubts by asking, "Now, would you rather have us be a second-rate nation or should we spend a little money?"[42]

Johnson gave a clear indication of the direction in which he was moving in an interim report to Kennedy on April 28, 1961. Stating that nothing less than "world prestige" was at stake in the space race, LBJ admitted that the Russians were still clearly ahead. But he added, "The U.S. can, if it will, firm up its objectives and employ its resources with a reasonable chance of attaining world leadership in space during this decade." The way to do this, he concluded, would be through "manned exploration of the moon," which would have "great propaganda value" as well as providing the United States with the chance to develop the experience and technology for "even greater successes in space." Then, following Dryden's recommendations, Johnson told Kennedy that a moon shot was possible by "1966 or 1967," at a cost of an additional $10 billion over a ten-year period.[43]

With the April 28 memo to the president, Johnson's role in the Apollo decision was essentially over. He had done precisely what Kennedy had wanted: LBJ had built a strong case for a moon landing and had produced a unanimous recommendation from the bureaucracy. On May 8, Johnson submitted a much-longer document to Kennedy; this was a detailed budgetary analysis, prepared by NASA and the Pentagon, of the costs that would be involved in an accelerated moon-landing program. Then Johnson left on a three-week trip to Southeast Asia. On May 25, two days after he returned, Kennedy announced his decision in a speech to the Congress. Citing the support of LBJ and the need to overtake the Russians in space, the president declared, "I believe this Nation should commit itself to achieving the goal, before this decade is out, of landing a man on the moon and returning him safely to earth."[44]

There has been considerable speculation about one final aspect of Johnson's contributions to the space program during his vice-presidency—the choice of Houston for the manned space center for Project Apollo. Johnson and Webb have repeatedly denied that the vice-president was responsible for building this $60 million facility south of Houston, claiming instead that any political influence could be attributed to Congressman Albert Thomas of Houston, who chaired the appropriations subcommittee that funded NASA. While undoubtedly Thomas did exert his influence independently of LBJ, a recently released memorandum from Webb to Johnson on May 23, 1961, two days before Kennedy announced his Apollo decision, offers new insight into Johnson's role. Bringing LBJ up to date after his return from Southeast

Asia, Webb pointed out that both Thomas and George Brown "were extremely interested in having Rice University make a real contribution" to the Apollo program. Noting that Rice had 3,800 acres of land available and that NASA needed to establish a new research facility for Apollo, Webb told Johnson that he believed it would serve the national interest to build up a strong science and engineering center in the Southwest, similar to those that had grown up around Harvard and the Massachusetts Institute of Technology in New England and around the University of California on the West Coast. Noting the availability of easy water transportation of heavy rockets by barge to Florida, Webb saw the Houston location near Rice as very attractive, adding, "George Brown has been extremely helpful" in bringing this possibility to his attention.[45]

On September 19, 1961, NASA announced that it had chosen a site south of Houston on which to build its manned spacecraft center for Apollo, on one thousand acres acquired from Rice University. Friendly journalists repeated NASA's explanation for the choice: "The availability of year-round water transportation between centers gives the United States a major advantage in the race for the moon with the Soviet Union." Johnson had wisely followed Webb's advice to keep a low profile: avoid any "end-runs," and let "the merit of this program" permit it to move through Congress "with minimum political infighting."[46] The choice of Houston for the manned space center was not the result of crude political pressure by Lyndon Johnson; instead it resulted from LBJ's foresight in involving George Brown in the Apollo decision and in choosing a man as sensitive to political considerations as James Webb to head NASA. In his own indirect way, LBJ played as important a role as Albert Thomas in making Texas the focal point of the nation's expensive new effort in space.

VII

After Kennedy's tragic death in 1963, Lyndon Johnson was in a position, as president, to carry through on the original Apollo decision. Yet once in the White House, he found that many other issues competed with space for both attention and funding. Johnson never abandoned his determination to beat the Russians to the moon, but the course of events, especially the Vietnam War, forced him to impose some very real limits on the American effort in space.

Within a month of becoming president, LBJ had to face up to the very high cost of the decision to land men on the moon. In December, 1963, Budget Director Kermit Gordon explained that an increase of

$583 million in the NASA budget for FY 1965 made up almost one-third of all budget increases proposed for that year. Although Johnson had promised Virginia's Senator Harry F. Byrd, whose support was vital for pending legislation to cut taxes, that he would hold NASA spending to no more than $5 billion in 1965, the president finally told Webb that he would receive $590 million in new funds, in order "to give NASA a 'fighting chance' to accomplish the lunar landing within this decade." Although NASA would exceed the $5 billion ceiling by nearly $250 million, Webb promised to keep actual expenditures in 1965 just under that magic figure. Congress finally appropriated $5.25 billion "to maintain the lunar landing program and other manned space flight programs on schedule," in the words of Budget Director Gordon.[47]

This expensive commitment made Johnson fearful that the Republicans would hammer away at the Apollo program in the 1964 presidential campaign. In June, before the GOP convention, Milton S. Eisenhower wrote to Johnson, on behalf of a Republican study group that Eisenhower headed, to urge that the 1970 deadline for putting a man on the moon be dropped so as to permit a "sounder program for manned lunar exploration" at a much lower annual cost. Johnson tactfully replied that while he would not let the target date become a "straightjacket," he did not see any reason "to slacken in our nationally approved effort to reach the moon as soon as we can."[48]

The nomination of Barry Goldwater led to considerable activity in the White House in regard to space issues. Aware that Goldwater had called Apollo "a terrible waste of money" and had declared that "all manned space research should be directed by the military," Johnson's aides, led by press secretary George Reedy, prepared long memos defending the space program and developed breakdowns of NASA spending by congressional districts to show its beneficial effect. Campaign statements that were prepared by the Space Council declared that under Kennedy and Johnson, the United States "has narrowed the space gap" inherited from Eisenhower; they also repeated Johnson's May 20, 1963, statement, "I do not believe that this generation of Americans is willing to resign itself to going to bed each night by the light of a Communist moon."[49]

In the fall campaign, Johnson stressed other themes, notably economic abundance and a responsible foreign policy, but he did make occasional references to the continuing space race with the Soviet Union. Citing the danger of letting "those who would destroy freedom" achieve mastery of the universe, LBJ told a St. Louis audience on October 21 that the United States "must maintain a leadership for the free world in outer space." A week later, he declared in Los

Angeles, "You cannot be first on earth and second in space." Yet earlier that month the Russians had once again surpassed the United States by sending the first three-man spaceship into orbit. Warned in advance of the upcoming Soviet feat, Johnson had declined to issue a public statement promising that the two-man American Gemini would be launched early in 1965.[50]

Once he had safely been returned to the White House, Johnson took full advantage of the successful Gemini program to reinforce his public image as the leading architect of the American space effort. His aides planned Rose Garden ceremonies honoring the astronauts and trips to space facilities as ways to achieve what one aide termed "visible identification with the Space Program at a period of conspicuous successes." When Virgil I. ("Gus") Grissom and John W. Young made the first Gemini flight in March, 1965, LBJ telephoned them after their safe return. In a later visit to the manned space center in Houston, Johnson claimed that the United States was no longer behind in space; but he then went on to stress his peaceful goals: "The race that we of this generation are determined to be first in is the race for peace in the world." By the time of the fourth and fifth Gemini flights in December, 1965, Johnson was telling the astronauts that they had taken the nation "one-step higher on the stairway to the moon" and that this effort not only increased "our knowledge of technology" but also would lead "to a better life for all."[51]

Despite this high-flown rhetoric, Johnson was aware of the danger of overplaying his role. When aides asked him to approve of White House ceremonies to honor the astronauts after each Gemini flight, LBJ responded cautiously: "Let's play it by ear." He refused to be pinned down by the television networks, which wanted to have cameras recording all of his telephone conversations with the astronauts while in orbit. As he told Reedy, "I don't want overexposure attached to me." Yet the president was aware of Trendex polls that documented the strong public interest in the space program, with 69 percent approving the commitment to put a man on the moon before 1970.[52] In his own shrewd way, LBJ was trying to continue to extract the maximum political benefit from a program that he still believed was serving the national interest.

VIII

Throughout his presidency, Lyndon Johnson faced two major and closely related questions concerning space policy. The first dealt with the future: What goal should the United States seek beyond the moon landing? The answer to that question increasingly came to depend on the available funding. Two developments in the mid 1960s—the expensive Great Society domestic programs and the unexpectedly high expenditures for the Vietnam War—caused a serious financial squeeze that tested LBJ's commitment to winning the space race and led to a sharp reduction in NASA's budget.

The issue of future space programs grew inescapably from the budget process itself. On January 30, 1964, the president asked James Webb to "review our future space exploration plans" and give him a progress report by May 1 and final recommendations by September 1. Johnson acted at the suggestion of his new science adviser, Donald F. Hornig, who pointed out the need to have a clearer idea of the nation's space goals in making decisions about specific budget items, such as a controversial nuclear rocket. The goal, Johnson told Webb, was to match "hardware and development programs to prospective missions."[53]

In his interim report in May, Webb began by stressing the progress that had already been made on a "ten-year $35 billion program" that was directed toward a moon landing by the end of the decade. Then in very broad terms, he sketched out possible future efforts, ranging from manned exploration of the moon to unmanned flights to the nearer planets, including "the landing of an instrumented payload on the Martian surface," a step that could help in "unraveling the long-term history and evolution of the solar system." Webb promised that in his September report he would evaluate these various possibilities and make some specific recommendations for the president to consider.[54]

After requesting several extensions, Webb sent LBJ his final report in February, 1965. It was brief, cautious, and quite conservative in its conclusions. There was no mention of manned flights to the planets or even of an orbiting space laboratory. Instead, Webb focused on two projects. The first would be "the exploration of Mars through the use of large unmanned soft-landing spacecraft." Calling this "a major undertaking" that would eventually cost more than $1 billion, Webb recommended aiming for a 1971 flight, with a possible fly-by of Mars in 1969. The second, which was soon termed Apollo Applications, was "a systematic program" of manned flights around the earth and to the moon, which would use the Saturn rockets and the Lunar Module that had been developed for Apollo. The result, Webb explained, would be "to extend into the new medium of space the leadership we now have an aeronautics."

Although Webb did attach a report by the Future Programs Task Force, which outlined longer-range missions for the 1970s and 1980s, such as orbiting space stations and the manned exploration of Mars, he limited his recommendations for the present to the unmanned Mars soft landing and the Apollo applications. These projects would not require any new rocket boosters, would "round out and strengthen our basic on-going space effort," and would do so "efficiently and at acceptable cost." This last consideration was clearly uppermost in Webb's thinking; presumably, it was what he thought Johnson wanted. White House aide Jack Valenti summed up Webb's report in an accompanying memo to LBJ in which he pointed out, "These recommendations require no major new launch vehicle systems . . . and assume that resources on the order of those currently programmed ($5¼ billion per year) will continue to be available."[55]

Webb's report reflected Johnson's determination to make the Apollo program his administration's primary goal in space and to avoid making any other commitments for the future. A report that was prepared by two Space Panels of the President's Science Advisory Committee in 1966 reinforced this position by calling simply for "a balanced effort" for the post-Apollo space program. While this report mentioned lunar exploration and unmanned planetary probes that would lead ultimately to manned flights to nearby planets, science adviser Hornig carefully added, "The Panels considered and rejected the idea of setting a new dominating space goal, such as a manned landing on Mars by a specific date."

Lyndon Johnson clearly had no interest in setting the agenda for the space program of the future. Instead, faced with growing budgetary pressures, he was intent on achieving the goal that he and Kennedy had set for the nation in 1961—landing men on the moon before the end of the decade. He would do everything he could to advance that goal through Project Apollo, even if it meant sacrificing vital first steps toward more ambitious space ventures.[56]

IX

The first financial squeeze on NASA came in the fall of 1965, when the administration began to plan its budget for the 1967 fiscal year. Space spending had reached its peak in newly appropriated funds in FY 1965 at $5.25 billion; the amount for FY 1966 was only slightly less, $5.17 billion. These figures were deceptive, however, for actual expenditures in FY 1966 were running at an annual rate of $5.6 billion as Project Apollo began to reach full stride, using money that had been committed but had not been spent in previous years.

The timing was unfortunate. The heavy NASA spending coincided with the far-larger sums that were suddenly needed by the escalation of the Vietnam War in 1965. On November 22, 1965, Budget Director Charles Schultze, who had replaced Kermit Gordon earlier in the year, informed Johnson that FY 1966 expenditures were running at a projected rate of $108.8 billion, more than $8 billion in excess of the $99.7 that had been budgeted. Vietnam accounted for more than half of this increase; but the space program, with an overrun of $500 million, was the next-largest contributor, costing much more than any of the domestic reform programs.[57]

Table 8.1. The United States Space Budget, 1959–69 (in $ millions)

Fiscal Year	Appropriations for NASA	Expenditures by NASA
1959	305.4	145.5
1960	523.6	401.0
1961	964.0	744.3
1962	1,824.9	1,257.0
1963	3,673.0	2,552.4
1964	5,099.7	4,171.0
1965	5,249.7	5,092.9
1966	5,174.9	5,933.0
1967	4,967.6	5,425.7
1968	4,588.8	4,723.7
1969	3,990.9	4,251.7

Sources: Homer Newell, *Beyond the Atmosphere* (Washington, D.C.: Government Printing Office, 1980), p. 382; Richard Hutton, *The Cosmic Chase* (New York: New American Library, 1981), p. 201.

On the next day, Johnson sent a memo to the heads of all departments and agencies. Citing "the current expenditure outlook and all the uncertainties in Southeast Asia," he asked them to hold spending "*to the absolute minimum* required for carrying out essential responsibilities." Equally important, he summoned these officials to his ranch in Texas in mid December to review their FY 1967 budget requests. The need for fiscal restraint was reinforced by a memo from Gardner Ackley, chairman of the Council of Economic Advisers, who told Johnson that the only way LBJ could avoid asking Congress for an immediate tax increase would be to keep spending for 1967 under $110 billion.[58]

The economy drive that was necessitated by the Vietnam War led Budget Director Schultze to propose a cut of approximately $300 million in NASA's requested allotment. Giving "the manned lunar landing schedule" the highest priority, Schultze made most of the cuts in post-Apollo programs, notably Apollo Applications and the 1971 Mars soft landing. Webb fought hard for these future programs, forcing the budget director to acknowledge that his cuts would have "political repercussions" with both Congress and the aerospace industry. Johnson backed Schultze by agreeing to the $300 million cut, which put the NASA budget at an even $5 billion, but the president drew the line there. When Schultze submitted a plan for reducing the total budget by another $2 billion that would include a $300 million further reduction for NASA, Johnson refused, because the additional cut would mean delaying the moon landing until the 1970s.[59]

The FY 1967 budget cuts put James Webb in a very difficult position. Within the administration, he fought hard for a large-enough NASA budget to fund unmanned flights to the planets and to conduct basic scientific research as well as to carry out Project Apollo. Yet the scientific community, which favored unmanned flights and was skeptical about the moon landing, pushed hard for more money for space science. And in Congress, advocates of the space program on the key appropriations committees sought even more funding, both out of conviction and out of political consideration for the economic stimulus that the space program was providing for their constituents.[60]

The situation became particularly difficult during the spring of 1966 as Webb sought to persuade Congress to approve the lower appropriations bills for NASA in FY 1967. Space "hawks" in Congress resented cuts in the unmanned Mars flights and feared that the Republicans would accuse the administration of permitting the Russians to move "permanently ahead in the space race." At the same time, Webb asked Johnson for guidance on how to implement the budget cut, since it would mean releasing "some 20,000 people . . . from NASA operations, plus 60,000 from research and development and an additional five to ten thousand from construction by July 1, 1967."[61]

Although the two men conferred, there is no evidence of how LBJ instructed Webb to handle these firings. By May, 1966, Webb was resorting to his ultimate weapon, the fear of Russia's beating the United States to the moon. Claiming that he had done his best "to minimize any political risk to your Administration" from the cuts in NASA's budget, Webb warned that it would be impossible to maintain "a forward thrusting effort in space" in view of the reduced budget. Apparently referring to Luna 9, an unmanned Russian spaceship that made a soft landing on the moon in early 1966, Webb added, "This is particularly true in light of what the Russians are doing and are going to do." The only way to regain the lead, he concluded, would be for the United States to increase spending dramatically. "My judgment is that the 1968 budget will be a major turning point," Webb concluded, "with indicated requirements on the order of $6 billion of new obligational authority."[62]

Although he must have known there was little chance of getting $6 billion in the FY 1968 budget for NASA, Webb fought hard for this goal. When Budget Director Schultze set a guideline of only $5.1 billion for NASA, Webb made his case for an additional $1 billion in a letter to the president on August 26, 1966. He reminded Johnson that in 1961, LBJ "had almost had to drive me" to recommend the expensive moon-landing program to Kennedy. Yet in just five years, with an expenditure of over $22 billion, they had built a space program that promised to reach the moon by 1969. Another NASA budget in the $5 billion range for 1968, however, would be disastrous, leaving Webb with "no choice but to accelerate the rate at which we are carrying on the liquidation of some of the capabilities which we have built up."

It was not the fate of Apollo that was at stake, Webb continued; rather, it was the future of the American space program. "There has not been a single important new space project started since you became President," he told Johnson. Although Webb was aware of the heavy burdens that were being imposed by the competing demands of the Great Society and the Vietnam War, he still felt that this failure to prepare new space ventures was "not in the best interests of the country." He regretted being so blunt, but the White House had recently asked him to draft a presidential speech on space, charting a course "that would constitute a ringing challenge for the next half century," and he felt that he had to let LBJ know his true feelings. If the president chose to make such a "ringing challenge," Webb would back him to the hilt; but such a commitment would require annual NASA budgets on the order of $6 billion for the next few years.[63]

Several weeks later, Charles Schultze sent to Johnson his rebuttal to Webb's August letter. He agreed with the director of NASA that the issue was future space programs, not the moon landing. Affirming the need to *maintain its capability in manned space,* including such possibilities as earth orbital stations and even a manned flight to Mars, Schultze still questioned the assumption that the United States, for fear of falling behind the Russians, should do everything in space that was technically feasible. Above all, he challenged the idea that it was necessary to strive to keep "the *peak level of industrial manpower*" that had been achieved during the Apollo build-up. "The space program," he reminded LBJ, "is not a WPA."

Schultze claimed that a continuation of a $5-billion annual budget for NASA would carry only a slight risk of delaying Apollo beyond 1969 by reducing the production of Saturn V boosters from six to three a year. It would involve a setback for what he termed "NASA's ambitious plans for unmanned scientific flights," pushing back the soft landing on Mars to 1973, but still permitting Apollo Applications to proceed on schedule. The budget director specifically denied that a $5-billion figure would force "the liquidation" of some NASA capabilities, as Webb claimed. Instead, Schultze compared this sum to the $2 billion that was being budgeted in 1968 for elementary and secondary education and the meager $1.8 billion for the war on poverty. "I don't believe," Schultze concluded, "that in the context of continued fighting in Vietnam we can afford to add *another* $600 million to $1 billion in the space program in 1968."[64]

Johnson finally resolved the dispute over the space budget in December in a meeting at his Texas ranch, which was attended by Webb, Schultze, and White House aid Joe Califano. This conference was held after Webb had told Califano that out of loyalty to LBJ he was ready to "fit the space program" to whatever "budget number" that "Charlie [would] give him." In fact, the two antagonists had narrowed down their differences from approximately $1 billion to less than $300 million. Schultze and Webb agreed that "we must continue our manned space flight capability, . . . that we should *not* announce a major new goal—like sending a man to Mars, that we can mount, at a reasonable cost, a useful series of Post-Apollo flights" involving "a number of important long-duration earth-orbit experiments."

They disagreed on two issues—namely, the cost of these future programs and the budgetary margins that would be required in order to ensure success. Schultze proposed limiting the amount that would be budgeted for post-Apollo efforts in 1968 to $455 million, while Webb wanted an additional $182 million for further tests of the equipment and for more scientific experiments. Webb placed ever greater emphasis on his request for $100 million more for Apollo. He wanted the money for insurance, as a cushion to provide financial flexibility in case of any unexpected setbacks in the moon-landing program. All the space flights to date, he pointed out, including the ten Gemini missions, had gone well, but "the margins between success and failure in these flights had been very thin." The budget cuts in 1966 and 1967 had forced NASA to "steadily draw down our margins." He pleaded for the extra $100 million for Apollo, as well as the $182 million for future programs, so as to build in a greater margin of safety. "I realize that these additional amounts are large," he concluded, "but I believe that the impact of an unsuccessful space program—which we would be risking unless they are provided—would be even more costly."[65]

Despite this ominous warning, Johnson sided with Schultze and held the NASA budget for FY 1969 to just over $5 billion. Webb took this setback gracefully, telling LBJ that he would "strike a very positive note" in explaining the administration's decision to the press and to Congress, calling it part of a continuing effort "to deny the USSR a hostile hegemony in space." Webb then sent the president the outline of a proposed public statement, which referred to "a strong space program of which Americans can be proud." But the future, Webb explained, was not so certain. "The manned lunar landing schedules must today assume the virtually total success of each test, each delivery, each flight if we are to meet the target date." And unless the administration were to begin building more Saturn boosters than was currently planned, "we will have, at best, a costly gap; at worst, a lack of space flight capability in the years to come." Thus Webb raised the specter of a space gap in the 1970s, reminiscent of the very situation that Johnson had warned the nation about after Sputnik.[66]

Webb's fears reflected the zeal of the bureaucrat, not a measured assessment of the Johnson space program. Despite the onset of the Vietnam War in 1965, the amounts spent on space, as opposed to the budget figures, actually rose in 1966 to $5.9 billion and remained at a relatively high level of $5.4 billion in 1967. The editors of *Aviation Week and Space Technology* recognized this fact in praising Johnson in January, 1967, for having resisted growing pressure from Congress to make sharp cuts in space spending.[67]

In fact, Johnson was pursuing what he perceived to be the continuing national consensus on space. A White House survey of the views of congressional leaders in late 1966 revealed strong sentiment for cutting NASA's budget, especially the post-Apollo program. But no one wanted to limit Apollo. Thus, Republican Congressman Gerald Ford commented, "Do not touch the moon program," while Democrat Carl Albert warned that the administration could not "take the risk of losing the race to the moon." Webb told associates that he thought LBJ was beginning to lose "his original enthusiasm" and even had "become indifferent" to the space program under the strain of Vietnam and the resulting antiwar turmoil.[68] But LBJ's commitment to Apollo never wavered. As a realist, he was forced to sacrifice the less-popular post-

Apollo program in order to preserve his enduring priority—sending an American to the moon ahead of the Russians.

X

What Webb had feared most finally occurred on January 27, 1967—a fire swept through the Apollo command module during a stationary test at Cape Kennedy, killing astronauts Roger B. Chaffee, Edward H. White III, and Virgil I. Grissom. Johnson learned of the tragedy that evening from Webb, who then took charge of the subsequent investigation and report, which was critical of NASA's procedures. By letting his agency shoulder the blame, Webb spared the president from political damage, but the space program never fully recovered. From this time forward, there was growing resistance from the public and Congress in regard to heavy spending for NASA, and there was increasing skepticism about the need to beat the Russians to the moon.[69]

A crisis in fiscal policy during the summer of 1967 proved to be an even greater problem. Faced with a potential budget deficit of $29 billion as a result of the Vietnam War, Johnson decided to ask Congress for a 10 percent increase in income taxes. Even then, warned economic adviser Gardner Ackley, without corresponding cuts in spending, the nation would face a runaway inflation that "would make it *almost impossible . . . to sustain prosperity and job opportunities after Vietnam.*" Aware that Congress would not raise taxes without making major reductions in spending, Johnson decided to pare down the FY 1968 budget, which was still in the appropriations stage in Congress.[70]

Johnson and Schultze quickly agreed that NASA spending in 1968 should be held to just under $5 billion, almost $600 million less than the 1967 expenditure for space. To accomplish this goal, Schultze said it would be necessary to reduce the 1968 appropriation by $500 million, cutting it from $5 billion to $4.5. Webb at first resisted, claiming that Apollo was "just now getting back to speed" after the fatal fire and warning that the Russians would be "flying vehicles larger than the Saturn V by next year." But once he understood that Johnson was giving the tax increase highest priority, the NASA director agreed to go along with the reduced appropriation, though he still hoped to receive at least $4.6 billion.

Two issues remained to be settled. First, there was the question of where to make the reductions in NASA's budget. Charles Schultze outlined two alternatives: abandoning the 1969 target date for the moon landing or cutting back sharply on all of the post-Apollo programs. The budget director favored the first alternative, arguing that it would be better not to sacrifice long-term goals in order to land on the moon in 1969 when "technical problems" might make achieving this goal impossible. "Why not make a virtue out of necessity," he asked. But for Johnson there could be no abandonment of his and Kennedy's pledge to put men on the moon before the end of the decade; at the president's insistence, the half a billion dollars that was cut from NASA's budget came from such future programs as Apollo Applications and the soft landing on Mars.[71]

There was even more disagreement on how best to handle the cuts in Congress. In the House, strong pressure had built up over the summer to reduce NASA's budget by $400 million. Democratic leaders were willing to fight against such cuts, but Budget Director Schultze advised LBJ against such tactics, pointing out that the administration itself now planned to pare NASA spending by $500 million in 1968. "If the space program has to be cut this much," Schultze argued, "it would be better to have the Congress do it." Moreover, the administration's acceptance of congressional cuts would "help in the fight over the tax bill" by winning over conservatives who insisted on reductions in spending and even by pleasing "some of the liberals who have urged cuts in the space program rather than in the Great Society program."

Webb once again found himself in opposition. He claimed that any administration statements approving congressional reductions in NASA's budget would be viewed as a betrayal by those who had loyally supported Johnson's space program from the beginning. "The friends of the program," such as Republican Senator Margaret Chase Smith of Maine, would deeply resent it if the president " 'knifed' the very activities he had previously been urging them to support." At the very least, Webb wanted the administration to remain silent and let NASA "make the cuts internally."

Johnson sided with Schultze, issuing a public statement endorsing the congressional cuts. Citing the threatened deficit of $29 billion and the need for a 10 percent tax surcharge, LBJ declared, "The times demand responsibility from us all." Much as he regretted the circumstances, he agreed that "we must now moderate our effort in certain space projects," but he reaffirmed his ultimate goal: "to master the challenge of space."[72]

The $500 million slice in NASA's budget caused Johnson great personal anxiety. In late September, when Webb was about to go before congressional committees to endorse the budget cut, LBJ sent him a confidential telegram. "Be sure to make abundantly clear that

I do not choose or prefer to take one dime from my budget for space appropriations for this year," the president told Webb. He only did so because Congress "forced me to agree to effect some reductions or lose the tax bill."[73]

The outcome confirmed the conflicting views of Johnson's advisers. As Webb had predicted, space advocates in Congress felt betrayed by the administration's about-face, with Senator Smith declaring that LBJ had "literally pulled the rug from under those who direct the space program." But after some delay, Congress did enact the 10 percent income-tax surcharge, which Schultze felt was so crucial to the economy. When Congress appropriated $4.59 billion for NASA, Webb was able to cut enough from the future programs to hold actual 1968 expenditures down to $4.83 billion, a reduction of almost $500 million from his original estimate. And although Webb felt that "confidence" in the achievement of the moon landing before the end of 1969 had been lowered by the cuts, Johnson could still take comfort in Webb's assurance that "the goal of the manned lunar landing in this decade is preserved."[74] Despite the Vietnam-induced increase in taxes, LBJ's commitment to Apollo had survived intact.

XI

Lyndon Johnson's last year in the White House witnessed both the continued decline in the space budget and the first tangible sign that the United States would, in fact, land men on the moon by the end of the 1960s. With little debate, the administration accepted congressional cuts that reduced NASA's funds in FY 1969 from $4.3 billion to just under $4 billion. Although these reductions further weakened future space programs, they did not affect the moon-landing schedule. Before the end of 1968, two NASA flights put that effort on target: in October, Apollo 7 successfully tested the spacecraft for the moon shot on 165 orbits of the earth, and in December, Apollo 8 saw three astronauts fly around the moon and return to the earth without incident.[75]

James Webb, unfortunately, was not able to preside over these triumphs. In mid September, frustrated by growing opposition in Congress and by continuing budget cuts, he submitted his resignation to President Johnson, who quickly accepted it. For the first time, Webb felt free to make public his fear that cuts in the post-Apollo programs would enable the Russians to win the space race. Commenting on a recent unmanned Soviet flight to the moon, Webb claimed that it proved that the Russians were developing capabilities in space "that could change the basic structure and balance of power in the world."[76]

Two of Johnson's assistants voiced sharp disagreement to the president. Donald Hornig, the president's science adviser, called Webb's statement "grossly exaggerated," arguing that the Russians, who had not yet developed a booster as large as Apollo's Saturn V, were at least a year behind the United States. Edward Welsh, head of the Space Council, was almost as blunt, calling Webb's comment on the Russian lead "inaccurate" and maintaining that "the U.S. has had more successful missions to the Moon and to the planets than has the USSR and has obtained more information about outer space in these missions."

The president, who realized that his own role in cutting back on NASA's budgets was involved, backed Webb to the hilt. His response to Hornig's suggestion that the President's Science Advisory Committee make a public report in regard to Webb's charges was negative: "Drop it! That is my feeling," he instructed his staff. He sent both Hornig's and Welsh's memos to Webb for a "prompt reply," suggesting that he have "all his scientists . . . support him and me." In his responses, Webb reiterated his belief that the cuts that Congress had forced upon the president, coupled with evidence of Soviet advances "across a broad spectrum," meant that "the present trends are against the United States." Johnson echoed this argument in his formal reply to Hornig on October 10, in which he turned down a public report by the Science Advisory Committee and defended Webb for loyally submitting to budget cuts which had been dictated by "overall fiscal requirements."[77]

No one knew better than did Lyndon Johnson how hard Webb had fought to preserve the post-Apollo programs; it was the president, not the director of NASA, who had decided to sacrifice future space programs to ensure the success of Apollo. The attacks on Webb served only to strengthen the bond between the two men. In his formal letter of resignation, Webb expressed his appreciation for LBJ's trust and then added, "You never failed to base your actions on a deep understanding that the space program, perhaps more than any other, opens mankind's door to the future." LBJ was equally appreciative. At a ceremony marking the success of Apollo 7, he awarded to Webb NASA's Distinguished Service Medal, and after the flight of Apollo 8 to the moon and back, Johnson termed Webb "the single man most responsible" for the success of the space program and "the best administrator in the Federal Government."[78]

Apollo 8 did in fact mark a triumphal finale for Johnson's contributions to the American space effort. During the six-day flight to the moon, the president spoke both to the astronauts and to their wives by telephone, as TV cameras recorded the scene in the Oval Office. On December 26, with the Apollo spacecraft on its way back to earth, Joe Califano told LBJ that this mission indicated "the near certainty that we will be the first to land on the moon." Johnson apparently agreed, telling Webb the next day that "I have never been more proud of American scientific accomplishment than I am today." Apollo 8 touched off what one NASA official described as an "unprecedented wave of popular enthusiasm"; *Time* magazine even scrapped its original choice for "Man of the Year" in favor of Frank Borman, James A. Lovell, Jr., and William A. Anders, the three astronauts who had flown around the moon.

For Johnson, Apollo 8 was a fitting climax to all of his endeavors since Sputnik. In a White House ceremony on January 9, 1969, honoring Borman, Lovell, and Anders, LBJ recalled the early days of the struggle: "There were those men in our government who ten years ago fought to guarantee America's role in space. . . . I am glad that I was one of them." Noting that this was the last time he would take part in a space ceremony as president, Johnson concluded, "I am proud that I have stood with the space effort from its first days—and I am so glad to see it now flower in this most marvelous achievement."[79]

His pride was justified. From the time that he chaired the Preparedness Subcommittee hearings through his service as head of the Space Council under Kennedy, he had set forth the goal of achieving American preeminence in space. One can question the sincerity of his initial motivation, mixing, as it did, political expediency with concern for the nation's welfare. And one can also argue that Johnson placed too strong a nationalistic emphasis on the new frontier of space, reducing a vital scientific quest to a Cold War cliché. But Johnson's steadfast dedication to the goal of putting a man on the moon can never be doubted. His determination overcame all the obstacles, even the competing claims of the disastrous Vietnam War, to making good on the pledge that he and Kennedy had made to the nation.

In addressing Congress after Apollo 8, Frank Borman said that Archibald MacLeish had best captured "the feelings that we all had in lunar orbit" in a prose poem that MacLeish had written for the *New York Times* in December, 1968, as Borman, Lovell, and Anders were circling the moon. Lyndon Johnson must also have appreciated the poet's tribute to his finest achievement:

To see the earth as it truly is, small and blue and beautiful in that eternal silence where it floats, is to see ourselves as riders on the earth together, brothers on that bright loveliness in the eternal cold—brothers who know now they are truly brothers.[80]

Notes

1. Lyndon Baines Johnson, *The Vantage Point: Perspectives of the Presidency, 1963–1969* (New York: Holt, Rinehart & Winston, 1971), passim; George Reedy, *Lyndon B. Johnson: A Memoir* (New York: Andrews & McMeel, 1982), p. 13; George Reedy oral history interview, Dec. 20, 1983, by Michael Gillette, tape 11, p. 36. All cited manuscripts and oral history interviews are in the Johnson Library unless otherwise noted. Alfred Steinberg, *Sam Johnson's Boy: A Close-up of the President from Texas* (New York: Macmillan, 1968), pp. 479–80.

2. Johnson, *Vantage Point*, p. 272; transcript of interview with President Johnson by Walter Cronkite, July 5, 1969, pp. 2–3.

3. Telegram, Symington to Russell, Oct. 5, 1957; telegram, George Smathers to Russell, Oct. 7, 1957, Richard Russell Papers, University of Georgia Library, ser. 15, box 403; transcript of telephone conversation between LBJ and Neil McElroy, Oct. 21, 1957, Reedy: Subcommittee, Senate papers, box 433.

4. Russell to Carl Marcy, Jan. 9, 1958, Russell Papers, ser. 1, J. General, box 9.

5. Solis Horwitz to Russell, Oct. 7, 1957, Russell to Symington, Oct. 7, 1957, and Russell to Smathers, Oct. 7, 1957, Russell Papers, ser. 15, box 403.

6. Enid Curtis Box Schoettle, "The Establishment of NASA," in *Knowledge and Power: Essays on Science and Government*, ed. Sanford A. Lakoff (New York: Free Press, 1966), pp. 185–86; Solis Horwitz oral history interview, June 9, 1969, by Paige Mulhollan, pp. 15–16; Horwitz to Neil McElroy, Oct. 11, 1957, and Horwitz to Johnson, Oct. 11, 1957, Preparedness Subcommittee, Senate papers, box 355; Johnson-McElroy telephone transcript, Oct. 21, 1957, Senate papers, box 433.

7. Reedy to Johnson, Oct. 17, 1957, Reedy: Memos, Senate papers, box 420.

8. Johnson speeches, Tyler, Texas, Oct. 18, 1957, and Austin, Texas, Oct. 19, 1957, Statements file, box 22.

9. Russell to Robert B. Troutman, Nov. 9, 1957, Russell Papers, ser. 15, box 403; Reedy to Johnson, undated, Reedy office files, Senate papers, box 421; telephone conversation, Johnson and Styles Bridges, Nov. 5, 1957, Congressional file, LBJA (Lyndon Baines Johnson Archive), box 40.

10. Johnson press release, Nov. 4, 1957, Statements file, box 23.

11. Telephone transcript, Johnson and Bridges, Nov. 5, 1957, Congressional file, LBJA, box 40; Dulles to Johnson, Oct. 26, 1957, and Johnson to Dulles, Oct. 31, 1957, Famous Names, LBJA, box 3.

12. Rowland Evans and Robert Novak, *Lyndon B. Johnson: The Exercise of Power* (New York: New American Library, 1966), pp. 204–5; Donald C. Cook oral history interview, June 30, 1969, by Thomas H. Baker, p. 25; Edwin L. Weisl, Sr., oral history interview, May 13, 1969, by Joe B. Frantz, p. 10; Cyrus R. Vance oral history interview, Nov. 3, 1969, by Paige Mulhollan, pp. 1–2;

Horwitz oral history, p. 17; Reedy oral history, tape 11, p. 34; Johnson to Russell, Nov. 8, 1957, Russell Papers, ser. 15, box 403.

13. Reedy to Johnson, Nov. 23, 1957, Reedy: Memos, Senate papers, box 421.

14. Reedy to Johnson, undated, Preparedness Subcommittee, Senate papers, box 355; Reedy to Johnson, undated, Reedy to Johnson, Nov. 11, 1957, and Rowe to Johnson, Nov. 21, 1957, Reedy: Memos, Senate papers, box 421.

15. Minutes of Preparedness Subcommittee meeting, Nov. 22, 1957, Preparedness Subcommittee, Senate papers, box 405.

16. Reedy to Johnson, Oct. 17, 1957, Reedy: Memos, Senate papers, box 420; Johnson to Eisenhower, Dec. 6, 1957, Famous Names, LBJA, box 1.

17. "Inquiry into Satellite and Missile Programs," *Hearings* before the Preparedness Investigating Subcommittee of the Committee on the Armed Forces, U.S., Senate, 85th Cong., 1st and 2d sess. (Washington, D.C.: Government Printing Office, 1958), pp. 1–3.

18. Ibid., pp. 22–23, 505–6, 614–15.

19. Press releases, undated, Preparedness Subcommittee, Senate papers, box 355; Johnson to E. L. Kelly, Jan. 23, 1958, Johnson to John L. Dore, Jan. 9, 1958, and Johnson to Mrs. Thomas E. Whitehead, Jan. 16, 1958, Armed Services, 1958 Subject files, Senate papers, box 588; speeches to Dallas Chapter, American Jewish Committee, Nov. 29, 1957, to Wichita Falls Junior Chamber of Commerce, Nov. 30, 1957, and to Waxahachie Luncheon Clubs, Dec. 10, 1957, Statements file, box 23.

20. *Washington Post*, Jan. 1, 1958, Estes Kefauver Papers, University of Tennessee Library, Knoxville, Tenn., ser. 11, box 5; Johnson to Russell, Dec. 23, 1957, Russell Papers, ser. 15, box 403.

21. Johnson speech to Democratic Caucus, Jan. 7, 1958, Statements file, box 23.

22. Edwin L. Weisl, Jr., oral history interview, May 23, 1969, by Joe B. Frantz, p. 2; Steinberg, *Sam Johnson's Boy*, p. 482; Herbert York, *Race to Oblivion: A Participant's View of the Arms Race* (New York: Simon & Schuster, 1970), p. 120; unsigned and undated memo, Siegel office files, Senate papers, box 405; Vance oral history, p. 6; Booth Mooney, *LBJ: An Irreverent Chronicle* (New York: Crowell, 1976), p. 102.

23. Evans and Novak, *Lyndon B. Johnson*, p. 208; Edwin Weisl, Sr., oral history, p. 13; Weisl to Johnson, Feb. 3, 1958, Famous Names, LBJA, box 9.

24. Johnson to Russell, Jan. 29, 1958, Congressional file, LBJA, box 53.

25. Johnson to Anthony Marcus, Nov. 19, 1957, Satellite, 1957 Subject files, Senate papers, box 355; Johnson to Vic Lindley, Jan. 28, 1958, Armed Services, 1958 Subject files, Senate papers, box 588.

26. Alison Griffith, *The National Aeronautics and Space Act: A Study of the Development of Public Policy* (Washington, D.C.: Public Affairs Press, 1962), pp. 19–24; Gerald W. Siegel oral history interview, May 26, 1969, by Thomas H. Baker, p. 40; Record of Organization of Special Senate Committee on Space, Feb. 20, 1958, Space Committee, Senate papers, box 357.

27. Johnson to Eisenhower, Mar. 25, 1958, 1958 Subject files: Space, Senate papers, box 630.

28. Robert L. Rosholt, *An Administrative History of NASA, 1958–1963* (Washington, D.C.: Government Printing Office, 1966), pp. 10–11; Schoettle,

"Establishment of NASA," pp. 229–39; Analysis of S.3609 with Proposed Modifications, May 8, 1958, Russell Papers, ser. 9, A, box 3.

29. Edward C. Welsh oral history interview, July 18, 1969, by Thomas H. Baker, p. 3; Edwin Weisl, Sr., oral history, p. 13; Reedy, *Lyndon B. Johnson*, p. 13; Reedy oral history, tape 11, p. 39.

30. "National Aeronautics and Space Act," *Hearings* before the Special Senate Committee on Space and Astronautics, 85th Cong., 2d sess. (Washington, D.C.: Government Printing Office, 1958), pp. 91, 258; Griffith, *National Aeronautics and Space Act*, p. 93.

31. Siegel oral history, p. 45; Walter Jenkins to Johnson, June 25, 1958, 1958 Subject files: Space, Senate papers, Box 630; Johnson, *Vantage Point*, p. 277; James R. Killian, Jr., *Sputnik, Scientists, and Eisenhower: A Memoir of the First Special Assistant to the President for Science and Technology* (Cambridge, Mass.: MIT Press, 1977), pp. 137–38.

32. Killian, *Sputnik*, p. 138; Johnson, *Vantage Point*, p. 277; Rosholt, *Administrative History of NASA*, p. 170.

33. Griffith, *National Aeronautics and Space Act*, p. 18; "NASA," Senate *Hearings*, pp. 6–7; Johnson to Ben F. Smith, Apr. 27, 1958, 1958 Subject files: Space, Senate papers, box 630; Johnson speech to United Nations, Nov. 17, 1958, Space Committee, Senate papers, box 359. For further information on the background and reaction to LBJ's UN speech see Statements file, box 27.

34. John M. Logsdon, *The Decision to Go to the Moon: Project Apollo and the National Interest* (Cambridge, Mass.: MIT Press, 1970), pp. 35, 64–66.

35. Ibid., pp. 67–68; Johnson, *Vantage Point*, pp. 278–79; Ken BeLieu to Johnson, Dec. 17, 1960, Vice Presidential Security file, box 17; Welsh oral history, pp. 5, 10.

36. Steinberg, *Sam Johnson's Boy*, p. 559; Leonard Baker, *The Johnson Eclipse: A President's Vice Presidency* (New York: Macmillan, 1966), pp. 127–29; Cronkite interview transcript, p. 25; Tom Wolfe, *The Right Stuff* (New York: Farrar Strauss & Giroux, 1979), p. 226; James E. Webb oral history interview, Apr. 29, 1969, by Thomas H. Baker, pp. 3–10.

37. Evans and Novak, *Lyndon B. Johnson*, pp. 326–27; Reedy, *Lyndon B. Johnson*, p. 133; Kennedy to Johnson, Jan. 28, 1961, John F. Kennedy, 1961, White House Famous Names file, box 4.

38. Welsh to Johnson, Mar. 22, 1961, and Agenda for NASA-BOB Conference with the President, Mar. 22, 1961, Vice Presidential Security file, box 15; Webb oral history, pp. 14–15; Johnson, *Vantage Point*, pp. 279–80; Logsdon, *Decision*, pp. 88–91, 95–100; Jay Holmes, *America on the Moon: The Enterprise of the Sixties* (Philadelphia: J. B. Lippincott, 1962), pp. 195–97.

39. Logsdon, *Decision*, pp. 101–6; Hugh Sidey, *John F. Kennedy, President* (New York: Atheneum, 1964), pp. 117–23.

40. Logsdon, *Decision*, pp. 108–10; Kennedy to Johnson, Apr. 20, 1961, John F. Kennedy, 1961, White House Famous Names file, box 4.

41. Logsdon, *Decision*, pp. 59–61, 112–14; Welsh oral history, pp. 11–12; Dryden to Johnson, Apr. 22, 1961, Vice Presidential Security file, box 17.

42. Logsdon, *Decision*, pp. 120–21; Holmes, *America*, pp. 199–200; Cook oral history, p. 27; Welsh oral history, p. 14.

43. Johnson to Kennedy, Apr. 28, 1961, John F. Kennedy, 1961, White House Famous Names file, box 4.

44. Holmes, *America*, pp. 201-2; Welsh oral history, pp. 16-19; Logsdon, *Decision*, pp. 123-28.

45. Baker, *Johnson Eclipse*, pp. 126-27; Webb oral history, pp. 18-21; Webb to Johnson, May 23, 1961, Vice Presidential Security file, box 17.

46. Rosholt, *Administrative History of NASA*, p. 214; Holmes, *America*, p. 32; Webb to Johnson, May 23, 1961, Vice Presidential Security file, box 17.

47. Gordon to LBJ, Dec. 14, 1963, and Jan. 23, 1964, White House Central Files (hereafter cited as WHCF), Ex FI 4, box 21; Webb oral history, pp. 38-39; LBJ to Gordon, Dec. 23, 1963, WHCF, Ex FI 4/FG 260, box 30; Edward Welsh to LBJ, Aug. 14, 1964, WHCF, Ex OS, box 1.

48. Milton Eisenhower to Johnson, June 2, 1964, and Johnson to Eisenhower, June 29, 1963, WHCF, Ex OS, box 1.

49. "Statements of Barry M. Goldwater on Space Exploration," George Reedy office files, box 29 (1498); undated memos by Reedy, "Space 1963-1964," Reedy office files, box 19 (1404); Richard Callaghan to Paul Southwick, Mar. 16, 1964, Space, Fred Panzer office files, box 519; Welsh to Southwick, Apr. 27, 1964, Space, Panzer office files, box 516; Space Council brochure, undated, Space (Outer), Bill Moyers, office files, box 134.

50. *Public Papers of the Presidents: Johnson, 1963-64*, 2 vols. (Washington, D.C.: Government Printing Office, 1965), 2:1397, 1496 (hereafter cited as *Public Papers*); Hayes Redmon to Moyers, Oct. 11, 1964, C.F. OS 2, box 75.

51. Horace Busby to Johnson, Feb. 24, 1965, NASA Visit, Horace Busby office files, box 31; transcript of telephone conversation between Johnson and Grissom and Young, Mar. 23, 1965, Space, Panzer office files, box 493; Jack Valenti to Johnson, June 15 and Sept. 13, 1965, WHCF, Ex OS 4-1, box 8; text of LBJ speech, June 11, 1965, Astronauts, Busby office files, box 35; Johnson to Webb, Dec. 15, 1965, WHCF, Ex OS, box 1.

52. Webb to Johnson, May 25, 1965; William Monroe to Reedy, May 18, 1965; Reedy to Johnson, undated; LBJ to Reedy, undated; Julian Scheer to Moyers, Oct. 11, 1965—all in WHCF, Ex OS, box 6; Welsh to Johnson, Oct. 24, 1964, WHCF, Ex OS, box 1.

53. Johnson to Webb, Jan. 30, 1964, and Hornig to Johnson, Jan. 29, 1964, WHCF, Ex OS, box 1.

54. Webb to Johnson, May 20, 1964, Space (Outer), Moyers office files, box 134.

55. Webb to Johnson, Feb. 16, 1965, and Valenti to Johnson, Feb. 17, 1965, WHCF, Ex OS, box 1.

56. Hornig to Johnson, Dec. 22, 1966, Donald Hornig papers, box 4; Welsh oral history, p. 31.

57. Homer E. Newell, *Beyond the Atmosphere: Early Years of Space Science* (Washington, D.C.: Government Printing Office, 1980), p. 381; Schultze to LBJ, Nov. 22, 1965, WHCF, Ex FI 4, box 22.

58. Johnson memo, Nov. 23, 1965, Joe Califano to Johnson, Dec. 8, 1965, and Ackley to Johnson, Dec. 17, 1965, WHCF, Ex FI 4, box 22.

59. List of Major Dollar and Politically Sensitive Items, WHCF, Ex FI 4/FG 260, box 30; Schultze to Johnson, Jan. 14 and 24, 1966, WHCF, Ex FI 4, box 22.

60. Newell, *Beyond the Atmosphere*, pp. 380-81; John Noble Wilford, *We Reach the Moon* (New York: Norton, 1971), pp. 147-50; Welsh oral history, pp. 29, 31.

61. Edward Welsh to Johnson, Mar. 18 and Apr. 8, 1966, WHCF, Ex OS, box 2; Joe Califano to Johnson, June 25, 1966, Henry Wilson to Johnson, Mar. 25, 1966, and Marvin Watson to Johnson, Mar. 16, 1966, WHCF, Ex FI 4, box 22.

62. Webb to Johnson, May 16, 1966, WHCF, C.F. OS, box 74; for information on the lunar soft-landing program see Clayton Koppes, *JPL and the American Space Program: A History of the Jet Propulsion Laboratory, 1936–1976* (New Haven, Conn.: Yale University Press, 1982), pp. 172–84.

63. Webb to Johnson, Aug. 26, 1966, WHCF, Ex OS, box 2.

64. Schultze to Johnson, Sept. 1 and 20, 1966, WHCF, Ex OS, box 2.

65. Califano to Johnson, Dec. 15, 1966, WHCF, Ex FI 4, box 23; Schultze to Johnson, Dec. 16, 1966, and Webb to Johnson, Dec. 14, 1966, WHCF, Ex FI 4/FG 260, box 30.

66. Webb to Johnson, Dec. 17, 1966, WHCF, Ex FI 4/FG 260, box 30.

67. Preliminary Expenditure Figures for 1968 Budget, Dec. 17, 1966, WHCF, Ex FI 4, box 23; clipping, "The Aerospace Budget," *Aviation Week and Space Technology*, Jan. 30, 1967, in WHCF, EX FI 4/FG 260, box 30.

68. Survey of congressional opinion by Charles Schultze and Sam Hughes, undated, WHCF, Ex FI 4, box 23; Webb oral history, pp. 39, 42; Newell, *Beyond the Atmosphere*, p. 380.

69. Jim Jones to Johnson, Jan. 27, 1967, President's Appointment file, box 53; Bob Fleming to Johnson, Jan. 28, 1967, WHCF, Ex OS 4-1, box 8; Wilford, *We Reach the Moon*, pp. 119–33.

70. Ackley to Johnson, Aug. 3, 1967, WHCF, Ex FG 11-4, box 62. For the debate and decision to seek a tax cut see Chapter 2.

71. Schultze to Johnson, Aug. 11 and 14, 1967, WHCF, Ex FI 4/FG 260, box 30; Webb to Johnson, Aug. 10, 1957, WHCF, Ex FI 4/FG 200, box 29.

72. Schultze to Johnson, Aug. 14 and 19, 1967, and Webb to Schultze, Nov. 6, 1967, WHCF, Ex FI 4/FG 260, box 30.

73. Johnson to Webb, Sept. 29, 1967, WHCF, C.F. FI 4/FG 260, box 43.

74. *New York Times*, Oct. 7, 1967, in National Aeronautics and Space Administration, Panzer office files, box 384; Schultze to Johnson, Nov. 3, 1967, WHCF, Ex FI 4/FG 260, box 30.

75. Edward Welsh to Johnson, May 10 and Sept. 20, 1968, WHCF Ex OS, box 3; Wilford, *We Reach the Moon*, pp. 193–96, 215–29.

76. Newell, *Beyond the Atmosphere*, p. 285; *New York Times*, Oct. 1, 1968, and *Greenville* (S.C.) *Herald Banner*, Sept. 24, 1968, in National Aeronautics and Space Administration, Panzer office files, box 384; Donald Hornig to Johnson, Sept. 26, 1968, WHCF, Ex OS, box 3; Thomas Paine oral history interview, Mar. 25, 1969, by Harry Baker, p. 8.

77. Hornig to Johnson, Sept. 26, 1968, Welsh to Johnson, Sept. 30, 1968, William Hopkins to Webb, Oct. 1, 1968, Webb to Johnson, Oct. 1, 2, and 5, 1968, and Johnson to Hornig, Oct. 10, 1968, WHCF, Ex OS, box 3. The president's memo to Webb was never sent; instead, White House aid Larry Temple read it to Hornig's assistant over the telephone (Temple memo, WHCF, Ex OS, box 3).

78. Webb to Johnson, Oct. 7, 1968, WHCF, Ex FG 260/A, box 294; unsigned memos, Nov. 2, 1968, and Jan. 9, 1969, President's Appointment file, boxes 114 and 120.

79. Tom Johnson to Johnson, Dec. 26, 1968, Califano to Johnson, Dec. 26, 1968, and Johnson to Webb, Dec. 27, 1966, WHCF, Ex OS 4, box 4; Wilford, *We Reach the Moon,* pp. 230–31; Thomas Paine to James Jones, Dec. 26, 1968, and text of Johnson remarks, Jan. 9, 1969, President's Appointment file, box 120.

80. Wilford, *We Reach the Moon,* pp. 231, 232.

About the Contributors

Charles DeBenedetti received his Ph.D. from the University of Illinois and taught at the University of Toledo from 1968 until his death in early 1987. He had a special interest in the relationship between domestic peace and antiwar movements and U.S. foreign policy. He was the author of *The Peace Reform in American History* (1980) and the editor of a volume of essays entitled *Peace Heroes in Twentieth Century America* (1986). The essay in this book was part of a larger study of the antiwar movement in America from 1955 to 1975 that he had been working on for many years.

Robert A. Divine is the George W. Littlefield Professor in American History at the University of Texas at Austin, where he has taught since 1954. A specialist in American diplomatic history, his publications include *Blowing on the Wind: The Nuclear Test Ban Debate, 1954-1960* (1978) and *Eisenhower and the Cold War* (1981). He is presently working on a study of Eisenhower and the Sputnik crisis.

Lewis L. Gould is the Eugene C. Barker Centennial Professor in American History at the University of Texas at Austin. His most recent book is *Reform and Regulation: American Politics from Roosevelt to Wilson* (1986). He is at work on a book about Lady Bird Johnson and her beautification campaigns in the 1960s, which grew out of the research for his essay in this volume.

Burton I. Kaufman received his Ph.D. at Rice University in 1966. He is presently Professor of History at Kansas State University, where he has taught since 1973. His areas of specialization are American foreign policy and post–World War II America. Among his publications are *Trade and Aid: Eisenhower's Foreign Economic Policy, 1953-1961* (1982) and *The Korean War: Challenges in Crisis, Credibility, and Command* (1986). He is currently working on a history of the Carter presidency and a study of U.S. foreign economic policy during the Kennedy and Johnson administrations.

Donald F. Kettl is Associate Professor of Government and Foreign Affairs at the University of Virginia. He earned a Ph.D. in political science from Yale University; his publications include *Government* *by Proxy: Performance and Accountability in American Government* and *Leadership at the Fed* (1986). His research interests include public administration and economic policy. Kettl currently is working on as book investigating the management of the Pentagon and its relations with defense contractors.

Clarence G. Lasby is Professor of History at the University of Texas at Austin and the author of *Project Paperclip: German Scientists and the Cold War* (1975). He is currently at work on a history of coronary heart disease in twentieth-century America and a book about Lyndon Johnson's health policies.

Martin V. Melosi is Professor of History and Director of the Institute for Public History at the University of Houston. His major research fields include urban technology, environmental studies, energy history, and public-policy history. His most recent book is *Coping with Abundance: Energy and Environment in Industrial America* (1985). His current research projects include a biography of Thomas Alva Edison and a study of hazardous waste in the United States.

Index